THE BRAIN ALWAYS WINS

THE BRAIN ALWAYS WINS

Improving your life through better brain management

John Sullivan and Chris Parker

URBANE
Publications

First published in Great Britain in 2016 by Urbane Publications Ltd

Suite 3, Brown Europe House, 33/34 Gleaming Wood Drive, Chatham, Kent ME5 8RZ

Copyright ©John Sullivan and Chris Parker, 2016

The moral right of John Sullivan and Chris Parker to be identified as the authors of this work has been asserted in accordance with the Copyright, Designs and Patents Act of 1988.

All rights reserved. No part of this publication may be reproduced, stored in a

retrieval system, or transmitted in any form or by any means, electronic, mechanical, photocopying, recording or otherwise, without the prior permission of both the copyright owner and the above publisher of this book.

A CIP catalogue record for this book is available from the British Library.

ISBN 978-1-909273-73-3

EPUB 978-1-909273-74-0

KINDLE 978-1-909273-75-7

Design and Typeset by The Invisible Man

Cover by The Invisible Man

Printed and bound by CPI Group (UK) Ltd, Croydon, CR0 4YY

URBANE
Publications

urbanepublications.com

MIX
Paper from responsible sources
FSC® C013604

The publisher supports the Forest Stewardship Council® (FSC®), the leading international forest-certification organisation. This book is made from acid-free paper from an FSC®-certified provider. FSC is the only forest-certification scheme supported by the leading environmental organisations, including Greenpeace.

This book is dedicated to my mom, dad, and beautiful new bride.
John Sullivan -

For Mairi.
Chris Parker -

The Brain Always Wins

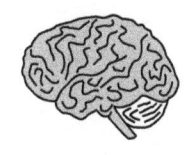

Contents

Preface *xi*
Introduction *xxiii*

1 The Governor 1
2 Physical Activity 27
3 Rest and Recovery 56
4 Optimum Nutrition 93
5 Cognitive Function 125
6 Emotional Management 165
7 Socialization & Communication 202
8 Synergy 242

About the Authors *247*
References *251*
Index *265*

The Brain Always Wins

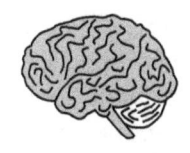

Acknowledgements

Accomplishments are not solitary activities and for that reason I would like to acknowledge the following:

Daniel Fabian, Julian Saad, and Caitlin Malone for their efforts, spirit, and youthful enthusiasm for the exploration of the brain and science;

Dr. Antoinette Minniti for her love and support as well as her keen eye for science and narrative combined;

Dr. David Coppel for his collegial support, professionalism, and mutual interest in the brain;

Kim Bissonnette for his professionalism, ethics, and shared vision;

Family and friends who have always supported me; and, to all those in sport and tactical environments who are open to learning about the brain.

John

My thanks to Alan Barnard for his critical and thought-provoking insights, Mairi for her endless support, and Matthew who is everything a Publisher should be – bold, creative, caring and collaborative.

Chris

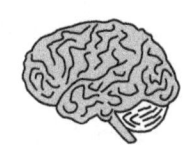

Preface

The first conversation

'The best ideas start as conversations.'

Sir Jonathan Ive

(i)

My name is Chris Parker. Since the age of nineteen I have been fascinated with Communication and Influence. It's a topic I study, practise, teach and write about. I became involved in meditative practices at exactly the same time as I began my fascination with Communication and Influence. In many ways, the two have gone hand-in-hand ever since. I didn't fully appreciate when I was nineteen that I was making decisions and beginning things that would shape and direct the rest of my life. The year was 1976.

Thirty-seven years later, in October 2013, I met John Sullivan. My life was about to change again.

John is an applied Sport and Clinical Psychologist with many years' experience working at the most elite levels of the military, law enforcement and sport. He has trained some of the very best in the world, teaching them how to manage their brain to achieve excellence, proving time and time again it is the brain that ultimately decides what happens in the heat of activity, when those involved have to make and then execute high-pressure decisions. His work, from the most specialized front line military personnel to the NFL, gives him a unique perspective about how and why the brain matters – and just how to make the most of it.

We met for lunch in a Chinese restaurant in Nottingham, England. My plan was to find out everything I could about his philosophy, experience and skills. Unfortunately – or, fortunately, as things turned out – he had the same plan with regard to me. It became a very long lunch in which food was lost behind conversation and conversation quickly gave way to possibilities.

John's focus, not surprisingly, was on the brain. He said, 'We have learned much about the interconnection of the brain and its functions through scientific research and through injury to the brain or peripheral systems - typically these discoveries have come from the military and the sacrifices of war.'

He paused and reflected momentarily. He was, I knew, firmly committed to providing support for military personnel. It was a topic close to his heart.

After a sip of his tea he went on, 'Our brain leads, directs, and facilitates all our actions and reactions. Research shows that brain resiliency is influenced by our daily habits including rest and recovery, emotional management, physical activity, socialization and nutritional intake. This is important because the human brain is inherently resilient; it's the most sophisticated survival tool. Through our consistent, habitual behaviors we either reinforce or challenge that resiliency.'

I didn't realize at the time just where those sentences would eventually take us. It was only in hindsight I saw their significance and potential. When I first heard them I was too busy wanting to know more. I began by asking John about the difference - and the relationship - between our brain and our mind. His answer was instantaneous.

'Often we hear people using the words 'brain' and 'mind' as if they are interchangeable, but they are not. A colleague of mine, Dr. David Coppel, a Clinical, Sport, and Neuro-Psychologist from the University of Washington, explains the differences brilliantly. He says that the brain works in the background whilst the mind is our experience in the present moment. Although they work together they are independent; the brain is working constantly to keep us safe, even when the foreground of the mind experience is not. Our mind can be engaged in so many ways, oblivious to many of our needs, yet our brain is always working to meet them - to give us the best chance of survival.'

As John continued to explain his work, and the incredible science that underpinned it, he returned repeatedly to the same phrase, 'The brain always wins.'

Within seconds of asking him precisely what he meant by that I realized I had touched the very heart of his work and world view.

'Firstly,' John began, 'I need to define what I mean by "winning". We both know that words have great power, so it's important to provide clarity here.

'I'm defining "winning" as the innate and expansive ability of the human brain to adapt and overcome. Of course, our brain has its limits but pound for pound it is the most advanced adaptive system in the known universe. I would not bet against the human brain when it comes to survival, over-coming difficult odds, and problem solving, because the brain is fabulously designed to survive.

'This is a most important point. At the core of our existence is, and has been, our ability to survive and adapt and, simply put, the brain is our ultimate survival system and tool. For millions of years there have been many threats to our survival as human beings. What has enabled us to survive and see the other side of another day, what has enabled us to "win" so consistently and for so long? Our brain! Not muscle or any other system or part of the human anatomy, it's our brain.

'It's clear from the examination of other animals we are neither the strongest nor the fastest but, because of our brain, we are the best at problem solving which has been a key factor in our survival and evolution.

'In fact without a healthy brain, strength does not matter. You see, the ability to use strength is based upon a whole host of brain processes and without brain health these processes do not synchronize as practiced and mastered. We ascended to the top of the food chain because we are the best at survival, problem solving, and learning to cooperate socially, all of which are dependent on a healthy, functioning brain.

'On the physical level, the brain is the control center for all the body's functions, including body temperature, blood pressure, heart-rate and breathing, how we walk, talk, taste and smell. Connected to this, the brain runs systems that enable the body to repair. It also determines how we interpret and respond to every piece of stimuli we encounter throughout our life!

'Our brain controls all of our thinking functions, intellectual activities and emotions. It is the brain that gives us the power to speak, imagine and dream. It processes information and protects us, governing all of our behaviors, working usually subconsciously in conjunction with other sub-systems in our body, whether we are awake or asleep. And the brain itself is adaptive. It actually changes in response to experience.

'So why do I say, "The brain always wins"? Quite simply because how you perceive, understand and respond to the world, how you literally move through your life day after day, how you communicate, feel, learn and remember, how you survive and adapt, are all determined by your amazing brain. However, it's also important to stress that the brain is our servant. We have to take care of it because it takes cares of us.

'The implications of this are really significant, because although our brain can do all of these things surprisingly well with very limited support by way of nourishment and rest, if we actually give it the nourishment, rest and stimulation it needs to be healthy and function optimally we will reap incredible benefits in terms of health, productivity, performance enhancement and, even, social engagement.

'We are who we are, and we have the role we have in the world because our brain always wins. If we actively manage and support our brain - our unique adaptive, survival system - we will all improve the quality of our lives. Now, why wouldn't we want to do that?'

John paused giving me time to answer his question in the only way possible - 'Of course we would want to do that!' - before moving on to his conclusion.

'Think of all the things we know are good for us, such as nutrition, exercise, rest, emotional management, socialization, whilst they all add value in their own right and in different ways, they are ultimately good for us because they are good for our brain! In fact, given that the brain always wins, this should be our primary reason for doing them. All of the other benefits are secondary. If we all focused more on brain health and performance, and acted accordingly, the overall quality of our lives would be so much better!

'And we can do this, if we choose to. We actually know enough now to behave in ways that enhance brain health and function and, therefore, by extension, enhance the quality of everything we do. The problem is most people don't realize this fact. It's time for that to change!'

How right he was...

(ii)

My name is John Sullivan. I'm a Sport Scientist and Clinical Sport Psychologist. For the last 20 years I've been privileged to work with some of the most amazing people. I work to optimize high performance environments and develop both individual and team performance especially when under the most extreme pressure.

How do I do this? By prioritizing the brain because it's the ultimate decider on the quality of human performance.

Why do I do this? Because, for me, people come first. We matter. We are capable of so much. And the brain is at the center of our capability and our humanity. It is our wondrous brain that makes us who we are, that makes us so special.

The tragedy for me is two-fold:

1. So few people know enough about their brain.
2. So many myths about the brain still abound.

They are myths that actually get in the way of our learning. They are myths such as:

Preface

'We only use 10% of our brain.'

and

'We know so little about our brain that we might as well just ignore it.'

Both, of course, are utter rubbish.[1] And the danger is that people who believe such myths use them as behavioural guidelines – and why wouldn't they? After all, if they haven't been taught differently they have to act on what they've got, and by doing so they unwittingly limit the quality of their life, of what they do, how they feel and how they live.

I want to change this, not just for the elite men and women with whom I work but for everyone else, too.

That's why I'm writing this book. It's become a very important part of my life's work. I now know it's the first of several books I'm going to write about the brain and how we can all learn to understand and manage it better, and so have a better life experience.

I didn't always know I was going to write this book. Or the others I am now planning. I didn't know until I met Chris Parker in October 2013. I heard that he'd spent his life studying interpersonal communications and influence, that he was a teacher and a trainer, a novelist and a poet, a martial artist who had been practicing meditation for decades. He certainly wasn't a Scientist. As I soon discovered, he didn't have the inclination to be. He was interested only in what he could make work, rather than in the science of why it worked. It was clear that Chris's plan for our first lunch was to fill the time asking me all about my background, skills and work, and to say next-to-nothing about himself. Over time I came to

---

[1] We use all of our brain and we certainly know enough about it – and are learning more every day – to create and implement a deliberate brain management process.

xvii

realize that, like myself, he was a person who preferred asking the questions rather than answering them. Fortunately, for both of us, we quickly came to an unspoken agreement to take it in turns. What might have been an interview session turned instead into an exciting and meaningful dialogue.

I began by asking him about a phrase he used in many aspects of his teaching, 'Chris, explain to me what you mean by the term "The Wisdom of The Village"'.

'Ah,' he stopped eating and half-smiled. I thought for a moment he was going to ask me how I knew the phrase was so important to him,[2] but he didn't. Instead he looked briefly as if he was recalling a distant memory and then he spoke. '"The Wisdom of The Village" is the way I think, write and talk about the knowledge that elders in olden times – and maybe to some degree today, but probably less so in Western societies - passed down to the next generation. It's knowledge that grows out of a lifetime of continual learning and experience, and is based on an understanding of what works. It's the knowledge of the most important things in life, those things that keep individuals and communities safe, that make relationships work, that enhance wellbeing and, generally, make life worth living. It's knowledge that ultimately is based on an understanding of Self and others.

"The Wisdom of The Village" is the sum total of the lessons learned through awareness and questioning, through engaging with the environment and quiet contemplation. It's a reflection of a time when elders dedicated the last stages of their life to furthering their own understanding; when, having looked after their families, they were able to give even more time to their own learning and offer this as their final gift. It's also, therefore, a reminder that we are always standing on the shoulders of those who have gone before

---

[2] I'd been doing my homework.

us, that no matter what we achieve we owe a debt of gratitude to those who led the way.

'In many respects, 'The Wisdom of The Village" is the opposite of the scientific approach. It's not driven by a desire to understand how something works, but rather to simply identify what works and to use that in daily life.

'From my simple perspective, many scientists – especially those like yourself who study how human beings function and interact, how we learn, change and grow, how we perform at our best and, sometimes, get in our own way, - are explaining the underpinning systems, mechanisms and processes of "The Wisdom of The Village". You are teaching us why things work.'

'Do you think, then, that science has now replaced this older approach?'

'No. It one sense it never will, because we are talking about the difference between subjective and objective experience. Also, we might say everything that happens in our world that we don't fully understand – everything that works and remains as yet unexplained - can be seen as aspects of "The Wisdom of The Village". And science continues to explore them for us.'

I understood exactly what Chris was saying. I also understand that one factor critical to success is collaboration. It was only halfway through lunch and I was already wondering how I could turn this first meeting into a meaningful, long-term collaboration. I was sure we had much more in common than Chris appreciated. I was confident we could do some useful work together – and have fun doing it. At that moment I just didn't know what form that work would take.

It didn't take long to find out. Our conversation moved on a pace. By the end of lunch, we had agreed to begin our work together by writing this book. We agreed the title, created an outline of the contents, and settled on three commitments that would serve as the book's very foundation. These are:

The commitment to share with you the work of leading scientists and researchers in the hope that this book will not only help you, the reader, to understand and manage your brain better, but will also play a role in promoting the importance of on-going brain-related research. There are no absolutes in science; knowledge and understanding are always being developed and we aim to acknowledge and support this.

The commitment to use a structure and style that makes the science and associated content engaging, informative and motivational. After all, for science to be truly influential it has to be shared in ways that make it easily understandable to the rest of us, making clear how the lessons it offers can be used to enhance our lives.

The commitment to providing you with a practical, personal-to-you brain management Process in which we will:

1. Provide specific recommendations, introducing certain behaviors we urge you to incorporate in your daily life
2. Provide choices, giving you a range of options to select from based on your own needs and starting point
3. Provide direction beyond the book, highlighting various sources including technology that will further your understanding and/or increase your ability to manage your wellbeing.

I work primarily with elite performers in different domains, however I realized talking to Chris that we could write a book everyone can benefit from; a book that will help us all squeeze every drop of the-best-we-can-be out of this process we call Living.

You see, it doesn't matter who you are, how old you are, or how you spend your life, your brain always wins. And you can improve your life experience in all aspects by knowing how to fuel, rest and stimulate your brain in the most positive of ways, and how to avoid mismanaging it.

In the Introduction, which is coming up next, we outline and explain the reasons for the structure and sequencing of the book, and identify the all-important component parts of our - your - brain management Process.

The Brain Always Wins

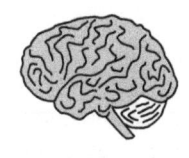

Introduction

'There is no scientific study more vital to man than the study of his own brain. Our entire view of the universe depends on it.'

Francis Crick

A winning partnership

Right now, something truly amazing is sitting above your shoulders. Not only is it truly amazing, it's all yours.

What is it?

The human brain.

Your brain.

And the great thing is as you stand or sit there now, creating meaning out of these agreed shapes we call *words*, your brain is doing the work. It's helping you to make sense of this. Just as it does everything else.

What many of us tend to forget as we go about our daily business is that the brain is the central, most important factor in all of our lives. It's our brain that allows us to function on a daily basis. It's our brain that controls the multiple independent systems within our body, and helps to shape our understanding of ourselves and the environment around us.

The human brain – our brains, *your* brain – runs our particular life-show. It influences us every step of the way. It helps us to make sense of the chaos of daily life. It plays a vital role in determining our level of physical and/or mental performance in every context. As Neil deGrasse Tyson, the American astrophysicist, emphasised, 'Everything we do, every thought we've ever had, is produced by the human brain.'

However, too often – and for too long – many have chosen to accept the myth that the human brain is so complex and mysterious that it's essentially unknowable; better, therefore, to just ignore it in favour of those other aspects of ourselves that we do have some understanding of.

Such thinking is seriously flawed.

> *Our knowledge about the brain is growing daily and at a significant rate.*

This is a really important point.

People have been studying and learning about the brain throughout history. Now we are learning more quickly than ever before. We know more than we ever have about how and why the brain always wins. We certainly know enough to be able to actively manage our relationship with it. Indeed, we know enough to say that we should prioritise this relationship.

We should, therefore, all be thankful to the dedicated academics, applied scientists, and researchers who work so hard to make this possible. We're committed to sharing their work with you and encouraging you to seek out more.

As we will explain the level and quality of our performance – in anything, from work to sport, to the management of the relationships in our personal lives and, even, how we communicate with our self! – is ultimately determined by our brain. Of course, it's important to keep other parts of our body healthy and well. However, as we'll show, by doing this we are actually *serving the brain*; giving it what it needs to run the show, *our* show, to the best of its ability.

Perhaps you have never thought of yourself as a performer before. Yet each and every day we are asked by others, or ask of ourselves, to be mentally and/or physically alert and able to perform for at least for some portion of time.

You don't need to be an elite athlete, play in a world cup match, drive on the track at Nuremberg, attempt to return a serve at 125 miles per hour or appear on stage to be a performer. When you lead a business meeting, take part in a business presentation, or share an important update with a colleague, you are performing. In fact, every time we act out our *professional self* we are performing in one way or another. Then, of course, there is also the precious time we spend with the people we love most in the world. Performance is part of being a partner or parent, of being a supporter or a soul mate. Indeed, for most of us the results and relationships we create in our personal lives are even more important than those we develop at work.

To be honest, we nearly called this book *Your Brain Always Wins* because your brain is uniquely your own. Indeed, your individuality is a result of your brain function. And, although there are some universal truths we'll share about the human brain, when it comes to optimizing performance we know that most training is only truly impactful when individuality is taken into account. That is why we're providing you with a brain management Process that provides you with everything you need to create your own customized program based on your individual needs and contexts.

The benefits of increased brain health and performance are truly significant. Not just for us as individuals, but for the societies in which we live. Through better brain management we can, for example, change the status of economies (by reducing negative health expenditure and improving output), develop the quality of our education (by applying the latest cognitive science to the learning and evaluation process of students), improve sporting performance (by assisting with training, talent identification and rest and recovery) and raise the standards of medicine and health care even higher (through targeted prevention and targeted treatments).

Conversely, the costs of getting our brain management wrong are great and take many forms. Sadly, we experience and witness examples of these all too often. Soldiers returning from war suffering from post-traumatic stress disorder, people unhappy and underperforming at work because of inappropriate negative stress, students limited in their learning by nervousness, self-doubt or fear, economies losing literally billions of dollars every year due to physical and mental illnesses that limit productivity and demand costly resources.

So, you might ask, if the brain always wins how is it that we can experience such pain and negativity?

The answer relates to the brain's dominant role in determining how we perform in every aspect of our life and its primary purpose in ensuring our survival.

We use the phrase *the brain always wins* as a reminder that it's our brain that ultimately determines how we feel, think and behave. It drives our ability to avoid or manage threats to our wellbeing, solve problems, and adapt. It does this by responding to the stimuli – the feedback - we present. Inevitably, if our interpretation of a situation is flawed then our response will also be flawed. If, for example, we constantly perceive threats where none exist our brain will automatically shift us into flight or fight mode, and it will keep us there until we can acknowledge our safety. In this respect our brain is *winning*. It is governing how we are feeling and acting based on the stimuli it is receiving, on our perceived needs.

That's why we need a Process to manage our relationship with our brain well, to ensure brain health and performance. Science teaches us that if we get our brain management right, we are far more likely to get everything else right.

Our brain is what separates us from every other living thing on Earth. It is the most amazing organ we are aware of. It has enough computing power to put most super computers to shame. It is made up of 100 billion neurons. It is only 3% of our overall weight and yet consumes 30% of our calories at rest and 50% of our daily oxygen intake! It does this without asking. It fuels itself without our conscious awareness. It is amazing and complex. Yet, despite its complexity, there are three vitally important things we do know for certain:

1. The human brain – our brains, *your* brain – is the most amazing thing on planet Earth.
2. If you want to perform optimally and repeatedly, you need to know how to make the most of this most amazing thing.
3. There are things we can do deliberately to achieve this. There are ways we can manage our brain that both support brain health and enable us to perform repeatedly at our physical and mental best.

Although we still have much to learn about the human brain, we do now know enough to enter into a deliberate and successful working partnership with what Professor Michio Kaku calls 'the most complicated object in the known universe'.

We can become partners with our brain in a way that once, not too long ago, would have been impossible. Now we have scientific evidence that proves it is possible to manage brain health and performance and to identify and measure the outcomes. We also know that doing this creates the most positive results.

Better yet, this works for everyone not just those seeking to be the elite in a particular domain. We can all play a conscious role in supporting what until relatively recently has been only a subconscious process.

This book will teach you how. That's why it's here. This is how it works:

Building blocks, skipping and the opportunity to take what you need when you need it

This book is designed with you and your brain – specifically how your brain works – in mind.

We make learning easier by engaging with your brain in the way it most naturally works. So we have written a summary at the start and end of each chapter. This will prime your memory and engage your brain with regard to the take away messages each chapter contains. We also include:

- Illustrations that are detailed for easy exploration
- Quotes that highlight key points
- A wide range of practical activities

The chapters are ordered as independent building blocks. If you wish to start at the beginning and work your way through the book in the usual, linear fashion, we provide a clear route. Yet if skipping around the book is the way forward (and maybe sometimes the way backwards) for you, the content and sequencing will still work.

Next, we introduce you to your brain. We explain its structure and function and, importantly, the role it plays in governing everything we do. In the main body of the book, we address each aspect of our brain management Process and highlight the value of combining them. The Process incorporates:

Physical activity
Rest and recovery
Optimal nutrition
Cognitive training
Emotional management
Socialization
Synergy.

Each chapter is divided into two parts. In the first part we provide essential knowledge, giving you an overview of the associated science and relevant influencing factors. In the second part we provide the training, making specific recommendations before giving you options to choose from.

Too often health and performance programs adopt a 'one size fits all' approach. However, we know that we are all in many ways unique; we have different starting points, different ways of learning and operating and different end goals. It follows, then, that although there may be certain principles or practices that benefit us all, we also need the guided freedom necessary to create our own personal Process for success. This is why, although we are prescriptive at times, we provide a wide range of activities and resources for you to choose from based on your understanding of yourself, your lifestyle, your values and your purpose.

Although each aspect of the Process can be addressed and managed independently, and benefits will be realized by improving any one, we encourage you to think and act systemically. The Process is interactive and synergistic in nature. We experience the best results, therefore, by ensuring that eventually we develop all aspects.

The Nobel Prize-winning Scientist and Educator, Santiago Ramon y Cajal wrote, 'Any man could, if he were so inclined, be the sculptor of his own brain.'

If you are so inclined keep reading and, no matter what other skills you have, we will help you to become a proficient brain-sculptor! The process is both enlightening and fun. The reward is great. It's the quality of your life.

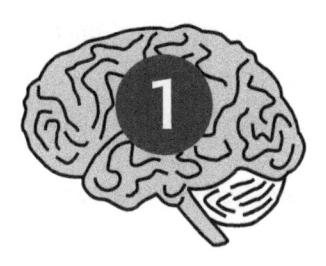

The Governor

'Your brain is the command and control center of your body.'

Daniel Amen.

Brain Priming – This chapter in focus

Here are the key facts and messages:

- Your brain is the result of millions of years of evolution – and it continues to evolve.
- Your brain is a collection of billions of inter-connected neurons working together.
- The average human brain weighs three pounds.
- The average adult brain at rest consumes 30% of all calories taken in.
- The average infant brain consumes 64% of all calories.
- 50% of all oxygen is used by the brain.

- Both the structure and function of the brain is important.
- There are seven sections or lobes and two sides of the brain.
- Information is processed by our feelings first and then by our thoughts.
- Management of emotion is critical to resiliency and decision making.
- Brain function governs every aspect of your life.
- Your brain always wins.

It's all about the connections

Our brain governs everything we do. Like every governor, our brain's power comes from its network and associated connections. Like every governor it fulfils its role best when it's given the support it most values. We will talk about how to support it in later chapters. Right now get ready to be introduced to your brain. We'll begin with its evolution and anatomy.

The human brain has been around for a very long time. Not only has it been around for a very long time, it has been evolving throughout. Over almost seven million years the human brain has tripled in size. Along the way it has developed its structure and functions. Our modern-day brains have 100 Billion neurons, 100,000 km of interconnections and 1 quadrillion connections wired within. They are big numbers. There is a heck of a lot of zeros involved – in the way that creates a quantity that is, for most of us, unimaginable.

The human brain has evolved because of its limitations and the ever-changing environmental stresses our ancestors encountered. As they developed they needed to process more and more information and store it for learning. In that respect they were exactly the same as us. In our modern world we too must be able to use our big brains to keep improving the quality of our lives and to keep up with the changes that are always happening around us.

Thankfully our brains were designed to adapt and grow, enabling us to connect, problem solve, and grow more resilient. Indeed, the work of physicist Dmitri Krioukov and his colleagues reveals that the structure of the human brain has evolved to the point where it has an almost ideal network of connections. Our brain is optimally efficient, capable of using the smallest number of connections necessary to create the best possible output.

Here's just a quick overview of how our brain has evolved throughout our history:

Human Brain Evolution

Date	Characteristics	Brain size
4-2.75 million years ago	Our most recent ancestor – Australo-pithecus afarensis. The remains are known as Lucy.	380-450cc
3-1.6 million years ago	Australopithecus africannus	380-450cc
2.3-1.3 million years ago	Australopithecus africannus	500-600cc
1.8-1 million years ago	Homo erectus	800-1300cc
200,00-300,00 years ago	Homo sapiens	1350cc
100,00-40,00 years ago	Neanderthals	1500cc
35,000 years ago	Cro-magnon	1600cc

Human brain evolution

Over time humans have evolved one of the largest brains relative to body size of any living animal, with an average brain volume about four times that of our closest cousins, Chimpanzees. In addition, crucial organizational differences further distinguish humans from Chimps.

The illustrations on the following page provides a brain anatomy comparison between similarly scaled endocasts of a human, a chimpanzee and 2 members of the hominid family, Australopithecine: Australopithecus sediba and Australopithecus africanus. The former lived in southern Africa between 1.98 and 1.977 million years ago. The latter lived in southern Africa between 3.3 and 2.1 million years ago and was the first early ape-form species to be classified as a hominin – the group made up of modern humans, extinct human species and our immediate ancestors.

An endocast is simply a cast made of the cranial vault. It shows the size and shape of the brain and is often used in the study of brain development.

The top illustration provides an inferior view of the endocasts. You will see that the orbitofrontal organization in the Au. sediba endocast resembles the human condition more closely than do the Au. africanus endocasts.

The bottom panel provides a left lateral view of the same endocasts, enabling you to notice similarities in surface configuration of australopithecines and chimpanzees.Note similarities in surface configuration of australopithecines and chimpanzees.

Just as our brain has evolved, so has our understanding of it. The first known writing about the brain dates back to 4000BC. Since then we have learnt a tremendous amount about the brain, how it functions and the essential role it plays in shaping our lives.

Human

Au. africanus
(Sts 5)

Au. sediba

Au. africanus
(Sts 60)

Chimpanzee

Human

Au. africanus
(Sts 5)

Au. sediba

Au. africanus
(Sts 60)

Chimpanzee

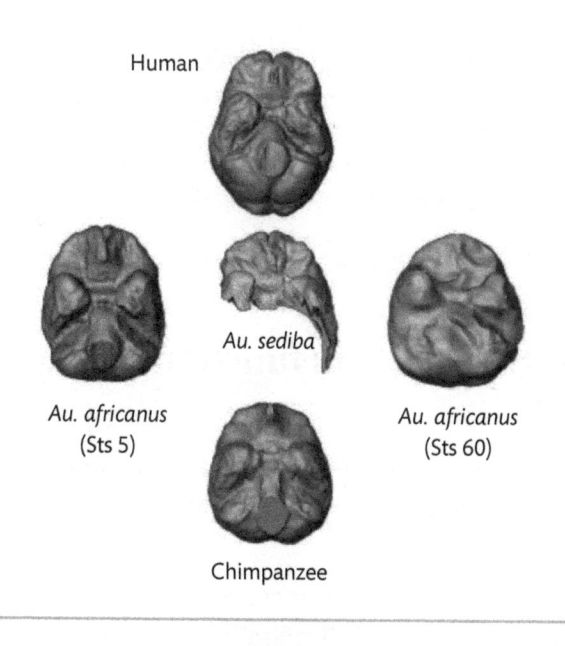

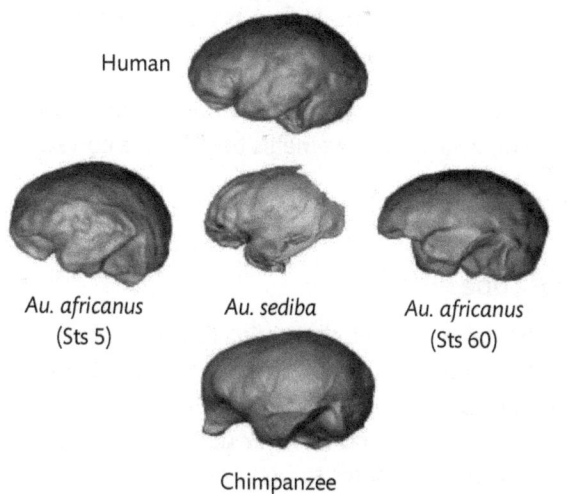

Taken from http://www.esrf.eu/UsersAndScience/Publications/
Highlights/2011/imaging/ima7]

As the 20th century has progressed the study of the nervous system – neuroscience - has come to be acknowledged as an academic discipline in its own right. As with so many other topics of study, our knowledge and understanding of our all-controlling, brilliant brain has grown – and is growing - rapidly.

Given that, we are going to introduce you to the governor:

The structure and functions of our brain

There are two sides of the brain and seven sections, or lobes. As we will see shortly, both the structure and function of the brain are important.

Like all governors, your brain is protected. Your skull (or cranium) plays a very obvious role in this regard. Next is the dura. It's the first of three layers of membrane known as the meninges that surround the brain and spinal cord.

The outermost layer of brain cells is known as the cortex. All of our thinking and voluntary movements begin in the cortex.

Your brain is structured like this:

Frontal Lobe

This is the front part of the brain, located right behind your forehead. It controls planning, organizing, critical thinking and the attention process. It also interacts with other areas of the brain to process both emotion and complex decision-making. The frontal lobe is vital when it comes to brain health and optimization. So we'll explore this area in more depth later in the book.

Brain diagram with labels: Cortex, Cranium, Parietal Lobe, Occipital Lobe, Frontal Lobe, Temporal Lobe, Basal Ganglia, Brain Stem, Spinal Cord, Cerebellum, Dura.

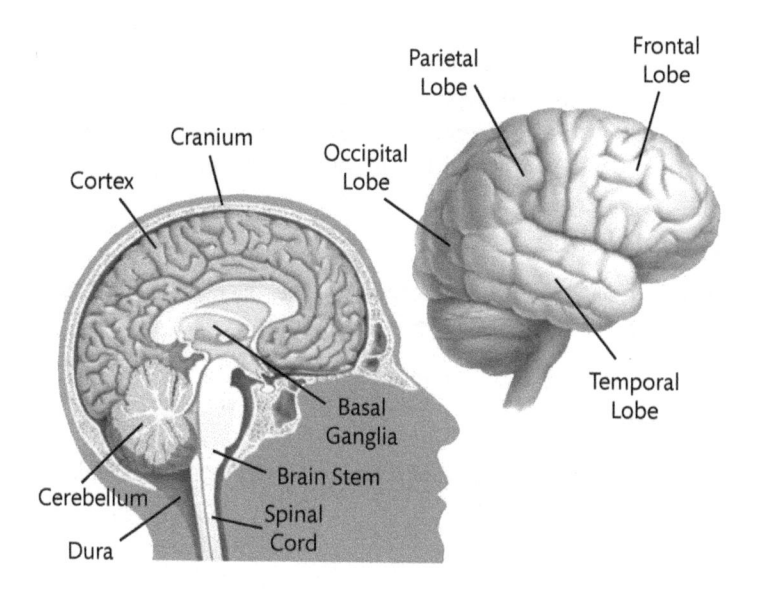

Parietal Lobe

The parietal lobe is found just behind the frontal lobe at the top of the brain. It's divided into 2 sections. The right parietal lobe manages visual spatial information, enabling us to navigate our way from place to place. The left parietal lobe facilitates our ability to use language.

These two sections also coordinate the primary sensory cortex, which controls sensations such as touch and pressure. Near the primary sensory cortex is an area that controls fine sensation. This allows us to judge texture, weight and size of items, and shape.

Temporal Lobe

This has two sides and is located just above your ears. The right temporal lobe is essential for our visual memory, being able to remember faces, places and pictures for example. The left temporal lobe assists with verbal memory, enabling us to remember such things as words and people's names. These areas also allow us to make sense of different smells and sounds, and to sort new information, as well as assisting in short-term memory.

Occipital Lobe

This part of your brain is located at the back and is primarily responsible for our visual processing systems.

Cerebellum

Also found in the back of your brain, this is responsible for balance and muscle coordination.

Brainstem

This is where the spinal cord first interacts with the brain. Its primary functions include breathing, digestion, heart rate, blood pressure, and alertness.

Basal ganglia

This is a cluster of structures in the center of your brain that coordinates messages between multiple other brain areas. It's involved in the formation of habits. The following diagram shows some of the key roles and responsibilities of different parts of your brain:

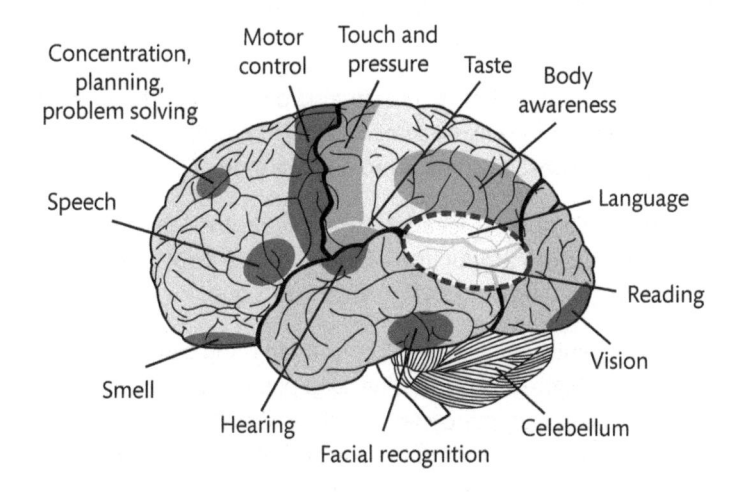

Example from: http://ipwebdev.com/hermit/brain.html

A brain in 3 parts

Our brain consists of the following 3 regions:

1. The forebrain
2. The midbrain
3. The hindbrain.

1) The forebrain

The forebrain is made up of the limbic system, the thalamus, the hypothalamus, the basal ganglia, and the cerebral cortex. We'll be discussing the limbic system in a minute and, as we've already mentioned the basal ganglia,[1] we'll now introduce the other elements.

The thalamus is a small structure situated on top of the brain stem. It relays motor and sensory information to the cerebral cortex. It also regulates consciousness, sleep and alertness.

The hypothalamus is located just below the thalamus. It's responsible for the production of many of our body's hormones and acts to maintain our physiological status quo.

The most recently evolved part of our brain is the cerebral cortex. It's where our high-level processing takes place. Looking something like crumpled paper, the cortex is a thin layer of tissue that caps most of the brain. The part of the cortex that covers the cerebrum is known as the cerebral cortex. It's often referred to as grey matter because the nerves here do not have the insulation that makes the other parts of the brain appear white.[2]

The cerebral cortex is made up of bulges and furrows. The bulges are called gyri and the furrows, sulci. This folded structure adds to the overall surface area and so increases the amount of *grey matter*. This, in turn, allows for more information to be processed.

2) The midbrain

Situated between the forebrain and the hindbrain, the midbrain relays information between the two. It's the smallest of the 3 regions of the brain and is made up of the tegmentum at the front and the tectum at the rear. The midbrain serves an important role in motor movement, particularly that of the eyes, and in auditory

---

[1] And we will again in Chapter 5.

[2] That's why these other parts are referred to as *white matter*.

and visual processing. It's also involved in the regulation of sleep, alertness and body temperature.

3) The hindbrain

This is situated at the rear of the brain and is the lowest part. It incorporates the medulla, the cerebellum, the pons and the brain stem.

The medulla is the place where our spinal cord enters our skull. It's responsible for helping us maintain our upright posture and for controlling breathing. It's also important in regulating reflexes.

The cerebellum is found beside the medulla. It is thought to play a role in such cognitive functions as attention and language, and is also significantly involved in coordinating, but not initiating, movement.

The pons is situated above the medulla and below the midbrain. It acts as a bridge connecting different parts of the brain including the cerebellum and cerebrum. It also plays a part in some of our automatic and essential functions such as breath control, and is thought to be associated with the control of sleep patterns.

The brain stem sits at the base of the brain and connects to the spinal cord. This connection allows the flow of messages between the brain and the rest of the body. The brain stem is the oldest part of the brain and consists of the midbrain, pons, and medulla oblongata.

The limbic system

It's situated deep within the temporal lobe and is primarily responsible for the nature and quality of our emotional responses.

The limbic system, as shown below, is a complex set of structures that includes the hypothalamus, the hippocampus, the amygdala, and several nearby areas.

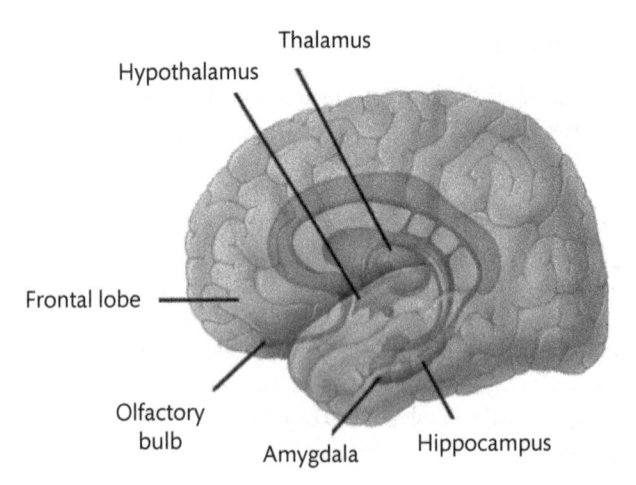

The limbic system receives information from the spinal cord. This information is processed by the amygdala, a small walnut-sized node. The amygdala is the relay station for emotional processing and, as such, is critically involved with our wellbeing and our decision-making. It has the power to protect us by detecting environmental and internal changes and informing our next actions. Although our brain has incredible capabilities that make it all too easy to describe it in the terms we reserve for super-technology, the truth is that because of the amygdala we feel before we think. We are emotional beings.

It is only *after* the amygdala has processed information that our Frontal Lobe, particularly the pre-frontal cortex, comes into play enabling us to make higher-order decisions.

So, you might ask, how does *my* brain process information? How does it make these connections? The answer is because of the incredible basic building blocks of our nervous system known as neurons.

Neurons

A neuron is a cell that uses both electrical and chemical signals to transfer information. Your brain has lots of them. Professor S. Ramachandran[3] explains it thus, 'There are 100 billion neurons in the adult human brain, and each neuron makes something like 1,000 to 10,000 contacts with other neurons in the brain. Based on this, people have calculated that the number of permutations and combinations of brain activity exceeds the number of elementary particles in the universe.'

We are back to numbers that for most of us are beyond comprehension. And we are back to the importance of connections. Each of our 100 billion neurons acts as a sender and receiver of information; they enable the brain to communicate throughout our body.

Neurons look like this:

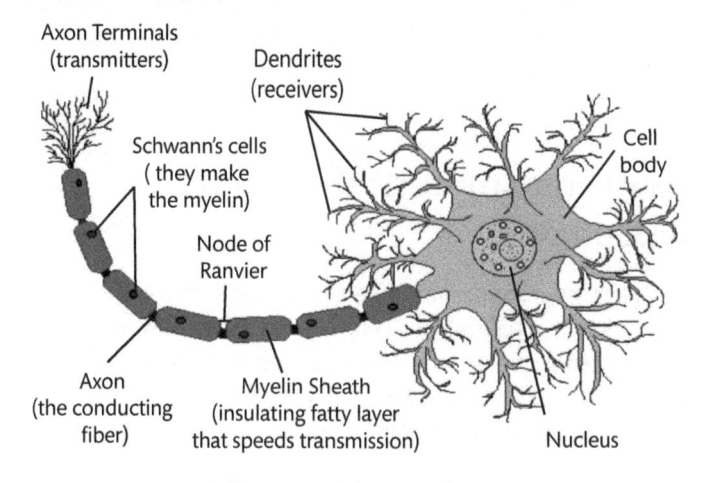

Example from: www.enchantedlearning.com

---

[3] Professor in the Department of Psychology and the Graduate Program in Neurosciences at the University of California, San Diego and Director of the Center for Brain and Cognition affiliated with the UC San Diego Department of Psychology.

A typical neuron possesses a cell body (known as the soma), dendrites, and an axon. Dendrites are thin structures that branch out from the soma. They can extend for hundreds of micrometres and develop multiple branches, creating in effect what looks like a 'dendritic tree'. An axon is a singular cellular extension that may travel for as far one meter in humans and even further in some other species! Although each soma only ever gives rise to one axon, that axon may branch hundreds of times before it ends.

Neurons use electro-chemical signals to move information from one neuron to another. These signals between neurons occur via synapses, specialized connections with other cells. Each synapse contains a small gap separating neurons.

Here's how the system works: dendrites receive messages from other neurons. The message then moves through the axon to the other end of the neuron, then to the tips of the axon and then into the space between neurons. From there the message can move to the next neuron. This transmission occurs because of the neurotransmitters in our brain.

Neurotransmitters: the brain's messengers

Simply put, neurotransmitters are the chemicals that communicate information throughout our central nervous system (comprising the brain and spinal cord) and our peripheral nervous system (made up of those nerves which leave the brain and spinal cord and travel to certain areas of the body).

Neurotransmitters send information that's necessary for us to perform everything from our most basic movements to our most complex functions, including our physical activity, decision-making, task completion, concentration, and mood state. Consequently, our brains must be dosed neurotransmitters every millisecond of every day. W part of the process breaks down we see mild to p disorders and nervous system dysfunctions, including depression, anxiety, autism, attention difficulties, schizophrenia, Alzheimer's disease, and epilepsy.

Neurotransmitters are released from a neuron at the presynaptic nerve terminal. They then move across the synapse to a specific site in the next neuron, known as a receptor.

There are two kinds of neurotransmitters: excitatory and inhibitory. Excitatory neurotransmitters stimulate the brain and inhibitory transmitters calm the brain. Inhibitory neurotransmitters act to balance our mood when the excitatory neurotransmitters are active.

Inhibitory neurotransmitters include the following:

Serotonin

Apart from balancing any excessive excitatory neurotransmitter, serotonin also regulates many other processes such as cravings for carbohydrates, our sleep cycle, pain control and digestion. Serotonin levels can be depleted by the continued use of stimulant medications or caffeine. Low levels are associated with decreased immune system function.

GABA

This is often referred to as 'nature's Valium-like substance'. Whenever an excitatory neurotransmitter is firing too often in the brain, GABA is released in an attempt to balance this over-firing.

Excitatory neurotransmitters include the following:

Dopamine

This is considered to be both excitatory and inhibitory. Dopamine enables us to focus and is also responsible for our drive or desire to get things done. Stimulants such as medications for ADD/ADHD and caffeine cause dopamine to be pushed into the synapse so that focus is improved. Unfortunately, stimulating dopamine consistently can cause its depletion over time.

Norepinephrine

This is responsible for stimulatory processes in the body. Consequently, low levels of norepinephrine are associated with low energy, poor focus, and sleep cycle problems. Norepinephrine also helps to make epinephrine:

Epinephrine

This regulates our heart rate and blood pressure. Elevated levels of epinephrine can cause feelings of anxiety; long term stress or insomnia can cause epinephrine levels to be depleted.

We know so much about neurotransmitters and their vital role in brain function because of the collaborative efforts of many scientists including Henry Dale, Otto Loewi, Wilhelm Feldberg and Walter Cannon working together to solve the difficult mysteries of the brain.

The following diagram highlights the relationship between some of the neurotransmitters mentioned and our performance:

Scientists have also discovered that some specific neurons fire not only when a person, or animal, performs a movement but also when they see the movement being performed by another. These are known as mirror neurons.

Venn diagram of three overlapping circles: Norepinephrine, Serotonin, and Dopamine.

- **Norepinephrine**: Alertness, Concentration, Energy
- **Serotonin**: Obsessions & Compulsions, Memory
- **Dopamine**: Pleasure, Reward, Motivation/Drive
- **Norepinephrine ∩ Serotonin**: Anxiety, Impulse, Irritability
- **Norepinephrine ∩ Dopamine**: Attention
- **Serotonin ∩ Dopamine**: Appetite, Sex, Aggression
- **All three**: Mood Cognitive Function

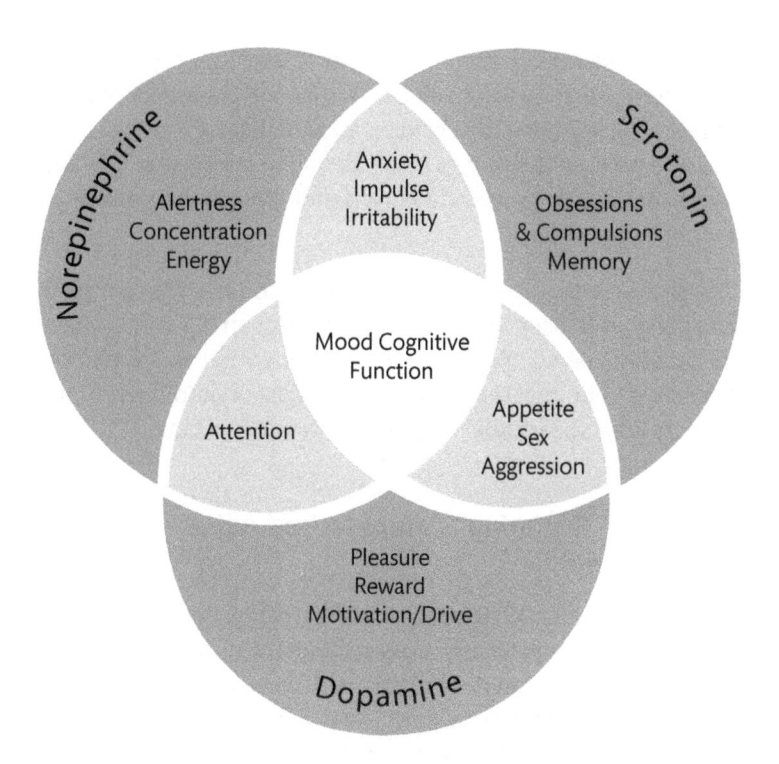

Mirror neurons

In humans, mirror neurons are believed to exist in different parts of the brain including the premotor cortex and the motor area both of which are in the frontal lobe, and the somatosensory cortex located in the parietal lobe. Mirror neurons may be important for understanding the actions of other people, and for learning new skills by imitation. They might also play a role in helping us to connect with others emotionally. Research has shown that the same area of the brain is activated both when we make a particular facial expression and when we see another person make that expression. Such findings lead some to argue that mirror neurons are the neural basis for our ability to feel empathy towards others.

Given the incredible complexity and capability of the human brain, it's no surprise that it has taken us literally thousands of years to reach the level of understanding about it that we now have. But how are we able to know so much about the brain's structure and associated functions, about neurons and the way information is shared and processed?

The answer is that it is certainly not down to luck. We can thank engineers and neuro-physicists for the fact that we now have technology that enables us to see and study what we have never been able to before. Here is a brief introduction into some of the primary ways we are able to gain insights into our brain:

CAT, or CT, Scanning (Computerized Axial Tomography)

Developed in the 1970s this combines many two-dimensional x-ray images to generate cross-sections or three-dimensional images. CAT scans can detect brain damage and changes in brain activity measured by blood flow. The drawback to this technology is that it delivers a high dose of radiation to the subject.

EEG (electro-encephalography)

This technique allows us to see the electrical impulses across the surface of the brain and observe changes over time. This is important because the different states we experience, such as being calm or focused, or awake or asleep, all have specific electrical patterns. This method allows us, then, to observe these states and their associated brain activity. As the necessary equipment has become much smaller over time, it can now be worn during activity. Its major drawback as a technique of measurement is that it can only provide surface readings; it cannot show the structures and anatomy of the brain in complete action.

ECoG (Electrocorticography) or iEEG (Intracranial EEG)

This involves placing electrodes directly on the exposed surface of the brain in order to record electrical activity from the cerebral cortex. This method increases the accuracy of the signal as the skull diffuses the electrical signal emitted in non-invasive EEG. However, for obvious reasons, this is not a procedure that is applicable in many situations.

MEG (magneto-encephalography)

MEG measures the very faint magnetic fields that emanate from the brain using coils bathed in liquid helium that are positioned over the patient's head. This method of measurement can give accurate resolution of nerve cell activity down to the millisecond. It is, however, expensive and rarely available.

MRI and fMRI (Magnetic Resonance Imaging and Functional Magnetic Resonance Imaging)

MRI scanners use strong magnetic fields and radio waves to form images of the body. fMRI adds even more detail showing blood flow changes in different areas of the brain. This procedure is highly favored because it does not require the subject to go through surgery or be exposed to radiation.

PET (Positron Emission Tomography)

PET scans allow us to see blood flow throughout the brain through the injection of a small quantity of radioactive glucose. Since brain cells use glucose as fuel, cells that are more active consume more of the radioactive glucose and are thus highlighted. This technique enables the study of cross-sectional slices deep in the brain that earlier measurement techniques could not provide.

SPECT (Single Photon Emission Computed Tomography)

SPECT scans like PET imaging use an injection of radioactive glucose and can provide 3D information presented as cross-sectional slices. Generally, SPECT radioactive injections last longer, giving the imaging team more opportunity to perform longer tests.

DTI (Diffusion Tensor Imaging)

DTI is a variation of MRI, using radio-frequency to track movement of water in the brain, enabling a clear picture to develop of axons and complex networks of nerve fibers.

It is these pioneering techniques and others that have brought us to our current understanding of the human brain. And the research is continual, collaborative and endless.

Here are just some examples:

1) Studies using PET and MRI brain scanning technology have shown that new neural cells and neural pathways are generated throughout life. This ability, for the brain to reorganize itself by forming new neural connections, is known as *neuroplasticity*. It was once believed that the human brain could not generate new neural cells and that it was unable to create new neural pathways. The realization that this was wrong was a significant breakthrough.

Neuroplasticity occurs in response to a variety of stimuli. For example, when practicing a new skill new neural connections are created in the brain as synapses that don't usually fire together do, enabling us to develop the required ability. Neuroplasticity can also come to our aid in response to severe injury or illness.

Perhaps the most incredible example of this is the case of U.S Representative Gabrielle ('Gabby') Giffords who, on January 8th

2011, was shot during a meeting held in a supermarket parking lot in Tucson, Arizona.

Gabby was shot in the back of her head with a 9mm bullet at point-blank range. The bullet travelled through her brain, exiting through her forehead. It was the type of injury that few survive. Gabby did. However, because the bullet passed through her left hemisphere it damaged her speech and language production. Gabby's medical team made the most of her brain's inherent neuroplasticity by encouraging her to sing rather than attempt to talk. As the brain's right hemisphere is recruited more for music than for language this engaged different neural networks and over time enabled her to regain many of her previous abilities.

Gabby's story is a powerful illustration of how the brain compensates for damage by forming new communications between intact neurons. It's a reminder too of its incredible capacity for growth, protection and resiliency.

As our understanding of neuroplasticity grows, so does our understanding of how to improve the quality of our life.

2) A team of neuroscientists and bioengineers at the University of Colorado Anschutz Medical Campus have created a miniature, fiber-optic microscope enabling them to see deeply inside the brain of animals as they roam freely and respond to various stimuli. Consequently, deeper parts of the living brain like the amygdala, which have been virtually off-limits to microscopes, will soon be seen in a real-time, high-resolution, 3-D image!

3) Researchers at the Max Planck Institute for Biological Cybernetics (Germany), VU University Amsterdam (Netherlands) and Max Planck Florida Institute for Neuroscience (USA) have succeeded in developing 3D modelling that provides unprecedented insight into how neurons within and across the sensory cortex are interconnected.

The British computer scientist, Sir Charles Antony Richard Hoare (commonly known as Tony) highlights this need for collaboration in his acknowledgement that, 'A computer program that throws light on the mind/brain problem will have to incorporate the deepest insights of biologists, nerve scientists, psychologists, physiologists, linguists, social scientists, and even philosophers.'

Now, though, it's time to move on from collaboration and talk about:

The brain and prediction

Neuroscientists are increasingly talking about the human brain as an advanced prediction machine. Research is suggesting that the brain doesn't just passively receive and classify information from our senses; rather it is continuously using that information to predict what is going to happen next and what behaviors and responses are most likely to be successful.

Through a process that some refer to as *predictive coding* our brain adapts in response to experience, making increasingly detailed predictions as our expectations are met and, importantly, when they are not. Errors lead to new predictions, new learning and fundamental changes in our brain. Writing more than 50 years ago W. Ross Ashby, the British psychiatrist and cyberneticist, stated, 'The whole function of the brain is summed up in: error correction.' It seems he was right. Our brain is working continually to determine the causes from the effects we experience and so limit the degree of surprise or unpredictability we encounter as we go about our daily lives.

This process is influenced by more than just sensory input. Our perception[4] is inevitably directed and affected by our current

---

[4] More about perception in Chapter 5.

beliefs, biases and past experience. It is only when these are challenged, when there are failures in prediction that information is processed higher up the neural hierarchy and our expectations are revised.

This ability to predict accurately and adapt as necessary plays an essential part in our success as individuals, communities and as a species. It's another example of the awesome nature of the governor.

Talking of which, let's end this chapter by considering the challenges we face when seeking to find the right words to describe the brain's incredible capability.

Talking about the brain

Our brain – *your* brain – is far more than the source of our intellect and rational thinking. Which is why, of course, we are far more than just the nature and capability of our intellect. We are physical, emotional, intuitive, *complex*. As author John Green notes, 'The vast majority of us imagine ourselves as like literature people or math people. But the truth is that the massive processor known as the human brain is neither a literature organ or a math organ. It is both and more.'

Which is why, perhaps, we find ourselves drawn to explain what we know about the brain by comparing it to high performance objects we have created.[5] It is why it is easy to compare it to a super computer. Or, in John's case, to a high performance car. Not surprisingly, he is a car enthusiast. If you heard a man drawn to make what are useful and relevant comparisons between the

---

[5] Objects we have created, of course, by using the same brain we are trying to explain.

human brain and a super car, you would find it easy to guess that he was at once a neuroscientist and a petrol-head, right?

In one of our very first conversations, John said to me, 'Chris, when you've got a few spare minutes take a good look at a Hennessey Venom GT or a Koenigsegg Agera R. You will see examples of what we all imagine when we think of fast cars. They are sleek, with a low profile. They even look fast when they are standing still! A super-fast, super car is a good comparison in some ways to our brain as nerve impulses travel to and from the brain at speeds of 268 miles per hour with more than 100,000 chemical reactions happening in the human brain every second!

'What is even more impressive is the way our brain manages to maintain its energy, balance, and peak capabilities. A fast car is only as good as its fuel, oil, and set-up – its center of balance and suspension. The brain, however, needs very little, but what it does need must be provided relatively consistently. In fact, the brain can make energy out of pastries as well as whole grains. We both know that not all calories are of equal value, but the fact is that the brain can produce in suboptimal situations. That's pretty impressive, right? '

'Yes, John. But I do have one question.'

'Which is?'

'How do you spell Koenigsegg...?'

The truth is that once we move away from the scientific language that describes and explains the human brain, we run the risks of creating misunderstanding and misinterpretation. Too often words that are easier to say, like 'super car' instead of 'Koenigsegg', become part of our common parlance simply because they are easier to manage and, too often, they bring with them misunderstandings that negatively affect both thinking and behavior.

John experienced what is, for him, a quite common example of this at a Sport Performance Conference recently when colleagues began talking to him about muscle memory. As John explained, 'The phrase is incorrectly used to describe the acquisition of motor movements and coordination, complex or otherwise. It's incorrect because muscles don't have memory. They are completely controlled by the brain and more specifically the cerebellum. So when talking about the muscle coordination of novice practitioners we should refer to immature motor patterns. And we should say that those who have mastered skills have mature motor patterns and coordination.

'These descriptions are not as sexy as muscle memory but notice the differences between the two. Muscle memory falsely leads you to believe that all you have to do is repeat certain movements over and over and then the skill will be acquired, which is not even partly true. Movements need to be repeated but not endlessly. As far as the brain is concerned, more is not better – better is better. The brain likes efficiency. If overtrained it gets dull and weaker. Along with it so do other sub systems, for example the cardiac and neuromuscular systems.

'This difference in terminology is significant because one emphasizes a process that seems like magic and the other a thoughtful process of working with the brain and learning. This is just one more example of how we distance ourselves from the actual truth that the brain matters. We have to ensure we avoid language that ignores or limits the brain's influence or that restricts our curiosity about it. Unwrap the brain and you have solutions, keep it closed and we end up with mysteries.'

Our purpose in this book is to unwrap the brain in ways that offer solutions to the problems we all face about maintaining or enhancing our wellbeing and performance.

We will end this part of the chapter as promised with a reminder of the summary we began with. Then we'll move on to Physical activity – the **P** in our brain management Process.

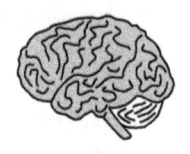

Summary

- Your brain is the result of millions of years of evolution – and it continues to evolve.
- Your brain is collection of billions of inter-connected neurons working together.
- The average human brain weight three pounds.
- The average adult brain at rest consumes 30% of all calories taken in.
- The average infant brain consumes 64% of all calories.
- 50% of all oxygen is used by the brain.
- Both the structure and function of the brain is important.
- There are seven sections or lobes and two sides of the brain.
- Information is processed by our feelings first and then by our thoughts.
- Management of emotion is critical to resiliency and decision making.
- Brain function governs every aspect of your life.
- Your brain always wins.

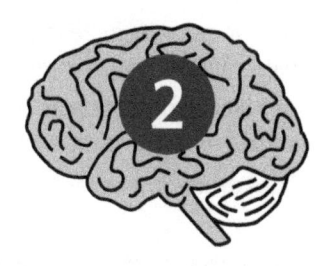

Physical activity

'Those who do not find time for exercise will have to find time for illness.'

Edward Smith-Stanley

Brain Priming – Chapter in focus

Here are the key facts and messages:

- Our brains were built for moving – from 5 to12 miles a day!
- Physical activity enables the creation of new connections throughout our central nervous system and restores and repairs existing connections.
- To improve your emotional management and thinking skills, *move*.
- Aerobic activity just twice a week halves your risk of general dementia and reduces your risk of Alzheimer's by 60%.

- Enhancing your aerobic capacity increases your ability to deal with stress – ultimately improving your resiliency.
- Physical activity gets blood to your brain, bringing it oxygen and glucose for energy, stimulating recovery and healing.
- Keeping fit stimulates proteins that keep neurons connecting over and over.
- Physical activity improves your memory capacity, memory recall, decision-making and overall processing speed.
- Regular physical activity is one of the principle factors in maintaining so-called mental toughness.

Made to move

We chose the chapter title Physical Activity rather than Physical Exercise so we can differentiate between the two and emphasize the importance of the former.

Your brain needs *movement*, any sort of physical activity that increases blood flow, because this increases the amounts of oxygen and glucose in the brain, which, in turn, enables the brain to grow and heal. The concept of physical activity includes, but is not restricted to, all types of formal exercise and sport.

People who, through the nature of their work, or other daily routines are physically active inevitably need to do less additional exercising than those who are more sedentary. Simply put, the more physical activity you do during the day, the less formal exercising you need to undertake.

Although so many people around the world have lapsed into a sedentary lifestyle, in evolutionary terms this is still abnormal behavior. As our hunter-gatherer ancestors demonstrated, we were made to move. Our capacity to sustain and grow was determined by our ability to walk anything from nine to fifteen kilometers or more every day.

In many modern societies this requirement no longer exists. Our hunter-gathering instincts are demonstrated in different ways, requiring different capabilities. Our brain though still needs us to be physically active. We can accommodate it by choosing the type of activity, the exercises or sports that best supplement our daily needs. Given that, as we progress through this chapter, we will use the terms *activity* and *exercise* interchangeably.

So the message is that movement however it is achieved – whether it is through formal exercising or not - is vital for our wellbeing. It is a message we have probably all heard many times before. Despite that, the evidence suggests it is one many of us find easy to ignore, even though we know that a lack of relevant physical activity can result in an increased risk of any of the following:

- Accelerated aging
- Coronary heart disease
- High blood pressure
- Stroke
- Metabolic syndromes (including obesity and abnormal blood cholesterol levels)
- Diabetes
- Cancers of the breast and colon
- Mental Health related difficulties (including depression and anxiety).

We might also have heard that inactivity has become a major public health issue. In fact, such a large proportion of the world's population is inactive much research suggests the problem is of pandemic proportions!

Not surprisingly, the messages that are conveyed about exercise and activity focus on the benefits to heart and body and the avoidance of illnesses. All of which are appropriate. None of which make explicit the vital role that physical activity plays in ensuring brain health and optimization.

In this chapter we will explain to you why exercise is more about preserving and serving our brain's needs than it is about toning muscles or shrinking waistlines.

As we will show, activity and exercise serve as both healer and fuel for the brain, developing our information processing speed, our memory, our emotional management, and that elusive quality so casually referred to as 'mental toughness'.

When we fail to exercise, we fail to give the brain the stimulation it needs to maintain and develop the story of our lives. Just consider the fact that regular physical activity can reduce the risk of Alzheimer's and Vascular Dementia by up to 60%.

Indeed, the previous list of health issues are all symptoms of our brain losing capacity, rather than just weaknesses created in specific sub-systems.

If we accept that the brain is the seat of what and whom we are – the source of what makes us unique - it follows that without appropriate physical activity we are damaging this uniqueness. As human beings we are integrators of memories and these do not remain fixed, rather they grow by stimulation.

Our ability to gain or maintain on a day-to-day basis is largely based on the quantity and quality of this stimulation and, of course, our recovery cycles. Insufficient physical activity results in insufficient stimulation for our brain, with inevitable negative knock-on effects: when we don't move we lose. Without exercise our stimulation for brain growth slows and in some cases it stops altogether.

In contrast, there is overwhelming evidence that exercise produces both welfare and performance gains. For example, an analysis of more than 1,200 participants who were tracked for more than 20 years showed that those with lower fitness levels at midlife had signs of accelerated brain aging in their sixties. More recent research suggests that people who are fit in their forties seem to retain more brain volume two decades later and also perform better on decision-making tests.

Physical activity also triggers the release of influences within the brain that support continued health and growth. One such, known as BDNF, Brain-derived neurotrophic factor, also starts the chain of events that creates neuroplasticity, or neural growth. The positive effects of such a chain of events include:

- Increased production of nerve-protecting compounds.
- Improved and increased blood flow to your brain.
- Improved development and survival of neurons.
- Increased production of growth cells within the brain.

In some ways, then, exercise acts as multi-faceted medicine for our brain. It provides fuel for growth and it heals.

Hippocrates, the father of modern medicine, wrote, 'If we could give every individual the right amount of nourishment and exercise, not too little and not too much, we would have found the safest way to health.' He was right for many reasons, not least because exercise is so good for our brain.

Its impact on our memory and our ability to process information is significant.

Moving and learning

Exercise improves memory and processing speed on three levels: it optimizes our alertness, attention, and motivation. When we talk of our brain's processing speed we are referring to the rate at which we can take in information, reach a decision and then formulate an answer or response. Exercise prepares and encourages nerve cells to work and bind to one another, which is the foundation for both memory and managing new information.

The reasons why we often see an age-related decline and deceleration in information processing are not completely understood. There is some strong evidence, however, that such a decline reflects wear and tear of the brain, resulting in a slowing down of information transfer along axons.

Individual and lifestyle factors also a play a part. Risk factors include smoking, diabetes, high blood pressure, vascular issues that starve brain pathways of much needed oxygen and glucose, concussion, poor nutrition and lack of sleep.

Importantly, though, many of the individual factors are in our control.

Physical activity increases blood flow, and increased blood flow increases our cognitive capacity and our speed with both cognitive and physical processes. In fact, a person who exercises can sustain or even improve their information processing speed. This happens because by simply increasing the flow of blood, oxygen and glucose to the brain we are both enlarging the neural highway and improving its capacity and speed.

Recent research has demonstrated that after only 4 weeks of increased exercise, elderly adults experience positive brain changes resulting in improved processing speed, decision-making, and types of memory.

Indeed, exercise has such strong effects on our neuroanatomy that it is used as therapy for those diagnosed with some forms of cancer. Clinical research has established the efficacy of exercise and fitness regimes as a way of counterbalancing and counteracting the physical impairments caused both by the treatments and the cancer itself. These impairments include fatigue, functional decline, cognitive impairment, depression, and anxiety.

It isn't just in healthcare though that the benefits of exercise have been realized and applied. Several American schools experimented by having students exercise before class to see whether or not this improved their classroom performance. Not surprisingly, it did.

These findings were supported by a report presented in 2010 stating that college students who regularly engage in vigorous exercise get better grades.

Additionally, a study in Scotland looked at the relationship between physical activity levels and academic performance amongst approximately 5,000 children. When the children were eleven years old, the investigators measured the duration and intensity of their physical activity levels for periods of three to seven days, using a device called an accelerometer. They were measured again at the ages of thirteen and fifteen to sixteen. Those who demonstrated the positive effects of exercise on academic performance at the age of eleven were still doing so five years later, probably because teens who make exercise part of their day generally keep on being active.

This positive relationship between exercise and educational accomplishment was once again the source of a study in 2014, when Pivarnik, Danbert and their colleagues reviewed information obtained from 4,843 freshmen and sophomore students, and compared the Grade Point Average (GPA)/Grade Classifications of those who had purchased a membership at a fitness center with those who had not.

They found that the cumulative GPAs of those students who belonged to a fitness center were 0.13 points higher than their counterparts. Additional analyses revealed that 74% of freshmen with memberships went on to have successful sophomore semesters, compared to just 60% in the non-gym goers. The study also supports the argument that exercise helps develop the ability to manage the stress of transition and maintain or expand achievement levels.

Overall, the available research is sufficient to make those who argue for reducing time spent on physical education in schools to change their position. And to do so with the utmost haste. The qualities needed to study well – indeed, the qualities needed to do *anything* well – are dependent on brain health and optimization. For this reason, physical activity is as important in all levels of education as it is in every other aspect of our life. If leaders in education fail to understand this they are failing our children, because physical activity not only improves our ability to learn it also improves our emotional management and can even help in the treatment of serious illness.

Moving as medicine

Hippocrates recommended that, once you recognized you were not in a good emotional state, you should take a walk and if that didn't help change your mood you should take another. It's a truth that has stood the test of time. If walking isn't your thing, choose a different type of exercise. Once again, the advice echoing through the ages is, *Move!*

Physical activity is an effective way of interrupting the emotional patterns of the brain. It can ease threat responses into more manageable emotions. It releases endorphins in the brain, helping to relax the muscles and relieve tension throughout the body.

Dr. John Ratey author of the book, *Spark: The Revolutionary New Science of Exercise and the Brain (2008)* puts exercise in its rightful place – as a powerful brain intervention equal to, and in some cases more powerful than, medication. Dr Ratey states:

'Exercise isn't just about physical health and appearance. It also has a profound effect on your brain chemistry, physiology, and neuroplasticity (the ability of the brain to literally rewire itself). It affects not only your ability to think, create, and solve, but your mood and ability to lean into uncertainty, risk, judgment, and anxiety in a substantial, measurable way...'

Within *Spark*, Dr Ratey refers to a range of studies that highlight the connection between exercise and emotional control. These include:

> A 1999 Finnish study of 3,403 people that revealed those who exercised two to three times a week experienced less depression and fewer feelings of anger, stress and 'cynical distrust.'
>
> A 2004 study led by Joshua Broman-Fulks of the University of Southern Mississippi that showed students who walked at 50% of their maximum heart rates or ran on treadmills at 60% to 90% of their maximum heart rate reduced their sensitivity to anxiety.
>
> A 2006 study of 19,288 twins and their families in Holland that demonstrated those who exercised experienced less anxiety, depression and neuroticism, and were also more socially outgoing.

Further studies prove that aerobic exercise increases both the size of the prefrontal cortex and the functional interaction between the limbic system and the frontal lobe. This interaction is vitally important because the limbic system, as we discussed earlier, is the part of the brain that manages emotions and the frontal lobe is responsible for controlling our decision-making.

Furthermore, a study of 200 patients at eight memory clinics in Denmark has shown that intensive aerobic exercise can even have a positive cognitive effect in patients with Alzheimer's disease. The study found that participants who exercised for one hour, three times a week for 16 weeks improved both their mental speed and attention.

There is also significant evidence that exercise can aid in the management of cancer and that it can act as a counterbalance to the negative cognitive, emotional and physical impacts associated with the illness and its treatment. Exercise also has the added benefit of being an inexpensive, highly accessible intervention with few adverse side effects when appropriately applied.

Hugh Blair, the eighteenth century Scottish writer, proclaimed, 'Exercise is the chief source of improvements in our faculties.' Whether or not that is the case, it is certainly a most positive influence – even on that most misunderstood quality, mental toughness.

Exercise and so-called mental toughness

Exercise and what many people refer to as *mental toughness* go hand-in-hand, because exercise plays a pivotal role in the toughening process that helps develop the fortitude to keep going when times are difficult. This is why traditionally physical training has been a foundation of military and tactical training.

Having said that it's also a misused and misunderstood concept. Here's what John had to say on the subject during a New York workshop:

'Essentially I believe strongly that the term *mental toughness* has been hijacked to mean things it does not mean, to illustrate things it does not illustrate, and to be non-specific enough to be illusory to all but a few. Quite frankly, mental toughness has been a concept that, not unlike the brain itself, has been treated with some neglect over the years. Because the brain has been ignored to smaller and larger degrees, the truth of what mental toughness actually is has remained open to debate and interpretation.

'So let's be clear about it now: mental toughness is the process of training that includes stress inoculation and resiliency building through iterated stress and rest leading to an increased capacity for emotional understanding, energy maintenance, information input, and work output. Don't get this concept confused with winning and losing – mental toughness no more guarantees outcomes than having greater strength or being faster does.

'Exercise is one of the principle factors in maintaining mental toughness, because stress is the stimulus for growth whilst rest is where it all comes together. An under-rested brain and central nervous system is weakened or degraded and the more it is under-rested the more it is unable to be mentally tough. We are born mentally tough – a lack of training or too much training and inadequate rest disturbs that balance.

'Exercise is the toughening process, the work cycle, that if done correctly creates a process of stress inoculation because of the challenges that increase blood flow and glucose to the brain, refining the vitality of the wiring and rewiring of responses, and finally stimulating increased capacities emotionally and cognitively. But, let me say again, all of this stress inoculation is based upon *the rest we give our brains*. We are products of pulsation and oscillation; if we behave in a linear fashion for too long, the level of our mental toughness and the quality of our performance inevitably diminish.

'Fatigue, however, is not necessarily a completely undesired consequence of training; it is the intensity of the fatigue that is critical. If our level of fatigue is not acknowledged, observed, and managed, an overdose is applied. I use this language purposely because if we overdose on medication we have side effects and those effects impact our brain first and foremost. It is precisely the same with fatigue. Work, work, work is not an approach any of us can maintain indefinitely. Once you add in sufficient rest however you have the makings of mental –emotional –physical toughness.

'It's important to understand that training in all arenas is brain based and the interplay between training fatigue and recovery is a vital factor in attaining consistent results.

'Moving on from this, many of us have grown up believing in the truth of the phrase *no pain no gain* when it comes to physical activity or exercise. This is most especially connected to the practice of building muscle. I have to say that the notion of *no pain no gain* is more a culturally supported myth than an absolute truth.

'The belief held by many is that muscles will not grow unless they are damaged via physical activity or exercise, and that this damage then starts a cascade of events that result in the brain restructuring, healing, and growing muscle. Now our brain and our muscles certainly do work in concert and muscle is indeed adaptive, because it is governed by the most adaptive system in the universe - the brain.

'What we have come to know from research is that, rather than causing damage or overtraining, *stimulation* is the key. This is good news for us all in terms of brain health and even high performance in sport. No pain no gain is far from true. In fact, the research demonstrates just how sophisticated our brain is in having the ability to use stimulation of various degrees of intensity to achieve the same end - our growth and adaption!'

Before we hear more from John at his workshop, let's highlight some of the key symptoms of overtraining. They can be categorized in four ways:

1. Underperformance
2. Physiological changes
3. Mood disturbance
4. Sleep disturbance/Insomnia

Underperformance

Symptoms include lethargy, muscle 'heaviness' and/or soreness, and the inability to complete training routines.

Physiological changes

Symptoms are many and varied. They include weight loss, or gain, increased resting heartbeat, constant minor infections, loss of menstruation, gastrointestinal disturbances and swollen lymph glands.

Mood disturbance

Symptoms include depression, loss of appetite or libido or competitive drive, irritability and apathy.

Sleep disturbance

Symptoms include difficulty in falling asleep, waking in the night, nightmares, waking feeling un-refreshed.[1]

---

[1] We talk more about mood and emotional management in Chapter 6 and about sleep in Chapter 3.

In his talk, John went on to speak about inappropriate attitudes towards mental toughness and their effect on consistency of performance.

'I have witnessed many times in high level sport a coach say that a player is not mentally tough and every time that notion has been incorrect. More often than not the player has been placed in a situation where adaption is needed and the brain is seeking more refined stimulation or rest to make the leap to the next level of stress. But due to a lack of knowledge about the brain, pressures to win, and or sociopolitical factors within the organization it's easier to move on and regard the person as lacking.

'Let me be clear I am well aware that the managers and coaches who lead high level sporting organizations are doing a very difficult job and, to be honest with you, I regard them as performers just as I do their players. Yet, by not using the latest cognitive science we are recycling nothing but myths and inconsistencies. The result is we produce occasional excellence as opposed to sustained excellence. Sustained excellence is rooted in deliberate, appropriate, on-going brain management.

'Nowhere is this seen more clearly than in the elite military. When matters of life and death are always on the line things are always specific and accurate. By which I mean training and rest are determined, delivered and measured according to individual needs. Operatives are highly valued, non-disposable human assets and by training their specific needs they continue to develop and toughen.

'You see, in the final analysis, training and toughening is an *individual process* not a team process because at each and every point our individual brains are either responding or not responding – and this is what is measured for elite adaption.

'In simple terms, the elite military understand that the brain always wins. That's why they do.'

To help you plan your own physical activity we offer our recommendations, guidelines and tips in the next part of the chapter. First though a reminder of the key points.

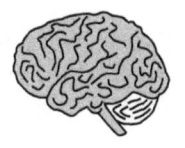

Summary

- Our brains were built for moving – from 5 to12 miles a day!
- Physical activity enables the creation of new connections throughout our central nervous system and restores and repairs existing connections.
- To improve your emotional management and thinking skills, *move*.
- Aerobic activity just twice a week halves your risk of general dementia and reduces your risk of Alzheimer's by 60%.
- Enhancing our aerobic capacity increases our ability to deal with stress – ultimately improving our resiliency.
- Physical activity gets blood to your brain, bringing it oxygen and glucose for energy to stimulate recovery and healing.
- Keeping fit stimulates proteins that keep neurons connecting over and over.
- Physical activity improves our memory capacity, memory recall, decision-making, and our overall processing speed.
- Regular physical activity is one of the principle factors in maintaining so-called mental toughness.

The Process

Our recommendations

Make physical activity, incorporating exercise, an integral part of your routine. Manage and monitor it, ensuring that it increases your daily energy levels and performance quality.[2]

Do this by:

1. Assessing your readiness for exercise and physical exercise.
2. Creating and following a program of regular exercise *in addition* to the usual activity of your daily life. [3]
3. Ensuring your program incorporates cardiorespiratory, resistance, flexibility, and neuromotor training.
4. Measuring your performance and results continually.

Cardiorespiratory training

Helps improve lung and heart condition, thus improving the ability of the respiratory and circulatory systems to supply oxygen to the skeletal muscles and increasing feelings of wellbeing.

Resistance training

Is that which causes the muscles to contract against an external resistance, leading to an increase in strength, tone, mass, or muscular endurance.

---

[2] Remember John's points about the importance of rest and recovery, so combine this with your Process planning from Chapters 3 and 4.

[3] Ensure the nature and amount of exercise is determined by the level of physical activity within your daily routine.

Flexibility training

Is made up of those exercises and activities that develop the range of motion of joints and/or their ability to move freely. In this context range of motion relates to the distance and direction in which joints can move and mobility relates to their ability to move without restriction.

Neuromotor training

This is sometimes called *functional fitness training* and incorporates and develops a variety of motor skills, including (but not limited to) balance, coordination, gait and agility.

Remember:

- In general, anything that is good for your heart is great for your brain.
- If you work your heart you make your brain more efficient and vice versa.
- Not only does physical activity improve your brain function, it also repairs damaged brain cells.
- Exercising in the morning before going to work primes the brain for any mental stresses that may occur for the rest of the day and stimulates better retention of new information and problem solving.
- Incorporating coordination through such activities as yoga, tai chi and dance along with cardiovascular exercise cross-trains your brain.
- If your time is short opt for condensed physical activity with a high intensity. This will quickly spike your heart rate and start a cascade effect of positive stress.
- When you feel like you are hitting a wall in your day reboot your brain with a few simple exercises such as sit-ups, push-ups or a short walk.

Readiness for physical activity

Please use the Physical Activity Readiness Questionnaire (PAR-Q) below as a guide to assess your readiness for increased physical activity. If you answer "Yes" to one or more of the questions, consult your doctor before engaging in exercise. Tell your doctor about the questions you answered "Yes" to and, after an evaluation, seek their advice about what type of activity is suitable for your current condition.

Table 1. Revised Physical Activity Readiness Questionnaire (PAR-Q)

Yes	No	
		1. Has a doctor ever said that you have a heart condition and recommended only medically supervised activity?
		2. Do you have chest pain brought on by physical activity
		3. Has a doctor ever said that you have a heart condition and recommended only medically supervised activity?
		4. Have you onone or more occasions lost consciousness or fallen over as a result of dizziness?
		5. Do you have a bone or joint problem that could bre aggravated by the proposed physical activity?
		6. Has a doctor ever srecommended medication for your blood pressure or a heart condition?
		7. Are you aware, through your own experience or a doctor's advice, of any other physical reason that would prohibit you from exercising without medical supervision?

If you answer "yes" to any of these questions, consult your personal physician or healthcare provider before increasing your physical activity.

Getting Started

Avoid making the mistake of doing too much too soon. Remember, managing your physical activity is part of a *Process*. Use that to remind you of the need to make only appropriate changes – those that enable you to progress without difficulty or setbacks.

When planning your exercise program the three elements that matter most are:

Frequency: The number of days per week you exercise.

Intensity: The degree of effort required. (How hard your brain and body are working.)

Time: The duration of each activity and/or the overall training session.

These are easy to remember; just use the acronym *FIT*.

We recommend you only ever change these factors one at a time. This will help reduce any risk of injury and, equally importantly, ensure the correct balance between effort and rest.

Rest and recovery are so important for brain health and performance optimization we dedicate the next chapter to the topic. For now, suffice to say that rest is the time when growth happens. Successful management of an exercise program incorporates sufficient rest and recovery and, by doing so, maximizes the physical, emotional and cognitive benefits.

Frequency

Does it matter if you choose to exercise only one day per week for an extended period of time or five to seven days a week for shorter periods? Yes, actually it does.

Every time you are physically active, your brain gets health benefits that are shared throughout the rest of the body. More frequent, shorter sessions provide these benefits more frequently, reduce the likelihood of injury, and are often easier to plan in to a weekly schedule.

Intensity

The simplest way to determine the level of intensity at which you are working is to try holding a conversation at the same time. Moderately intense physical activity should allow you to carry on the conversation, whereas more rigorous activity will make it increasingly difficult.

A far more precise way to gauge intensity, however, is to measure your heart rate.

The basic way to calculate your maximum heart rate is to subtract your age from 220. For example, if you're 45 years old, subtract 45 from 220 to get a maximum heart rate of 175. This is the maximum number of times your heart should beat per minute while you're exercising. Once you know your maximum heart rate, you can calculate your desired target heart rate zone — the level at which your heart is being conditioned but not overworked.

Consider these categories of measurement and spend most of your time in the Mild Intensity category even if you are fit.

Mild Intensity is 50-65% of your maximum heart rate. If you are beginning an exercise program for the very first time this is a place to start. And it's an important zone to return to even when your fitness levels develop, as evidenced by the fact that many elite endurance athletes train most days of the week in this zone.

Moderate/Intermediate Intensity is 70-80% of your maximum heart rate. This zone is only for those who have at least six months experience of consistent physical activity with cardiorespiratory training as an integral part of their schedule. When your heart rate is this high, you will certainly feel that you are working 'very hard'.

Profound Intensity is 80-100% of your maximum heart rate. This training requires the most effort and preparation and can be maintained for only a limited duration.

Why measure your heart? Because it allows you to be specific, safe and progressive. It underpins the creation and implementation of a personalized training program that works best for you as an individual. As we will discuss in more detail, by deliberately measuring our performance and progress we seriously reduce the risk of falling into the *no pain no gain* mentality.[4]

Time

How much time you spend on each activity is determined by the intensity at which you are working and the nature of the activity itself.

We'll give you examples of this as we move on to consider the types of activity that comprise a well-balanced training program.

Your program:

Cardiorespiratory training

- Choose any activity that enables you to establish and maintain a heart rate between 50-65% of your maximum heart rate.
- Do 3-5 sessions per week, on different days. (If you are a beginner start with 3 sessions.)
- Ideally each session will last between 20-60 minutes. (Although two or three 10 minute sessions will also be of value.)

---

[4] Here are some additional resources related to measuring heart rate and intensity:
http://www.cdc.gov/physicalactivity/everyone/measuring/heartrate.html
http://www.cdc.gov/physicalactivity/everyone/measuring/exertion.html

Here are examples of excellent low-impact[5] options:
- Walking
- Hiking
- Snowshoeing
- Cross-country skiing
- Elliptical fitness equipment
- Stairmaster fitness machine
- Cycling or stationary bike
- Rowing Machine
- Swimming
- Water aerobics
- Running in water
- Kayaking or canoeing
- Skating or rollerblading
- Golfing (walking the course)

It is a misconception held by some that lower impact physical activity has only a very limited value. This is not true. Remember, we need stimulation, not annihilation, and we were made to move. Low impact, mild intensity activity does the job.

In fact even a short duration of physical activity over three weeks can result in a very favorable change to the brain. Even moderate physical activity can result in favorable brain, physiological, and biochemical outcomes, leading to better health in general and improvement in brain autonomic functions and antioxidant status in particular.

---

[5] Low impact training is usually defined as those exercises during which one foot stays on the ground at all times. These are great for beginners and/or if recovering from injury.

If new to exercise, we recommend at least 3 months of low impact, mild intensity activity before engaging in any high impact exercise.[6] Examples of high impact training include:

- Running
- Skipping
- Basketball
- Plyometrics
- Regular aerobics

Resistance training

- Adults should train each major muscle group two or three days per week using a variety of exercises and equipment.
- Very light or light intensity is best for older persons or previously sedentary adults starting exercise.
- Two to four sets of each exercise will help adults improve strength and power.
- For each exercise, 8-12 repetitions improve strength and power, 10-15 repetitions improve strength in middle age and older persons starting exercise, and 15-20 repetitions improve muscular endurance.
- You can use bodyweight exercises[7] or weight training equipment. (If you choose the latter, we recommend you seek guidance from a professional trainer.)
- Adults should wait at least 48 hours between resistance training sessions.

---

[6] High impact training is usually defined as those exercises during which both feet leave the ground at the same time.

[7] The 7 Minute Workout shown in the coming pages is a great example of a training routine based on using only bodyweight.

Flexibility/Neuromotor training

- Adults should do flexibility exercises at least two or three days each week to improve range of motion.
- Flexibility exercises are most effective when the muscles are warm. Try light aerobic activity or a hot bath to warm the muscles before stretching.
- Each stretch should be held for 10-30 seconds to the point of tightness or slight discomfort.
- Repeat each stretch two to four times, accumulating a total of 60 seconds per stretch.
- Static stretching involves assuming a position and *holding* the stretch. Dynamic stretching involves controlled movements that take you safely and gently to your full range of motion.
- Proprioceptive Neuromuscular Facilitation (PNF) is a more advanced form of flexibility training that involves both the stretching and contraction of the muscle group. (We recommend that PNF stretches should only ever be conducted under the guidance and supervision by a health professional.)
- The activity or exercises should promote motor skills. For example, balance, coordination, agility and gait.
- Disciplines such Yoga, Dance and Tai Chi incorporate neuromotor training in combination with resistance and flexibility training.

Note: Whatever type of training you are doing, always warm up and cool down well. Warming up prepares the body for the stress of exercise. Cooling down starts the recovery process, which includes addressing the need for hydration and food.

Warming up

Spend several minutes gradually increasing the intensity of your activity. For example, if you are warming up in readiness for a run begin by increasing your walking speed from slow to fast before jogging and, finally, breaking into a run. If you are preparing for a weight training session, go through a series of exercises using only light weights.

Once your muscles have been warmed up, do some dynamic stretching. This might include swinging your arms and legs or twisting your torso. It's important, too, to create a deliberate mental state and focus. Forget what has happened before, or what you are going to do after your session. Remind yourself of the training targets you have set. Become aware of your body, how it is feeling and responding.

Cooling down

Spend several minutes gradually decreasing the intensity of your activity. If you are running, for example, reverse the process you employed when warming up. Do some static stretching. As your heartbeat comes down and you relax your body, ease your focus back into the rest of your day.

High intensity activities

We appreciate that finding the time to exercise on a regular basis can be a challenge. However, shorter more intense physical activity can be an effective component of an exercise plan. In fact, shorter, higher intensity activities done three times a week produce the same improvement as sixty minutes of cardio five times a week.

This training method, known as High Intensity Interval Training (HIIT) has been part of elite endurance training in running, cycling, rowing, and Nordic skiing for a number of years. HIIT sessions generally consist of the obligatory warm up followed by several repetitions of high intensity physical activity performed at near maximum intensity separated by some low-medium intensity activity enabling recovery, followed by a cool down period.

The entire session may last from less than 10 minutes up to as many as 30, making it an excellent way to maximize a workout when time is limited.

It has other benefits, too. HIIT training burns calories, boosts metabolism, increases the efficiency of the heart and lungs, stimulates muscle and, of course, brain growth and can positively influence mood, memory and problem-solving abilities for several hours afterwards. Remember, though, if considering HIIT to ensure that your training program reflects your current fitness levels and abilities.

Here's one example for you to consider:

The Scientific 7 Minute Workout

This workout involves doing a series of 12 exercises using bodyweight only. The exercises are performed in rapid succession, with only 30 seconds rest between each. This workout combines cardiorespiratory and resistance training. Scientists have determined that adherence to the 7 Minute Workout leads to:

- Decreases to body fat
- Improved insulin sensitivity
- Improvement to VO2max[8]
- Increased muscular fitness

Measuring your performance and results

Measuring performance is also important no matter what type of exercise you do because, as a general rule, what gets measured tends to get done. Measuring increases your awareness of your strengths, progress, and areas of development. It also protects the

---

[8] VO2max is the maximum rate at which your heart, lungs, and muscles can effectively use oxygen during exercise.

Physical Activity

Jumping Jacks → Wall sit → Push-up → Abdominal crunch

Step-up onto chair → Squat → Triceps dip on chair → Plank

High knees running in place → Lunge → Push-up and rotation → Side plank

Image from www.myfoxdetroit.com

effort you put into your training by informing you when to work and when to rest.

Without measuring the essential aspects of the training and recovery process it is quite easy to over-train. This can actually undo the positive effects of exercise by decreasing the resiliency of the central nervous system.

This is why elite athletes who are being trained well and the highest-level military operatives (who are always trained well) measure their training and recovery using the latest biometric devices. Those who are tasked with training the very best in the world know that what gives can also take away. Therefore, they measure accurately and frequently to ensure their programs create only sustained improvement.

The rest of us can benefit equally. We do not have to be working at the cutting edge of sport or involved in the ultimate challenges associated with the elite military to take advantage of such biofeedback.

No matter who you are or what your performance goals, if you really want to get to know yourself and your brain, *measure*.

Managing how and what you measure

As we have already mentioned, technology has its place in our daily lives and it is essential we ensure this is a useful rather than a useless, or even harmful, place.

To help you choose the fitness tracker that best suits your needs, remember to keep in mind these three factors:

1. Choose a device that is most wearable for you and your uses; consider the activities you are doing and how you will wear the device (e.g. on your wrist, ankle or clothing).
2. Be clear why – and what – you are measuring (e.g., goals, process measurements, outcomes).
3. Know what specific insights you are looking for; data should always drive insights!

Here are some other considerations once you make your choice:

- Make sure your wear your device! If it's not on you it can't measure.

Physical Activity

- If your chosen device has a test to assess your current fitness level do so, this will give you a baseline to compare to.
- If it is possible, calibrate your chosen device so that your profile is correct, as this will inform how some data will be estimated.
- Know your heart rate training zones to ensure you are working within the appropriate range; personalized data provides the basis for ever more effective sessions.
- Capture an additional five to ten minutes of your heart rate post exercise. The data you capture can reveal how your fitness is progressing over time. How quickly you return to a relative heart rate baseline is a sign of progress.
- Keep your training information so you can follow your trends on a daily basis.
- Set process goals daily, weekly, and monthly using features on your device.
- Synchronize and download your data daily because seeing your own progress can be motivational, and help you make informed changes to your program.
- Monitor your calorie count; know how much energy you need.
- If your fitness tracker has the option, set it to remind you when you have been sitting for anything from 45 to 90 minutes. Our maximal attention span is limited; by taking regular short breaks, moving around to increase blood flow to your brain, you can more easily maintain your focus.
- Monitor your training load (e.g., how often and what types) so you can determine and incorporate the necessary rest and recovery periods.

The topic of rest and recovery is the one we address next. It's the all-important yin to the yang of physical activity.

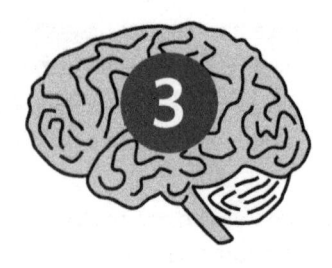

Rest & Recovery

'Your life is a reflection of how you sleep, and how you sleep is a reflection of your life.'

Edward Smith-Stanley

Brain Priming – Chapter in focus

Here are the key facts and messages:

- Sleep is your number one performance enhancer.
- Sleep impacts on our physical, psychological, social and economic well-being.
- During sleep growth hormone is released; you grow during sleep.
- Your brain is designed to rest and shut down; it's a primary drive we all have.
- During the sleep process your brain detoxifies, thus retaining

its day-to-day resiliency.
- During sleep your brain stores into memory what you have learnt throughout the day.
- The biological drive for a nap is universal – and napping is of great benefit to us all.
- Loss of sleep reduces the brain's abilities and those of all other systems.
- Sleep debt is a silent killer, eroding both well-being and optimal performance.
- Resting well is one of the factors to maintaining mental toughness.
- Consistent sleep patterns impact positively on mood, concentration, building and/or coordinating muscles, and decision-making.

The golden chain

Thomas Dekker, the English Dramatist (1572-1632) described sleep as 'the golden chain that ties health and our bodies together.' He was right[1] and if the chain is broken the consequences can be severe – or even disastrous – because the links that make up this golden chain combine to make us who we are and determine how we perform both personally and socially.

How can this be? Surely sleep is nothing more than obligatory time-out from living our lives, from managing the here and now and preparing for the future? Surely sleep is just a necessary evil that gets in the way for those who are ambitious and purposeful, and appeals seductively to those who are lazy?

---

[1] Chris here: Even though Scientists in the 16th and 17th centuries did not understand the purpose and value of sleep as they do now, Dekker's insight was accurate. It's a great example of *The Wisdom of the Village*.

Actually, nothing could be further from the truth. Even though it is true to say that sleep is obligatory, it's a serious error to regard it as passive time-out. Sleep is anything but a passive factor in our lives. In fact, we can argue that sleep brings us life by enabling us to recover, regroup and *grow* on a daily basis.

The links in the precious golden chain of sleep are many, each significant in their own right, all combining to create something greater than the sum of their parts.

Your brain is actually designed to shut down and rest; it's a primary drive no different to the need to eat and drink. As you sleep your brain stores into memory what you have learnt during the day. Consistent and appropriate sleep patterns are essential to help us maintain our emotional resiliency, concentration and decision-making abilities, and in the building of muscle. Remember, too, what we said in the previous chapter about the relationship between rest and mental toughness. Without sufficient sleep, over time we weaken mentally as well as physically.

However, that's not all. Researchers at the University of Rochester Medical Center (URMC) for Translational Neuromedicine have discovered yet another clue as to why sleep is mandatory for good health - especially brain health.

Their report reveals that as we sleep our brain actually removes toxic waste, including harmful proteins linked to brain disorders such as Alzheimer's or chronic traumatic encephalopathy (CTE),[2] by using what has been called the glymphatic system.

We also know that when the process of sleep is completed without disruption we actually grow, because the pituitary gland releases a growth hormone helping to repair, develop, and consolidate.

---

[2] This is a form of encephalopathy related to, amongst other things, repeated concussions.

The message, then, is that if you want to be at your best you need sufficient rest – and this isn't accomplished solely by sleeping through the night. Which is why we'll talk later about the great value of taking a daily nap, and how best to go about it.

Waves, stages and cycles

Given the sub-heading, you could be forgiven for thinking this next part tells you how a clown introduces and goes about their circus act. Actually we are going to consider the nature of sleep.

We'll begin with brainwaves.

These are synchronized electrical pulses sent from and between the billions of neurons in our brain.[3]

Brainwaves can be detected by using sensors on the scalp. Each type of wave is divided into bandwidths to describe its stated functions.

The type and function are as follows:

- Delta waves are the slowest and the loudest (low frequency and deeply penetrating) and can be seen and generated in the deepest of sleep and meditation. Healing and rejuvenation are stimulated in the state, which is why deep sleep is so essential to the day-to-day healing process.
- Theta waves also occur most often in sleep and are part of the process of learning and memory. In theta our senses turn inward, withdrawing from the external world. Within the sleep process we experience theta waves as we drift off into a dream.

---

[3] The efficiency of the brain is unparalleled. Consider just how much it does with such relatively little electrical output.

- Alpha brainwaves are present during very efficient flow states; those times we are relaxed and yet fully awake in the present moment. Alpha waves aid overall mental abilities, calmness, alertness, the integration of the central nervous system and the peripheral nervous system and learning.
- Beta waves are divided into three distinct bands, Low beta, Beta and High beta. These waves dominate most of our normal waking state, when we are engaged in cognitive processing and responding to the many internal and external demands we experience.
- Gamma waves are the fastest of all, facilitating simultaneous processing of information from different brain areas whilst also modulating perception and consciousness.

These different brainwaves look like this:

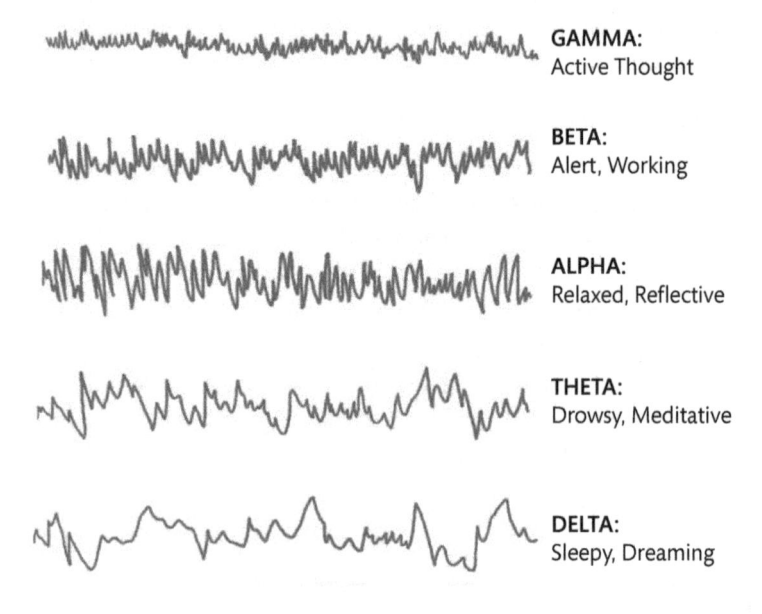

GAMMA: Active Thought

BETA: Alert, Working

ALPHA: Relaxed, Reflective

THETA: Drowsy, Meditative

DELTA: Sleepy, Dreaming

Example from: thisisartlab.com

Rest and Recovery

We sleep in stages and cycles. These, and the associated brainwaves, are:

Stage 1: This is the first 5 to 15 minutes of light sleep during which we experience both Alpha and Theta brain waves. During this stage we may enter into a dream-like state of consciousness and feel sudden muscle contractions followed by the sensation of falling.

Stage 2: The second stage lasts about 20 minutes. Our brain starts to produce short periods of rapid brain wave activity know as sleep spindles and our heart rate begins to slow down.

Stage 3: Now Delta waves begin to emerge and we make the transition from light to a very deep restorative sleep.

Stage 4: This stage lasts for about 30 minutes. It is a deep sleep where human growth hormone is released, the brain detoxifies, and memory is consolidated.

Stage 5 REM: This stage is marked by rapid eye movements and an increase in brain activity and respiration rate. Most of our dreaming occurs now because of the increased brain activity, although voluntary muscles become paralyzed. We enter this stage approximately 90 minutes after falling asleep.

Not surprisingly, we begin our sleep in Stage 1 and progress sequentially to stage 4. We then repeat stages 3 then 2 before we access REM sleep. Once REM is over, we usually return to Stage 2. We go through this process approximately four or five times every night.

The first cycle of REM usually lasts for only a relatively short period of time. However, as our sleep progresses each cycle becomes longer allowing us to reach and maintain the stages in which we heal and stay healthy. That's why we need to sleep for appropriate periods of time each night.

If you are wondering just how much sleep you need, the answer is it depends on your age and, to an extent, your lifestyle. However, researchers are pretty much in agreement that newborns in the first few months of life need between 14 and 17 hours a day. Teenagers in the 14-17 age range need between 8 and 10 hours and for adults the requirement drops slightly to between 7 and 9.

Disregarding individual differences based on age or, indeed, habit, most of us spend on average one third of our life asleep.[4] Yet it is only recently that sleep has become acknowledged as of great significance to all of us, and an important topic for scientific study.

Why is sleep so important? Because it is our number one performance enhancer! That's why we are designed to spend so much of our time doing it. As we've already mentioned, we grow during our rest and recovery periods.

Sleep is a natural part of every individual's life. Sleep is not just something to fill time when a person is inactive. Sleep is a required activity, not an option. We all recognize and feel the need to sleep and after sleeping we recognize positive changes that have occurred, as we feel rested and more alert. In contrast, the impact of poor sleep (of varying degrees) makes even the most mundane task more difficult and leads eventually to many of our human processes weakening considerably.

Of course our brain is adaptive and copes with some sleep deprivation. It's also true to say that the loss of one night's sleep is not the same as the loss of three. It's much easier for the brain and body to recover from the former. However, the brain's ability to manage is not a reason for disregarding the importance of your sleeping patterns.

---

[4] Just take a moment, consider a lifespan of 75 years and work out how much time that person probably spent sleeping. There was a good reason why.

Think of it this way, a favorite method of torture amongst those who practice such things is sleep deprivation! Why, then, would we ever willingly do it to our self? Yet the evidence shows that many of us do.

Research suggests that, for example, 56% of people in the USA and 51% of people in the UK get less sleep than they need on workdays. Not surprisingly, then, only 44% of Americans reported enjoying a good night's sleep every, or almost every, night. In the UK that figure is slightly less at 42% and in Germany it drops again to 40%.

The point is, if we don't get the right amounts of rest and recovery on a regular basis we not only don't grow, we actually go into deficit. And when our individual performance weakens there are inevitably knock-on effects. Here's a quick overview of some of the ways lack of sleep can harm us personally. After that, we'll talk about the social and global harm it can cause.

The costs of sleep loss

Dr. Rafael Pelayo, Associate Professor at the Stanford Sleep Disorders Clinic at Stanford University School of Medicine, highlighted the intimate relationship between our sleeping and waking states when he wrote, 'Your life is a reflection of how you sleep, and how you sleep is a reflection of your life.'

These are some of the personal costs of sustained sleep debt:

- Premature skin aging
- Irritability
- Memory lapses
- Gene changes negatively influencing immune and stress responses
- Increased risk of suffering a stroke
- Cognitive decline

- Decreased bone density
- Increased risk of obesity
- Increased risk of heart disease
- Increased risk of cancer
- Brain damage

More shocking still, researchers at Pennsylvania State University determined that, even after taking into account other variables including weight, alcohol and tobacco use, diabetes and hypertension, men who slept less than six hours per night were significantly more likely to die prematurely than those who slept longer.

It isn't necessarily just how much we sleep that influences our behavior and wellbeing, the consistency of our sleeping patterns is also important. In 2015 in a study funded by the National Institutes of Health and the Penn State Clinical Translational Science Institute, researchers in America analyzed the sleeping habits of 342 teenagers. Although on average their sleep fell within the healthy range, researchers found that sleep variations of at least one hour – sleeping either one hour more or one hour less than usual – were associated with the teens:

- Eating 201 more calories per day
- Consuming about 6 grams more total fat and 32 grams more carbohydrates per day
- Being 60% more likely to engage in nighttime snacking on school nights
- Being 100% more likely to engage in nighttime snacking at weekends.[5]

---

[5] Study co-authors were: Edward Bixler, Ph.D.; Jiangang Liao, DEGREE, Arthur Berg, Ph.D.; Yuka Imamura Kawasawa, Ph.D.; Julio Fernandez-Mendoza, Ph.D.; Alexandros Vgontzas, M.D.; Jeff Yanosky, Ph.D. and Duanping Liao, M.D., Ph.D.

It would seem, then, that adhering to a regular sleeping pattern is more beneficial than sleeping for significantly different periods of time from day-to-day. For many of us, though, that consistency in itself can be a challenge. Especially given the often-demanding pressures of managing our daily lives.

Sleep and stress management

Our stress levels influence both the quality and the quantity of our sleep. This, in turn, creates a vicious cycle because the less well rested we are, the less resilient we become in the face of stress.

A Stress in America™ survey carried out in 2013 by The American Psychological Association (APA) concluded that stress may be interfering with Americans' sleeping habits; preventing many from getting the sleep they need to be healthy. The survey of nearly 2,000 people revealed that only 20% of adults felt that the quality of their sleep was very good to excellent. And that those who reported lower stress levels slept on average almost one hour per night longer than their more highly stressed counterparts.

The findings also showed that adults who slept fewer than eight hours a night were more likely to report that in the previous month they had experienced:

- Symptoms of stress, such as feelings of irritability or anger
- Feeling overwhelmed
- Feeling a lack of motivation and energy
- Loss of patience
- Shouting at their partner and/or children
- An increased willingness to avoid exercise

These same people were also more likely to declare that their level of stress had increased during the previous year.

This is a problem that is not limited to one country, however. In the UK 22% of people surveyed acknowledged that stress negatively affected their sleep almost every night. 19% of Germans reported the same. As did 14% of Canadians, 25% of Japanese and 30% of all Mexicans.

One of the major causes of this problem is cortisol hyperactivity. Cortisol is called the *stress hormone* because it is secreted increasingly during times of fear or stress, whenever our body goes into the fight or flight response. Given that a constant state of stress is so commonplace in many societies, the negative effects of cortisol are reflected in the sleep problems identified above.

Increases in cortisol can lead to fragmentation of sleep, decreased slow-wave sleep, and shortened sleep time. To make matters even worse, sleep disturbances can themselves condition the cortisol process before and during sleep, thus worsening the cycle. Both insomnia and obstructive sleep apnea are specific sleep disorders that are associated with cortisol. Depression and other stress-related disorders are also associated with sleep disturbances caused potentially by elevated levels of cortisol.

In summary, cortisol hyperactivity can impact negatively upon both the nature and duration of our much-needed sleep.

We might all know some individuals who are sure they can maintain their optimum performance and wellbeing on far less than eight hours sleep per night, however researchers estimate that the real number of people who can do this successfully is probably as low as one in a thousand. In America alone, The Institute of Medicine estimates that 50 million to 70 million adults suffer from chronic sleep disorders and that most people would be happier, healthier and safer if they were to sleep an extra 60 to 90 minutes per night.

Sleep and emotional management

It's pretty easy to tell when someone we know hasn't been sleeping well and we certainly recognize the symptoms in our self. Now, though, researchers at the University of California Berkeley are suggesting that loss of sleep not only impacts our mood but also our ability to read the emotions of others.

Being able to recognize and read the emotional expressions of others influences the decisions we make about how and when to interact. Without it we might even experience unnecessary avoidance responses or even anxiety. It is, then, an ability that plays a vital role in helping us to manage the many and varied social interactions we experience on a daily basis.

For some, being able to accurately interpret facial expressions is an essential professional skill. For law enforcement officers or military personnel, for example, it may enable them to identify pre-fight indicators and de-escalate a potentially violent situation. For others such as medical professionals, educators, sportsmen and women and new parents, it is also of great importance.

In the study 18 young adults were asked to look at 70 images of faces showing expressions ranging from neutral to friendly and threatening. The participants viewed the images on two separate occasions, once having had a full night's rest and once having been awake all night.

The results were significant. fMRI scans revealed that, when sleep-deprived, the areas of the brain involved with emotional recognition did not activate, leaving participants unable to distinguish accurately between universal facial emotions such as friendly and threatening. Neither did the participant's heart rates change when looking at threatening faces. This is a worrying omission as the link between the brain and heart is critical for creating the necessary distress signals that allow the body to mobilize in response to threatening stimuli.

Overall the research suggests that consistent, appropriate sleep patterns not only underpin our ability to manage everyday social interactions, but also to respond in times of possible threat.

Sleep and storing memory

If you want to be able to recall particular information at some point in the future, you really do need to sleep on it. Sleep is one of the critical factors in determining the quality of our encoding, retention and recall process – what most of us tend to think of as *memory*.

We will talk about memory, and the different types of memory in more detail in Chapter 5. Now, though, we are going to ask you a couple of questions that will require you to exercise either your short or long-term memory:

Have you ever worked through the night, studying for an exam the next day, or preparing a speech or presentation, desperately trying to learn all the things you needed to remember? If you have, how successful were you?

The answer is almost certainly, not as successful as you could have been.

Why?

Because sleep is the state in which the brain optimizes memory consolidation at all levels. Lack of sleep reduces both the imprinting process and any hope of recall, especially under stress.

The usual result of such a last ditch, all-through-the-night effort is that although we have studied non-stop – actually *because* of it - we feel the need to study again just before the event. In other words, we double our work time and feel the pressure of doing so. The reason for this is that sleep is essential to both the encoding and the recall of information. Since the encoding could not occur we are obliged to keep studying just to keep the information fresh in our short-term memory.

This actually creates a two-fold problem, because not only are we negatively affected by our lack of sleep and the associated lack of encoding, we are also dependent on our sensory and short-term memory and that has only limited capacity. Consequently, we find ourselves redoubling our efforts and, usually, producing a sub-par outcome or performance.

The ability to create, store and recall memories plays a significant role in ensuring the quality of our life, our learning, and our professional performance. By managing our sleep well, we are, therefore, taking a vital step in ensuring that we learn, recall and perform to the best of our ability.

When we fail to do so the consequences in the workplace and beyond are really significant - and not just on a personal level. Sometimes the collapse of human capability due to sleep debt and deprivation lead to events of national and even global importance. Sometimes the consequences are less far-reaching, but equally devastating on a personal level. Here are just a few examples. We'll begin with two nuclear disasters:

Three Mile Island (1979)

Considered the most serious nuclear accident on U.S. soil, the catastrophe at Three Mile Island was attributed to human error due to sleep deprivation. Shift workers suffering from sleep loss failed to notice that coolant was needed for the reactor's core, resulting in a partial nuclear meltdown.

Chernobyl (1986)

The explosion at the Ukrainian nuclear power plant, the worst accident of its kind in history, released large quantities of radioactive particles over much of western USSR and Europe. It is still unclear how many people's lives have been affected by the disaster, but it is estimated the surrounding areas will not be liveable for thousands of years. The power plant exploded after engineers had worked for more than 13 hours and investigators linked sleep deprivation to the accident.

The Exxon Valdez Oil Spill (1989)

With the Third Mate allegedly asleep at the helm and the crew having put in a 22-hour shift, the oil supertanker ran aground in Alaska spilling 258,000 barrels of crude oil, destroying both wildlife and the shoreline. The effects of this accident continue to impact negatively on the Alaskan shoreline.

Canadian National Train Crash (2001)

Two Canadian National trains collided into each other, spilling 3,000 gallons of diesel. Two crewmen on one of the freight trains suffered from sleep apnea resulting in chronic sleeplessness. After investigation, the Canadian National Transportation Safety Board ruled that the disaster was the result of fatigue.

Air France Flight 447 (2009)

The flight going from Brazil to France crashed into the Atlantic Ocean, killing all on board. The official report concluded that the pilot had had only one hour of sleep the night before. He was taking a nap when the plane ran into a tropical storm.

Metro-North Derailment (2013)

The engineer on the Metro-North train taking large numbers of people to New York City fell asleep at the wheel and the train derailed, resulting in 4 people being killed and 61 seriously injured.

Driving when fatigued

In the USA The National Traffic Safety Administration has estimated that drivers who are overly fatigued cause approximately 1,550 deaths annually. Although the number of traffic accidents caused by tiredness is likely to be much higher.

Similarly, a study of 1,000 UK drivers showed that many drivers ignore signs of drowsiness when driving and that nearly a third choose to keep driving despite feeling drowsy.

An Australian Federal Government inquiry in 2000 estimated that the cost of fatigue-related road accidents was around $3 billion every year. Studies conducted by the Adelaide Centre for Sleep Research in Australia found that a person who has been awake for 17 hours is twice as likely to have an accident as a person who is not fatigued, and that drivers who have been awake for 24 hours are seven times more likely.

Fatigue and medical errors

Not surprisingly, research shows that physicians in training are more likely to make errors of judgment when in sleep debt caused by recurring 24 hour shifts. The findings show that the physicians:

- Make 36% more serious medical errors than those working 16 hour shifts.
- Make five times as many diagnostic errors.
- Make twice as many wrong decisions at night-time.

- Suffer 61% more sharp injuries after their 20th consecutive hour of work.
- Double their risk of being involved in a motor vehicle crash if driving home after 24 hours of work.

Given the cognitive demands placed on medical personnel these errors are, sadly, almost to be expected as those involved experience ever-increasing fatigue. The bottom line, no matter what the profession or context, is this:

Sleep loss impedes decision-making

Decision-making is a dynamic process. It requires a person to learn what is going on within changing circumstances. That involves being able to recognize and make sense of new information. Research undertaken by Dr. Paul Whitney and Dr. Hans Van Dongen of the Washington State University Sleep and Performance Research Center and Dr. Melinda Jackson, of the RMIT University, Victoria, Australia, revealed just how significantly sleep loss affects our decision-making ability.

In the experiment 13 healthy adults were required to go 62 hours without sleep, whilst another 13 were allowed to rest. For six days and nights, all the participants lived in a hotel-like laboratory where they performed a task designed to test their ability to use feedback to guide future decisions. In the task, participants were shown a series of numbers pre-assigned to have either a "go" response or a "no go" value. They had less than a second to decide whether or not to respond to each number shown. Every time they responded correctly to a number with a "go" value they received a fictitious monetary reward. Every mistake resulted in a loss. Eventually the individuals in both groups learnt how to manage the task successfully.

At which point the researchers introduced the real challenge by reversing the rules, with participants now having to withhold a response to the "go" numbers and instead respond positively to the "no go" numbers.

The results were clear. The 16 rested participants all responded to the switch within 8 – 16 numbers. The sleep-deprived participants, though, had almost zero success, even after being shown 40 numbers. The data showed that no matter how much a person wants to make the right choice and no matter how hard they try, sleep loss limits brain function preventing them from using feedback effectively.

The overall impact of this on national economies is startling:

Sleep loss and the economy

The Centers for Disease Control and Prevention (CDC) in the United States and the National Health Service in the United Kingdom both categorize insufficient sleep as a public health epidemic.

It's an epidemic that drains economies as the consequent lethargy, moodiness and poor decision-making of workers limits performance and productivity.

According to a report in The Journal of Occupational Environmental Medicine, fatigued workers cost American employers an estimated $136.4 billion per year in health-related lost productivity, over $100 billion more than the same costs related to non-fatigued workers.

In Canada a study estimated that employees with insomnia lost an estimated 28 days a year of work productivity because of their sleepiness. American researchers found that 15% of employees with severe insomnia admitted to having made errors at work in the previous month that could have had serious consequences, compared to only 6% of workers who got enough sleep.

In the UK a study by the private healthcare organization BUPA of 10,000 working adults determined that sick days and low productivity caused by lack of sleep costs the economy a total of £1.6 billion a year. Of those questioned, 27% admitted regularly going to work feeling tired and 24% admitted to low levels of productivity due to fatigue.

It isn't just lack of sleep that costs. A separate BUPA survey of 2,000 UK employees revealed that over 60% were not always able to take the 20-minute lunch break that is the national minimum requirement and 28% said that they didn't take a break at any time during their working day. 30% of the respondents reported that missing lunch made them feel physically ill and 40% said that it damaged their productivity.

We'll address the importance of nutrition in the next chapter. We'll close this section with a few words about the value of taking a nap.

We need to nap

Flying in the face of those business leaders and managers who expect their employees to work virtually non-stop day-in and day-out, the British author and journalist Sam Hodgkinson suggested that, 'When the going gets tough, the tough take a nap.'

If you feel that seems more like a cop-out than a positive opt-in, you'd be wrong. In all probability, you've fallen for the well-established myths that associate napping with lack of ambition or desire, something that is only acceptable when done by either children or the elderly.

The truth is napping is another one of those universal needs we discussed earlier. In fact, some of the most creative, powerful and influential figures in human history liked to nap. People such as Winston Churchill, John F. Kennedy, Albert Einstein and Leonardo De Vinci all liked to snooze – and understood the benefits of doing so. Which include restored alertness, reduced mistakes and accidents and overall enhanced performance.

A study at NASA, for example, found that a 40-minute nap improved pilots' and astronauts' performance by 34% and their alertness by 100%. In a related study it was found that pilots who had a 25-minute nap as their co-pilot took over were five times less likely to fall asleep than pilots who hadn't napped. They were also less likely to commit any errors during either take-off or landing.

Napping also seems to improve creativity, as long as the nap lasts for long enough to enable the person to experience REM sleep. When faced with a series of creative problems, volunteers who napped for a sufficient period of time before being tested did 40% better than those faced with the same problems but who were not allowed to nap. All of which begs the question, 'Is there a best way to nap and, if so, what is it?' We'll answer that and address a range of other practical issues in the next part of this chapter, when we discuss the Process of managing your rest and recovery.

Before that, here's the summary:

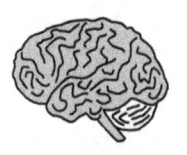

Summary

- Sleep is your number one performance enhancer.
- Sleep impacts on our physical, psychological, social and economic well-being.

- During sleep growth hormone is released; you grow during sleep.
- Your brain is designed to rest and shut down; it's a primary drive we all have.
- During the sleep process your brain detoxifies, thus retaining its day-to-day resiliency.
- During sleep your brain stores into memory what you have learnt throughout the day.
- The biological drive for a nap is universal – and napping is of great benefit to us all.
- Loss of sleep reduces the brain's abilities and those of all other systems.
- Sleep debt is a silent killer, eroding both well-being and optimal performance.
- Resting well is one of the factors to maintaining mental toughness.
- Consistent sleep patterns impact positively on mood, concentration, building and/or coordinating muscles, and decision-making.

The Process

Our recommendations

Manage your rest and recovery deliberately and consistently.

Do this by:

1. Creating and taking opportunities for both active and passive rest.

2. Knowing how and when to nap – and then actually doing so.
3. Taking short breaks from work at least every 90 minutes to rest and re-energize.
4. Discovering then implementing your optimum sleep schedule.
5. Creating a bedroom environment that encourages rest and sleep.
6. Learning and practicing relaxation techniques.
7. Having a 'winding down' pre-sleep routine.
8. Having a process for going back to sleep if you wake during the night.

The process of resting

Rest comes in many forms, both active and passive. Although sleep is the most obvious – and essential – form of rest, we can also recover from the demands of our daily activity in a variety of different ways.

Active rest involves physical movement. Passive rest does not. Activities such as walking, hiking, stretching, and even shopping, are all examples of active rest. Passive rest includes such things as watching TV, going to a movie, reading, listening to music, soaking in the bath, and laughing.

Your ability to rest well depends, in the first instance, on your willingness to *plan* periods of both active and passive rest into your daily and weekly schedules. Remember our levels of overall resiliency are determined by the consistency and quality of our rest and recovery. We have to be motivated to rest well, just as we have to be motivated to do anything well. To make it as easy as possible, incorporate into your daily routines those methods of rest that appeal to you the most and are the easiest for you to implement. If unexpected opportunities for some additional rest present themselves do what all great planners would do and make the most of them.

Remember, our aim is to use rest to create and enjoy full recovery – physical, mental and emotional – from the stresses of our day, whatever those stresses are and however they occur. If we do not address this in a deliberate and organized way, we risk forgetting its importance behind the increasing complexity and demands of our busy, multi-layered lives.

Planning your rest

In the previous chapter you considered your physical activity levels and planned your own personal training program. It's time now to do the same for rest and recovery.

Simply review the amount and nature of the active and passive rest you have in a normal working week. Then:

a) Determine whether or not you need more rest and recovery time in light of the activities you engage in.
b) Identify where/when you can add in those rest and recovery sessions.
c) Incorporate the types of active and passive rest you find most appealing, beneficial and easy to implement.
d) Put the plan into action.
e) Review and adapt if necessary in the light of feedback.

One of the most powerful and reinvigorating types of rest is napping:

How to nap well

To get the most out of napping, here are some tips:

- The best time for you to nap depends on when you wake up. If you rise at 5am, for example, plan to nap at 1pm. If you get up at 9am, nap at 3pm.
- Even if you can't always nap at the same time, aim to take your naps in the afternoon. According to research, our instinct as human beings is to sleep once for a relatively short period of time in the afternoon and for much longer during the night. So afternoon napping is a natural thing to do.
- Plan ahead. If you know you are going to get very little, or no, sleep during the night schedule a long nap of up to 2 hours into your day. Research suggests that such a lengthy nap can improve alertness for up to 24 hours, and that a preliminary nap counteracts the effects of sleep loss better than a subsequent nap.
- Create a restful environment; nap in a quiet, dark place, with a moderate room temperature, and few distractions.
- Use meditative, breathing techniques to help you relax deeply and quickly.
- As a general rule, keep your naps short, aim to nap for only 10 to 30 minutes to avoid sleep inertia.
- In order to avoid sleep disruption at night, never nap for more than 90 minutes.
- Set an alarm to wake you up. It's easier to relax and fall asleep during the day when we know we will be woken up at the right time.
- Give yourself time to wake up fully before resuming your day. Use deep, increasingly powerful breaths and simple movement such as walking to bring yourself back to full alertness.

Should everyone nap?

Napping is good for most people. If you find that you simply can't make the above tips work for you, then our advice would be to forget napping and ensure that you always have enough good quality sleep through the night.

If you suffer from insomnia, again, avoid napping during the day.

For the rest of us, napping can be a powerful part of our rest and recovery process. An obvious caveat, though, is that you can only enjoy napping at work if it is an accepted part of your organization's behaviour and routines. However, if you ever find yourself working night shifts an early evening nap before you go to work will improve your alertness for the rest of the night.

Taking short breaks throughout the day

If your environment and schedule allow it, take a short break of 5 minutes – or a little longer if you have the time - after every hour (and certainly after every 90 minutes) of work.

Why?

Because, no matter what we might believe about ourselves, our attention span is limited and, if the work is intense, even 45 minutes might be at the far end of our capability. In fact, if you can, you'd be well advised to take a break more frequently. Either way, by taking a regular and deliberately managed time-out you will optimize your brain function and enhance your overall performance.

Frequent breaks that provide positive distractions from our primary task not only enable us to perform well for longer, they also improve our decision-making by activating and directing our unconscious thought processes.

Researchers from the University of Illinois at Urbana-Champaign discovered that when groups were tasked with working on a brain-intensive activity, the groups that took the most breaks had the highest mental capacity at the end of the day.

In a different study carried out at the University of Amsterdam two groups of students were asked to choose a car to purchase based on a given set of specifications. One group was allowed to focus solely on the car-selection task. The other was deliberately interrupted and given a separate and completely distinct task to complete before being allowed to return to the original activity. Which group made the best decisions relating to the car? The one that had been interrupted. The researchers concluded that the distraction not only gave the students' conscious analytical processing skills a rest, it also – and importantly – enabled their unconscious thought process to take over. The results supported what the researchers called the deliberation-without-attention hypothesis.

Here are some activities you can choose to do in your short break:

Move!

Just walking for a few minutes, especially if you spend much of your working day sat in front of a computer screen, will energize you and increase blood flow to your brain. If you can, go outside and get some fresh air.

Perform breathing exercises.

If you need to calm yourself use diaphragmatic breathing; begin by relaxing your shoulders, your hands and your stomach. Then breathe in gently and deeply, *extending* your lower stomach as you do, imagining the breath going all the way down to the point about 2 centimeters below your belly button. Hold the breath there for just a couple of seconds before exhaling through your nose, gently *contracting* your stomach as you do so. As you exhale let your shoulders and the rest of your body relax even more. Perform in sets of 4 breaths as required. We'll talk more about diaphragmatic breathing in Chapter 6.

If you need to energize yourself, again relax your body first and then breathe strongly and deeply in through your nose raising your chest as much as you can, filling your lungs with air. Breathe out equally forcefully, this time through your mouth. Again, perform in sets of 4.

A simple and effective breathing routine that combines both benefits is based on a 1-4-2 count. Begin by selecting a low number - 3 or 4 for example - to assess your capability. If you are starting with the number 3, breathe in through your nose slowly and deeply for 3 seconds extending your stomach as you do so. Then relax your body and hold your breath for 12 seconds. Finally breathe out through your mouth continually for 6 seconds. This counts as one repetition. Breathe in and out once in normal fashion before doing the next repetition. Depending on the time you have available, we recommend you perform between 4 to 10 repetitions, increasing the value of the number you select for each repetition until you are working at your maximum capacity.

Meditate

We'll talk more about the benefits of meditation and ways to do it in Chapter 6. The only point to make here is that breath control, particularly slow, diaphragmatic breathing as outlined above, is central to most meditative practices. So if you are doing the calming breath we've just described you can add to it by closing your eyes, focusing physically on the intake, circulation and exhalation of breath as you mentally count the number of each repetition. Be particularly aware of the spot about 2 centimeters below your belly button. Feel it move out gently as you inhale. Imagine the breath reaching down to, and circulating in, this place, before you exhale. This will help distance you further from the work that has gone before and any thoughts you had about the work that is still to come.

Listen to music

This is another topic we address more fully in Chapter 6. We're sure that, by now, you won't be surprised to know that music affects your brain – and different types of music affect your brain in different ways. So if you are using your short break to calm down, listen to a piece of music that soothes and relaxes you. If you want to be energized, choose a piece that gets your toes tapping.

Do a different mental activity

Because, as we have already explained, this will allow your unconscious thinking processes to work on the task you are going back to, and it will help to re-energize you.

We suggest you choose just one, or a combination, of the above activities, determined by the time you have available and the purpose of your break. Whatever you do, though, make sure you stay away from your computer screen.

Managing your optimum sleep schedule

Our sleep rhythms, known as *circadian* rhythms, influence us powerfully. Many of us might already think of ourselves as a *morning person* or a *night person*. The more clear and precise we can be about our own personal sleeping preference, the more easily we can adhere to it at every available opportunity.

If you are able to have a week or two - and two might be needed - throughout which you can experiment to determine your circadian rhythm do the following:

1. Ban the use of alarm clocks.
2. Go to bed at the same time every night.
3. Sleep until you are naturally awake and ready to get out of bed.
4. Note your waking time and the length of your sleep.

The reason why we are suggesting it might take 2 weeks to identify your natural sleeping rhythm, is because if you are experiencing sleep debt when you start it will take some time for you to recover; you will only go into your natural rhythm once you have achieved equilibrium.

Alternatively, if you literally don't have the time for this, just ask yourself which hour do you instinctively prefer to go to bed (for example between 10pm and 11pm) and which hour do you prefer to wake up (e.g., between 7am and 8am.)?

The truth is that for most us our daily demands and the associated routines do not allow us to follow our preferred circadian rhythm. Recognizing the imbalance allows us to plan ways to compensate. For example, if your schedule requires that you have to wake early and you are not a morning person, do some exercise first thing and use light to increase blood flow and activity in your brain.

Light and sleep

Yes, we did say *use light*. Our brain and body react to the natural 24-hour cycle of daylight and nighttime. Light brings us and keeps us awake; darkness encourages sleep. Central to this process is melatonin, a hormone secreted by the pineal gland situated near the middle of your brain. In daylight when we need to be alert we produce less melatonin, when it becomes dark and we begin preparing for sleep we produce more.

Natural light during the day helps us to be active. Too much unnatural light in the evening can prevent us from becoming sleepy. Many aspects of our daily lives can disrupt our production of melatonin and with it our circadian rhythms. If, for example, you spend your working day in an office away from natural light you might find yourself becoming drowsy as your melatonin levels increase. If, on the other hand, you spend several hours in front of a bright TV or computer screen just before going to bed, you might find it harder to sleep as your levels rise.

Thankfully, there are many relatively easy things we can do to help manage our production of melatonin and regulate our sleep rhythms.

You can increase your exposure to natural light during the day by:

- Spending at least a few minutes outside, in daylight, first thing in the morning.
- Taking every other opportunity to spend time outside.
- Removing your sunglasses.
- Keeping curtains and blinds open.
- Positioning your work desk as close to the window as possible.

You can increase melatonin production at night by:

- Turning off your TV and computer earlier in the evening.
- Listening to soothing music prior to going to bed.
- Doing some relaxation exercises as preparation for sleep.
- Replacing bright light bulbs with low-wattage ones.
- Making sure your bedroom is dark.

Consistency is an important factor in determining the quality of our sleep and associated rest and recovery. Here are some additional tips:

Sleeping well

- Avoid dozing after dinner.
- If it's too early to go to bed and you are feeling sleepy do something to stimulate your brain.
- Use activities and stimuli that help you relax and unwind as you near bedtime.
- Invest in a comfortable, spacious and supportive bed.
- Keep your neck in a neutral position, as this helps keep movement to a minimum and reduces the chances of you waking up with a stiff neck.
- Keep the temperature in your bedroom at around 65° F (18° C). If the room becomes either too hot or too cold, it can interfere with sleep quality.
- Make your bedroom as quiet as possible. (If necessary, consider using earplugs.)
- Turn your alarm clock around so if you awaken you do not see the clock, because this is likely to start you thinking.
- Make sure your mobile phone is on silent or airplane mode.
- Create very deliberate mental and physical associations to your bedroom – use it only for sleep and sex.[6]
- Avoid eating large meals at night.
- Avoid alcohol, too. Although an alcoholic nightcap might put you to sleep quicker, you will spend more time in Stages 1

---

[6] Which is the only physical, stimulating activity that makes us sleepy.

and 2 of the sleep cycle and less time in the restorative Stages 3 and 4.
- Avoid drinking so much of *anything* at night that it results in you waking up because you have to go to the toilet.
- Limit your caffeine intake. Ideally avoid it in the second half of your day.
- Also, take a good look at any vitamins or nutrition supplements you regularly take, many contain stimulants which can interfere with a good night's rest.

Sleeping well and snacking

If you have to snack before going to bed – and you can do so without it disturbing your sleep – you need to choose the foods with care. Experiment with foods that contain a sleep-inducing amino acid called tryptophan. Tryptophan makes us sleepy because it helps produce serotonin, the chemical that influences our levels of relaxation, and serotonin, in turn, is used to create melatonin. Great late night snacks include:

- Cereal with milk
- Bananas
- Almonds
- A small muffin

Sleeping well and exercising

Yin and yang, that's how we referred to rest and exercise at the end of Chapter 2. Although the content of each chapter in this book can be addressed and acted upon in their own right and in any order, they do all interact. That's one of the reasons why we are calling this a Process. If you've read Chapter 2 you'll know that if you are physically active and exercise regularly, you're more likely to sleep deeply and well.

In the evening, exercise that can be used to relax and calm both mind and body, such as yoga, will help prepare you for sleep. Avoid strenuous exercise just before going to bed.

Sleeping well and managing anxiety

This is another topic that relates most clearly to another part of the book – in this case, Chapter 6 Emotional Management.

Negative emotions such as anger or worry not only make it difficult for us to go to sleep but also to sleep well. Sometimes we experience what we can think of as *residual stress*, left behind by the pressures of the day, manifesting itself as we review what has happened and evaluate our performance. Sometimes our stress is caused by thoughts of what lies ahead tomorrow.

If you are anxious about tomorrow you might write a list of what has to be done, ticking off all the things that are already in place and highlighting those you are prepared for; reminding yourself – *showing* yourself – that you are well organized and, therefore, ready to sleep.

No matter what the cause of your anxiety a well-established pre-sleep routine that encourages and enables you to relax and wind-down will increase your chance of a good night's rest.

Your pre-sleep routine

Just as warming up prepares you to exercise safely and well, so winding down and relaxing prepares you to sleep well. As with warming up, the key here is to prepare both mind and body for what is to come. Start slowing down at least thirty minutes before you intend to go to bed. Remember, your brain works at a super-fast speed and this is not conducive to sleep. We need a routine, therefore, to help us slow down.

The 'to do and already done' list we mentioned a moment ago can help you organize your thoughts. Gentle, relaxation exercises or breathing techniques can also help. A warm bath or shower will relax you and change your body temperature, which is a useful precursor to sleep. You might choose to listen to soothing music. Or find other ways to gradually *slow yourself down* as your approach bedtime. And do have a specific *bed time*. As we said earlier, consistency is a powerful ally when it comes to getting a great night's sleep due to your neural pathways firing in consistent patterns, so do have a deliberate sleeping and rising schedule.

By establishing a pre-sleep routine, you are creating a powerful brain-body association; a habit that, like all habits, becomes increasingly easy to do and ever more easily creates the associated outcome.

Sometimes, though, even if we become really good at going to sleep, we find ourselves waking up during the night. We need to know how best to manage this, too.

Going back to sleep

Just to be clear, the following tips are for use if you find yourself waking at night feeling unable to go straight back to sleep. It's common for even the best sleepers to wake briefly – sometimes though, it's for such a short period of time they don't even remember it. So, if you ever find yourself awake and struggling to sleep, do the following:

- Avoid trying to change the topic of your thoughts. Instead allow yourself to keep thinking about whatever is in your mind. (If you try to change the topic you risk creating internal conflict and/or other unwanted thoughts.)

- Gently slow down the speed of those thoughts; do this over 5-10 minutes.
- Deliberately slow down your breathing rate to assist with this.
- Deliberately yawn – maybe once every minute.
- Just ease yourself into slowing down and relaxing – focus on relaxing rather than telling yourself you must go back to sleep.

If you are asking yourself why the practice of counting sheep is not on our list, it's because sheep counting (or counting any other animal for that matter) can be a challenge on two fronts:

1. To focus on the sheep, you have to be able to stop thinking about whatever was in your mind when you woke up and that is usually difficult to do – hence our advice to simply slow down rather than attempt to change your thoughts.
2. If you do visualize sheep, they are likely to 'move' quickly – at the speed of your thoughts. So, if you do want to use this technique slow the sheep down gradually and deliberately whilst applying the other tips.

For people who work shifts there are usually two additional problems to face. These are sleeping during the day and staying awake throughout the night.

Sleeping well and shift work

Establishing a refreshing sleep schedule when required to work shifts can be tricky. Here are some things you can do to create the consistency you need:

- Ideally limit the number of consecutive shifts you work. Failing that, avoid changing shifts frequently so that you can at least create a regular sleep schedule.

Rest and Recovery

- Manage your exposure to light. Use bright light when you wake up at night and, if possible, use daylight-simulation bulbs in your place of work. If you are travelling home in the morning, when the sun is up, wear sunglasses to make things dark and so encourage melatonin release and sleepiness.
- Avoid drinking caffeine in the second half of your shift.
- Use your breaks at work to move as much as possible.
- Make sure your bedroom is silent and dark during the day.
- On your non-working days, prioritize sleeping to make up for any sleep debt.

It's not only shift work that affects our natural rhythms so, too, does travelling abroad.

Sleeping well when travelling

Here are some suggestions:

- If you are travelling Eastwards begin your preparations 3 or 4 days in advance by both going to sleep and waking up one hour earlier than is your usual routine.
- If you are travelling Westward, reverse this – sleep and rise an hour later.
- Sleeping for several hours during the flight can be also helpful.
- Avoid drinking too much alcohol during the flight.
- If possible, arrive in the afternoon; this will allow you to instigate your normal sleeping routine.
- When you arrive eat foods high in tryptophan to help stimulate melatonin.
- Exercising when you get to your destination will also help you to fall asleep more easily.

As we come to the end of the chapter, let's repeat our central point: the occasional bout of sleep deprivation is easily managed. However, on-going sleep deprivation is not a sustainable strategy for high-quality performance and wellbeing. Inevitably, it impairs our ability to perform by damaging our brain and all connected sub-systems.

Rest and recovery is a vital part of the Process of our lives. We need to ensure we manage it well. And we can.

With that said, we're both off for a much needed rest of our own.

Coming up next: optimum nutrition.

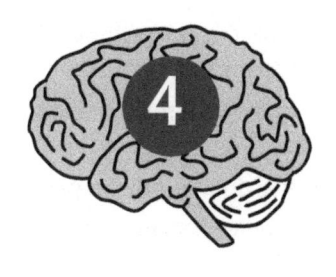

Optimum Nutrition

'The food you eat can be either the safest and most powerful form of medicine or the slowest form of poison.'

Ann Wigmore

Brain Priming – Chapter in focus

Here are the key facts and messages:
- Nutrition is brain fuel – your brain is dependent on the energy you take in.
- 30% of your calories are consumed by your brain at rest.
- A healthy brain is 60% fat.
- Large amounts of fat and sugar are detrimental to brain health and performance.
- The enteric nervous system – an interconnected system of

neurons that controls the gastrointestinal system - is often referred to as the second brain.
- There are tens of trillions of microorganisms living in your gastrointestinal tract.
- Nutrition is personal; food produces personal responses.
- Obesity equals cognitive decline, the pounds matter beyond your waistline.
- Foods that reduce inflammation assist one of the brain's primary functions of repairing and strengthening.
- States of dehydration cause the brain to work harder over time and limit our cognitive function.

Fat, gut and bugs

That's probably not the sub-heading you were expecting in a chapter titled *Optimum Nutrition*.[1] You might reasonably have expected us to begin with something like:

The brain is greedy

Because when we first introduced the governor we said that, despite weighing only approximately 3lbs, the average adult brain consumes 30% of all calories when at rest. Which does make it pretty greedy, right?

John weighs in at a fit and lean 180lbs. His brain, therefore, is only 1.6% of his overall weight. Yet that 1.6% uses nearly a third of the energy from his food input! It's a good reminder of just how much energy the brain requires as it processes, predicts and protects

---

[1] Chris here: To be fair, neither was I. When John first looked me in the eyes and said, 'Fat, gut and bugs' I thought he was making an uncharacteristic personal attack.

day-in and day-out. It's a good reminder, too, of how important our nutrition is. In one very important sense when we eat we are energizing our brain. To a greater or lesser degree.

We are what we might think of as a *closed energy system*. That means our brain is dependent on the energy we put in.[2] Earlier John made the point that the brain, unlike even the world's best cars, can create useable energy out of the most inappropriate fuel. However, the fact that it can do this, that it can keep performing regardless, is not a reason for ignoring the quality of our nutrition. Actually, it's a reason for doing the opposite. We can make small adjustments for short and long term gains.

What we eat and drink on a daily basis is one of the few things we can control to a significant degree. Our family, work and social commitments might limit the times we can do physical activity. At work we might be obliged to spend hours every day looking into a computer screen.[3] Our work schedule might not have sufficient rest periods built in. However, when it comes to what we eat and drink and how much of it we eat and drink we have a choice. We also have the personal power to exercise that choice.

It's easy to recognize the physical benefits of managing our nutrition well. You can choose a diet to help you lose weight. Or an eating plan designed to build muscle. We all know that what we eat directly affects how we look. However, our argument is that you - *we* - should do more than that. We should think of our nutritional input, along with all the other elements of our Process, as being of importance to our brain first and foremost. Of course, by managing our nutrition well we can, and will, achieve other benefits. Just as we will by engaging in sufficient physical activity, giving ourselves

---

[2] Which, we acknowledge, is pretty obvious. After all your brain can't go out and feed itself, can it?

[3] More about that in Chapter 5.

enough time for rest and recovery, and incorporating those other elements we talk about in future chapters. Top of the priority list, though, is the governor. And, even if fat, gut and bugs seems an unlikely sub-heading to most of us, it really does make sense when we start from the *nutrition is brain fuel* perspective.

Let's start by talking briefly about fat:

Your brain is nearly 60% fat. Recent research suggests that fatty acids play a vital role in determining our brain's level of performance, with some studies relating brain impairment to dietary intake lacking such fatty acids. It seems that by fuelling our brain with appropriate fats we can help protect against some brain diseases and positively influence learning and memory. For example, according to Fernando Gomez-Pinilla, Professor of Neurosurgery and Physiological Science at UCLA, Omega-3 fatty acids – found in foods as diverse as salmon and walnuts - provide just such benefits. Gomez-Pinilla says, 'Omega-3 fatty acids support synaptic plasticity and seem to positively affect the expression of several molecules related to learning and memory that are found on synapses...Omega-3 fatty acids are essential for normal brain function.'

It's important to note, however, that there are many different kinds of saturated and unsaturated fatty acids, and scientists are still working hard to understand how they all function in the body.[4]

Now it's time for gut and bugs:

The relationship between the brain and gut is a significant one. Actually, the relationship is so significant and the gut is so influential it is regarded and referred to by many as *the second brain*! When using this term people are actually referring to the *enteric nervous system*.

---

[4] We provide a guideline relating to fat consumption in the Process section of this Chapter.

The enteric nervous system, also known as the intrinsic nervous system, runs throughout the gastrointestinal system from the oesophagus, a muscular tube that connects throat and stomach, to the anus. The ENS is a complex network of approximately 500,000,000 neurons, neurotransmitters and proteins embedded in the sheaths of tissue that line the oesophagus, stomach, small intestine and colon. It's a network with extensive back and forth connections with the central nervous system. It appears to operate mainly independently of the brain and spinal cord and interacts with the brain by sending and receiving impulses and responding to emotions. It's because of this perceived independence and its significant role in our overall health and performance that the ENS is referred to as the second brain.[5]

It is true to say, then, that beyond the emotional and intuitive gut feelings most of us are familiar with[6], our gut really does play its part in determining the nature of our life experience. Not surprisingly, it's a topic of extensive research.

Our gut is made up of a huge microbe population known as microbiota. These are the bugs in your gut. They include over 1,000 different species of known bacteria, at least 10 times as many more viruses, and more than 3,000,000 genes – many times more than the number of human genes. There are, it is estimated, tens of trillions of microorganisms living in our intestine. To put it into a different context, there are 10 times more microorganisms living in your gastrointestinal tract than there are cells in your entire body!

This complex mix of microbiota weighs approximately 1kg in adults and its composition varies from person to person. Only

---

[5] It is worth pointing out that, despite the second brain analogy, our actual brain performs far more functions and roles than the ENS.

[6] And these are significant!

one third is common to most of us and the rest is as individual as our personality. In one sense, then, we have a unique mini-ecosystem operating inside us. The totality of this system is called the microbiome.

We share a symbiotic relationship with it. We provide the microbes in our gut with a regular supply of nutrition and they then influence our brain and, by extension, many aspects of how we function. For example, the microbiome serves to:

- Help the body digest some foods that the stomach and small intestine cannot.
- Help with the production of certain vitamins.
- Maintain the integrity of our immune system.

When this relationship – referred to as the gut-brain axis - works successfully we maintain a balance that enables us to perform well physically and emotionally. When it doesn't we risk imbalance and performance deficit. We know this because researchers are investigating just how the microbiome regulates our thoughts and feelings. The evidence is suggesting that the relationship between our gut microbes and our brain can influence both our perception of the world and our behavior. It seems that microbes in our gut influence:

- Neurotransmitters being released.
- Our immune system.
- Energy management.
- Emotional management.
- Brain communications.

Having said that, and despite the on-going research, it's not yet clear precisely how the microbiome influences the brain. There is, however, general agreement amongst researchers that there are probably several mechanisms at work. For example, the enteric nervous system uses over 30 neurotransmitters – just like the brain itself - including serotonin, dopamine and GABA all of which influence the moods we experience. In fact, 95% of all serotonin, which regulates feelings of happiness, is found in the bowels. Low levels of serotonin are also associated with a decrease in immune system function.

Also it seems there are some microbes capable of activating the vagus nerve, the longest cranial nerve, passing through the neck and thorax to the abdomen. It serves as the primary line of communication between the gut and brain. And the immune system itself acts as another important communication route between gut and governor.

This interaction between bugs and brain might seem surprising, yet it has been around for a very long time. After all, bacteria have lived inside people for as long as we have been around. That doesn't, though, answer the question *Why?* What is the benefit of their presence? What do we gain as a species? Well, we've already highlighted the fact that the microbiome influences our moods and, fairly obviously, this includes stress levels. There is also evidence suggesting that certain foods interact with our gut bacteria in ways that positively influence our brain and emotional states. For example, a study published in 2013 revealed the quite startling effects of simply eating yoghurt twice a day.

Yoghurt contains live bacteria known as probiotics that can also be found in dairy products. Probiotics are delicate in nature and can be killed by stomach acid before they can be of benefit.[7] Given the unique nature of our gut microbiology, when we ingest probiotics we're taking a chance that they will be good for us. According to the results of the study one of the benefits of eating just one cup of yoghurt twice a day seems to be that it can enhance feelings

---

[7] Probiotics might introduce good bacteria into your gut; prebiotics nourish the good bacteria that are already present.

of calmness. Out of a group of 25 healthy women, 12 ate the yoghurt every day for 4 weeks whilst the rest did not. All of the women were given brain scans before and after the 4-week period to gauge their individual response as they viewed a variety of different facial expressions, including anger and sadness. The differences were clear. The yoghurt eaters were calmer than their counterparts, leading the researchers to consider the possibility that the bacteria contained in the yoghurt influenced the women's gut microbes and that in turn affected their brain chemistry.

Another possible benefit of mood modification, according to Dr John Cryan a neuroscientist at the University College of Cork in Ireland, is that it enhances our sociability.[8] The argument being the happier the individual is the more likely they are to socialize and be welcomed for doing so. This is not only significant for the survival and success of the human race, but also for the survival of our gut microbes. The more we interact with others, the more opportunities our microbes have to spread. It's possible, then, that at least some of our gut microbes have played their part in developing our behavior for their own ends. If this were the case, it would be further proof of the symbiotic nature of the relationship we share with the bugs in our gut.

It's a relationship that might also influence the development of our cognitive abilities. Researchers are gathering increasing evidence that such processes as memory and learning are affected by, and perhaps to some extent even dependent upon, aspects of our microbiota. Which raises another question: If our cognitive capabilities develop over time, does this mean that the microbes in our gut also develop as the years pass?

The simple answer is *Yes*. The predominant view – although some research is now challenging this - is that at birth the newborn's

---

[8] More about Socialization in Chapter 7.

gut is sterile; initial colonization is determined therefore by the mother's microbes and other factors such as the mode of delivery, the nature of the environment, diet and any antibiotic use. As the baby ages its microbiota becomes more diverse and by its first birthday each baby has its own distinct microbial profile. This continues to develop until around two and half years of age by which time the child's microbiota resembles that of an adult.

The nature and make-up of each individual's gut environment determines which microbes survive and thrive. The speed with which food moves through the system and the amount of mucus lining the gut are two such important environmental factors. Both can be influenced by an increase in stress levels and, of course, by a change in diet.

We are what we eat

At least according to the adage. However, based on what we have already said a more accurate description might be: We are what our microbes eat. And, of course, what our brain consumes.

The transfer of energy from foods to communications throughout the body is fundamental to brain function. That's why dietary disorders can affect cognitive processes. It's why you notice your concentration levels dropping when you're hungry or when you're not hydrated.

Because our brain and gut communication is bidirectional any changes in communication can alter energy in either location. We'll define and discuss *communication* in more detail in Chapter 7. For now it's sufficient to say that it is absolutely appropriate to refer to the interaction between brain and gut as communication. They do exchange, one to the other.

Throughout this book we have, and do, refer to the brain as *the governor* and in Chapter 1 we began by highlighting the importance of connections. The connection – the communication – between our brain and gut is vital. It's a relationship that makes itself known in many ways. When an imbalance occurs we can experience any of the following:

- Bloating.
- Nausea.
- Canker sores, sores on the tongue.
- White coating on the tongue.
- Chronic heartburn.
- Diarrhea, constipation, or abdominal pain.
- Irritable Bowl Syndrome.
- Chronic yeast infections.
- Craving for sweets/carbohydrate.
- Chronic fatigue.
- Hives.
- Psoriasis or eczema.
- Acne or rosacea.
- Mood disorders like anxiety or depression.
- Autism or ADD/ADHD.

The simple message, as the following diagram shows, is that when we get the communication between our brain and gut right – as with every other type of communication – we create a positive dynamic. The more we get it wrong, the more negative the outcome.

The value of the small adjustments and long term gains we mentioned a few pages ago are highlighted in a study that monitored the diets, mental health and cognitive abilities of more than 27,000 people aged 55 and over in 40 middle-to-high income countries. The study ran for several years. It concluded with the

Healthy CNS function — **Abnormal CNS function**

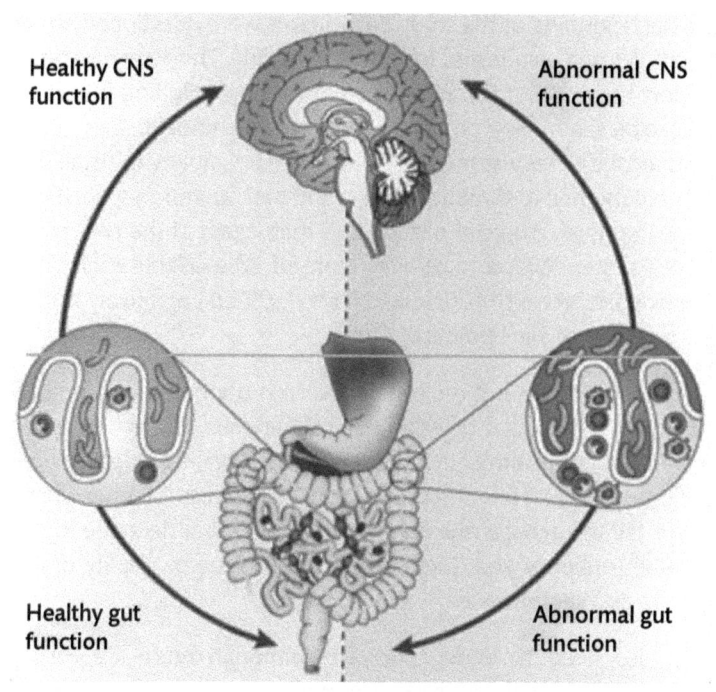

Healthy gut function — **Abnormal gut function**

Healthy status
- Normal behaviour, cognition, emotion nociception
- Heathy levels of inflammatory cells and/or mediators
- Normal gut microbiota

Stress/disease
- Alterations in behaviour, cognition, emotion nociception
- Altered levels of inflammatory cells and/or mediators
- Intestinal dysbiosis

Source: http://allergiesandyourgut.com/2015/07/04/psychobiotics-your-gut-bacteria-your-mood/

researchers reporting that, even when taking into account other factors that can influence cognitive performance such as physical activity, high blood pressure and a history of cancer, those who ate a healthier diet were 24% less likely to experience decline in memory, attention and reasoning ability than those who did not.

At the beginning of the study participants were questioned about their diet and also tested for cognitive ability. They were asked to report how often they ate a variety of foods including fruits and vegetables, nuts, soy proteins, whole grains and deep-fried foods and alcohol. The test measured each person's ability to recall lists of objects, their arithmetic prowess and their attention span. It was repeated 2 years into the study and then again at the end, some 3 years later. With a maximum score of 30 available each time, participants were considered to have declined cognitively if their score dropped by 3 points or more.

According to the authors of this research poor nutrition is likely to deprive the brain of vitamins and minerals that promote the generation of healthy new cells, help guard against inflammation, help break down fats and protect cells from stress. In other words, if we fail to manage our nutrition well we risk a decrease in our overall resiliency and, therefore, in the long-term quality of our health and performance.

We also need to understand that, although there are certain guidelines and behaviors we would all be well advised to follow, when it comes to what we eat and drink we do have our own specific requirements. This book is here to help you create your own individual, personal brain management Process; determining – and consistently meeting – your own nutritional needs is an essential and clear example of this. You see, despite the many common lessons we can all learn from the great research that's taking place, it's also true to say that:

Nutrition is Personal

Which, we admit, is a phrase that's in danger of reading like a cheesy Facebook post or a strapline for a new nutritional product. Thankfully it's neither. It's actually the conclusion drawn from a study carried out by a team of researchers led by Eran Elinav and Eran Segal.

The team studied the blood glucose levels of 800 people over a 7-day period. They collected data using a variety of common methods including blood tests, health questionnaires, glucose monitoring, stool samples and body measurements. By the end of the study nearly 47,000 meals had been measured providing more than 2,000 measurements for each participant and a grand total of more than 1,600,000 measurements overall.

Blood glucose, sometimes referred to as blood *sugar*, supplies energy to all the cells in our body. It is made from the food we eat. Our body seeks to regulate our blood glucose levels and if the balance is lost such health problems as diabetes and obesity can result. The team expected to find that the age and body mass index (BMI) of each participant would influence their blood glucose levels after eating. Indeed, it did.

What the team also discovered however was that different individuals responded very differently to the same food. For example, one participant who had tried unsuccessfully using diets to help manage problems of obesity and pre-diabetes, experienced sudden increases in her blood glucose levels after eating tomatoes. Her so-called *healthy* eating habits may well, it seems, have been contributing to her problems. According to Elinav, 'For this person, an individualized tailored diet would not have included tomatoes but may have included other ingredients that many of us would not consider healthy, but are in fact healthy for her. Before this study was conducted, there is no way that anyone could have provided her with such personalized recommendations, which may substantially impact the progression of her pre-diabetes.'

To gain greater insight into why these individual differences occur, the researchers studied the microbiome of each participant. They then created personalized diets for 26 individuals. In each case the new diet resulted in a reduction in post-meal blood glucose levels and a change in gut microbiota. Incredibly, other research suggests that a new diet can create microbial changes in our gut within 24 hours.

As a result of their findings Segal said, 'I think about the possibility that maybe we're really conceptually wrong in our thinking about the obesity and diabetes epidemic... People are actually compliant but in many cases we were giving them wrong advice... It's common knowledge among dieticians and doctors that their patients respond very differently to assigned diets. We can see in the data that the same general recommendations are not always helping people, and my biggest hope is that we can move this boat and steer it in a different direction.'

The obesity epidemic, as Segal referred to it, is a source of concern for many reasons. One of which is the relationship between:

Obesity and cognitive decline

Evidence is building to suggest that, beyond all the other detrimental effects of obesity, it can also impact negatively on cognitive performance. An 8-year long study of people who were in their early sixties when the research began revealed that the hippocampus of those who were obese shrank by almost 2% a year. The hippocampus is a brain region that plays a vital role in the processing of memory. A 2% yearly loss is similar to that experienced by people suffering from Alzheimer's disease and is nearly twice that found in people of normal weight.

The researchers used magnetic resonance imaging (MRI) to study the brains of over 400 people. It became clear from their very first measurements that those who were obese had smaller hippocampi than those who were not – even when other factors such as physical activity and education were taken into account.

The 2% shrinkage rate was, according to the co-author of the study Dr Nicolas Cherbuin, likely to cause other problems beyond memory loss including mood changes and difficulties with decision-making.

With many societies experiencing an ever-increasing elderly population and increases in obesity, such findings highlight the need for influential campaigns that change behavior. In the words of University of Pittsburgh neuroscientist Judy Cameron, 'Obese, sedentary people are aging without a lot of neural protection. By losing weight and exercising more, they would be much more protected against neurodegenerative diseases. It's a message that needs to get out to the public.'

Cherbuin agrees. 'If we don't do something now,' he says, 'we're going to pay so much in 20 or 30 years. We just can't let it happen.'

Before we move on to talk about hydration, we have two more messages we think it's important to share about food. The first is about:

The Myth of Superfoods

As you'll realize by now everything is a Process. In fact, to get the most out of our self and our life we are best advised to personalize that process - and to realize that it's an on-going, lifelong process. We have to get lots of little, yet important, things right. It's combinations and synergies that make the difference.

No matter how much we might wish for that single, magical cure-all that meets all of our physical, cognitive, emotional and social needs, the truth is it doesn't exist. If we want to optimize our performance, we have to consistently combine a number of elements. That's as true for the nutritional element as it is for our overall brain management Process.

Although some foods have been labeled as *superfoods* we strongly advise that you create a healthy diet based on variety rather than falling into the trap of thinking that specific foods are so good for us they limit, or end, our need for others.

Foods that have been elevated to superfood status in recent years include antioxidants[9] and Omega-3, 6, and 9 fatty acids. We are referring to them in this chapter within the context of an appropriately varied diet, as important parts in our personal nutritional jigsaw rather than as stand-alone superstars. Another important point to make when considering all food, not just so-called superfoods, is that diet is inevitably a part of culture and lifestyle. The environment we grow up in and the associated daily routines, behaviors, values and beliefs all influence us profoundly. Levels of activity, everyday stresses, the nature and types of our regular social interactions, are all factors that combine with our diet to determine our wellbeing and capability.

Let's aim, then, to base our nutritional intake on the understanding that:

1. There are no superfoods capable of offsetting a consistent pattern of unhealthy eating.
2. When we get our food combinations right we are supporting and protecting our brain and body in equal measure.

Which leads us on to our second message. It relates to:

Foods that fight inflammation

Whenever our body perceives a foreign invader our immune system goes on the attack. The process is called inflammation. It's

---

[9] We'll talk about those in the Process part of this chapter.

one important way we seek to protect our health. Occasional bouts of inflammation directed at a genuine threat are necessary for our wellbeing and we rely on our body to get this right. However, as with so many other aspects of our lives when an imbalance occurs problems can arise.

Sometimes inflammation can persist, even when there is no invading threat. When this happens the inflammation itself becomes the enemy. In fact, some of our most significant diseases, including cancer, heart disease and diabetes, have been linked to chronic inflammation.

There are, researchers tell us food and drinks that may have anti-inflammatory effects and those that can actually inflame. Once again we have to make some smart choices. If we get our nutrition right, we may reduce the risk of illness. If we get it wrong, we could be inadvertently accelerating the inflammatory disease process.

So which are which?

Well, it probably comes as no surprise to hear that many of the food types generally regarded as bad for our health are those that can also encourage inflammation. These include red and processed meat, fried foods, white bread and pastries and sugar-sweetened drinks. Many of these foods also contribute to weight gain, of course, which further increases the risk of inappropriate inflammation.

As a counter-balance there is a range of foods that appear to possess anti-inflammatory properties. These include fruits such as apples, strawberries and blackberries, vegetables such as leafy greens, fish and healthy oils and also nuts and whole grains. One relatively small study found that men who consumed flaxseed, or linseed as it is also known, for a 6-week period demonstrated a clear decrease in inflammatory markers compared with men who hadn't. In a separate study researchers found that eating ginger root extract seemed to reduce markers of colon inflammation.

Beyond the specifics, the overall message seems to be that a natural, less-processed diet incorporating fruits, vegetables, nuts, fish, healthy oils and grains will help reduce or limit unnecessary levels of inflammation alongside the other benefits it provides. It's important, too, that we keep well hydrated:

Hydration and Brain Health

Hydration is as important as air. It not only serves a neurophysiological need but also a psychological one. Our brain is approximately 80% water; we need to keep it well hydrated. Even slight dehydration can raise stress hormones that can damage our brain over time. It can also cause shrinkage of brain tissue and negatively impact such executive functions as planning and visual and spatial processing.[10] Insufficient hydration negatively affects the gut, too, by slowing the digestive process.

If you think that all you have to do to manage your water intake appropriately is to drink every time you feel thirsty, you are making a serious error. By the time we feel thirsty enough to drink we have already lost 2-3% of our body weight through dehydration! That means from a brain health and performance point of view we are already in a position of weakness. Even mild dehydration, reflecting a 2% loss in body weight, can impair our ability to concentrate, focus attention and recall.

If we create sustained periods of dehydration we make the situation even worse, increasing our chances of suffering from kidney stones, urinary tract infections, high(er) blood pressure and even a stroke. We said quite deliberately *if we create sustained periods*

---

[10] More about these topics in Chapter 5.

of dehydration because drinking is a behavior that's relatively easy for us to control. We can manage not only when we drink but also what we drink and how much. You'll notice that throughout this section we are talking about drinking water.

There is still some debate about the precise nature of our fluid requirements. In order to give you an introductory guideline we'll share the following recommendations from The European Food Safety Authority:

- 1,300 mL/day for boys and girls 2 to 3 years of age
- 1,600 mL/day for boys and girls 4 to 8 years of age
- 2,100 mL/day for boys 9 to 13 years of age
- 1,900 mL for girls 9 to 13 years of age
- 2.5 L/day for adult males 19-70 years of age
- 2.0 L/day for adult females 19-70 years of age

There's little debate however about the impact of hydration on cognitive function and brain performance. Some of the original studies, carried out amongst military personnel, found that dehydration caused a decline in short-term memory, motor coordination, sustained attention and working memory. Subsequent research has supported these findings.

Both hormones and neurotransmitters are influenced by our hydration status. For example, during periods of dehydration there seem to be increases in the so-called stress hormone cortisol, which can result in lower processing speed and memory difficulties. Neurotransmitters such as serotonin and dopamine are also influenced and, if either under- or over-regulated, can negatively impact our mood, attention, memory, sleep, and goal directed behavior.

Water consumption also helps us to maintain and even improve sustained visual attention. Our visual systems take a great amount of energy to sustain and are highly sensitive to our levels of hydration. So, if you want to keep reading this book for a while longer and you're realizing that you are probably currently dehydrated, go and get yourself a drink of water before carrying on.

We'll continue by outlining some other benefits of being well hydrated:

a) Brain cells are better supplied with fresh, oxygen-rich blood and the brain remains alert.
b) Hydration acts as a transporter of oxygen, carbohydrates, vitamins, minerals and other important nutrients to the cells. These then produce energy, enabling the body to function and helping to rid it of waste products.
c) Hydration plays an important role in the digesting of food, dissolving nutrients so they can be absorbed into the bloodstream.
d) Our heart and the associated circulatory system deliver a much-needed constant supply of oxygen to the brain, muscles and all other tissues. Correct regulation of water balance is essential in keeping blood pressure within the healthy range.
e) A well-hydrated healthy person's kidneys filter approximately 180 liters of water each day; an adequate water intake is essential to keep our kidneys working well.
f) Our muscles are made up of 70-75% of water, maintaining the right water balance is therefore essential for optimum muscle function. Water also acts as a lubricant for muscles and joints.
g) Hydration levels play an important role in regulating our internal temperature. When our body becomes too hot, water is lost through sweat as the body seeks to prevent itself from overheating.

As we come to the end of this part of the chapter we'll lead into our usual reminder of the key facts by making one small yet very important addition to a point we have already made: we are not just what we eat, rather we are what we eat *and drink*.

Here's the summary:

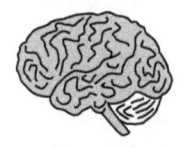

Summary

- Nutrition is brain fuel – your brain is dependent on the energy you take in.
- 30% of your calories are consumed by your brain at rest.
- A healthy brain is 60% fat.
- Large amounts of fat and sugar are detrimental to brain health and performance.
- The enteric nervous system – an interconnected system of neurons that control the gastrointestinal system - is often referred to as the second brain.
- There are tens of trillions of microorganisms living in your gastrointestinal tract.
- Nutrition is personal; food produces personal responses.
- Obesity equals cognitive decline, the pounds matter beyond your waistline.
- Foods that reduce inflammation assist one of the brain's primary functions of repairing and strengthening.
- States of dehydration cause the brain to work harder over time.

The Process

Our recommendations

Remember that the energy you take in through your food and drink serves as fuel for your brain; be brain-wise in what you choose. Remember, too, that responses to nutrition are personal so create a diet that works for you. Aim for consistency in your intake rather than perfection.

Do this by:

1. Emphasizing foods that your brain needs in order to function at its best.
2. Actively avoiding foods (and drinks) that are bad for your brain.
3. Maintaining a balanced diet that incorporates a variety of foods.
4. Consuming between 2,000 and 3,000 calories per day depending upon how active you are.
5. Keeping yourself well hydrated.

Create your own brain-healthy diet

This is a diet that encourages good blood flow to the brain and provides the optimal balance of nutrients. Basic guidelines are:

- Stick to a diet that consists of fresh rather than processed foods.
- Eat three meals or more every day, as both have been found

to be beneficial.
- Only skip meals if you are fasting.

Although many explanations of nutrition and dieting work from the premise of exclusion by highlighting what foods to avoid, we are taking a somewhat different approach. Our focus is on fuel for the brain.

Here's a list of foods to include:

Dark skinned vegetables and fruits

These are good for us because, generally speaking, they have the highest naturally occurring antioxidant levels. Antioxidants are chemicals that work to slow down and sometimes even prevent cell damage by protecting from the damaging effects of molecules known as *free radicals*. These are molecules that contain an unshared electron. It is thought free radicals might contribute to the development of cardiovascular disease and cancer. Examples of vegetables with such antioxidant properties are:

- Spinach
- Brussels sprouts
- Alfalfa sprouts
- Cauliflower
- Beets
- Lettuce
- Broccoli
- Kale
- Red bell pepper
- Onion
- Corn

- Eggplant.

Fruits rich in antioxidants include:

- Blueberries
- Prunes
- Raisins
- Blackberries
- Strawberries
- Raspberries
- Plums
- Oranges
- Red Grapes
- Cherries

Managing your fat intake:

Foods rich in Omega-3 fatty acids

These acids are essential for healthy brain function. They can be found in:

- Cold water fish like Halibut, Mackerel, Salmon, Trout and Tuna[11]
- Oily fish like Sardines and Herring

Nuts & Seeds rich in Vitamin-E/Antioxidants

Vitamin E is a form of antioxidant. It is found in the following nuts, seeds and non-hydrogenated nut butters:

---

[11] Note that Mercury acts as a neurotoxin, interfering with the brain and nervous system, and some fish, including Tuna and Mackeral, are higher in Mercury content. Choose appropriately the amount and frequency of fish in your diet.

- Walnuts, Hazelnuts, Brazil nuts, Pine nuts, Pecans, Filberts, Almonds, Cashews, Peanuts, Sunflower seeds, Sesame seeds, Flax seed
- Peanut butter, Almond butter, Tahini.

Foods rich in Vitamin C and Zinc

Vitamin C is another powerful antioxidant. It helps in the development and maintenance of connective tissue, including bones, blood vessels, and skin. Amongst other benefits, Zinc assists in keeping our immune system healthy, building proteins and triggering enzymes. It also helps the cells in our body communicate by functioning as a neurotransmitter.

Foods that offer a good source of Vitamin C include:

- Red peppers, oranges, grapefruit, kiwi, green peppers, broccoli, strawberries, Brussels sprouts, cantaloupe, cabbage, cauliflower, potato, tomatoes, spinach and green peas.

Foods rich in Zinc include:

- Oysters, beef, crab, fortified breakfast cereals, beans, yogurt, cashews, chickpeas, oatmeal, almonds and peas.

Vegetables rich in Betacarotene

Betacarotene is an antioxidant and a source of vitamin A, which plays an important role in ensuring good eyesight, a strong immune system and healthy skin. Vegetables that are a good source of betacarotene include:

- Carrots, sweet potatoes, spinach, Swiss Chard, pak choi, kale, Cos or Romaine lettuce and parsley.

Whole grains

They are a source of vitamins, minerals, fiber and plant-based protein and, as a regular part of your diet, can help reduce the risk

of chronic diseases including heart disease. Examples include:
- Oatmeal, whole-grain breads, and brown rice.

Beans
Help to stabilize glucose (blood sugar) levels. Our brain is dependent on glucose for fuel and, since it can't store the glucose, it relies on a steady stream of energy that such foods as beans and lentils can provide.

Avocados
Contribute to healthy blood flow and also help lower blood pressure.

Garlic
Incredibly, garlic may actually help stave off some forms of brain cancer! Researchers have found that the organosulfur compounds in garlic actually work to kill glioblastoma, the most common, aggressive primary brain tumor.

Dark Chocolate
If we told you dark chocolate is one of the best sources of antioxidants available anywhere, would you believe us? You'd be right to. Dark chocolate really does have powerful antioxidant properties. It also contains several natural stimulants, including caffeine, which enhance focus and concentration, and stimulates the production of endorphins that help improve mood.

Coffee and Tea
Coffee and green tea are both rich in antioxidants and modest amounts of caffeine have been shown to enhance memory, focus, and mood. Coffee is also a significant source of amino acids, which is important because the neurotransmitters in our brain and gut are

made from amino acids. As we mentioned in Chapter 3 serotonin is made from the amino acid known as tryptophan found in milk, oats and other foods.

Water

Be sure to get enough to keep your body and brain hydrated. When a person becomes dehydrated, their brain tissue actually shrinks. Hydration is essential to replace the water our body is constantly losing through breathing, perspiring, and using the bathroom. Water flushes toxins, helps carry nutrients around the body, and protects tissue.

Here's a reminder of how much water to drink on a daily basis according to The European Food Safety Authority:

- 1,300 mL/day for boys and girls 2 to 3 years of age
- 1,600 mL/day for boys and girls 4 to 8 years of age
- 2,100 mL/day for boys 9 to 13 years of age
- 1,900 mL for girls 9 to 13 years of age
- 2.5 L/day for adult males 19-70 years of age
- 2.0 L/day for adult females 19-70 years of age.

Remember our caveat though that nutrition is personal, so regard the above as guidelines only. Factors such as environmental conditions, intensity of your activity and how much you sweat can influence the exact amount needed. The following tips will help you manage your hydration:

1. Drink water – ideally warm water with a slice of lemon in it – first thing in the morning.
2. Carry a water bottle for easy access when you are at work or running errands.
3. Keep your water bottle visible so you remind yourself to drink throughout the day.

4. Use water bottles that allow you to track with some accuracy how much you drink daily.
5. Eat fruits and vegetables that have high water content. Your food provides an average of 20% of your daily hydration, so the higher the content of water in your food the more hydration it provides.
6. Choose water instead of other beverages when eating out. Generally, you will save money and reduce calories.

Before we talk about the now famous Mediterranean diet, here are a few more general tips:

1. Reduce your intake of foods high in salt, fat and cholesterol. People who have high cholesterol and high blood pressure have six times the risk of dementia. Also a high intake of saturated fat and cholesterol clogs the arteries and is associated with higher risk for Alzheimer's disease.
2. Avoid eating sugar and drinks with added sugar.
3. Bake or grill food instead of frying.
4. Eat only at the kitchen table.
5. Don't drive, watch television or talk on the phone while you eat.
6. Aim for eating more vegetables and fewer high-calorie foods.
7. Eat only because you're hungry, not because you're bored, tired or stressed.
8. Use alternatives to eating when you're not hungry: take a walk, play a game, read a book or call a friend.
9. Do your grocery shopping on a full stomach.
10. Eat a diet that is high in dietary fiber. Eat foods like fruits, vegetables and whole grains.
11. If you smoke: Stop. Smoking interferes with blood flow and oxygen to the brain and is a major risk factor for heart disease,

stroke and Alzheimer's.

12. Adhere to your countries guidelines for alcohol intake. For example in the UK the recommendation is to not regularly drink more than 14 units per week, and to spread the drinking over 3 days or more if you do drink that much.[12] A small amount of alcohol may be related to a healthy heart, and red wine may decrease the risk for developing Alzheimer's. The key word here is *may* so do be cautious.

The Mediterranean diet

Although Mediterranean cuisine, just like any other, varies from region to region common ingredients include fish, olive oil, vegetables, cereal grains, nuts, fruits and beans. Research has shown that this traditional Mediterranean diet reduces the risk of cognitive decline and heart disease along with other illnesses such as diabetes.

To follow the Mediterranean example:

1. Eat primarily plant-based foods such as fruits and vegetables, whole grains, legumes and nuts. On a daily basis eat 6 portions of vegetables, 3 pieces of fruit and such non-refined cereals as whole grain bread, whole grain pasta and brown rice.
2. Ensure that the majority of your meals are made up from a variety of plant foods. They should be processed minimally - fresh and whole are best.
3. Keep almonds, cashews, pistachios and walnuts on hand for whenever you want a quick snack. Nuts and seeds are good sources of fiber, protein and healthy fats.

---

[12] A single unit of unit of alcohol is 10ml or 8g. This is the equivalent of one 25ml single measure of whisky, or a third of a pint of beer, or half a standard (175ml) glass of red wine.

4. Choose natural peanut butter, rather than the kind with hydrogenated fat added.
5. Choose grass fed butter, or replace butter with healthy fats such as olive oil. Use raw extra virgin olive oil.
6. Flavor foods using herbs and spices instead of salt.
7. Choose low-fat dairy. Switch to skimmed milk, fat-free yogurt and low-fat cheese. Ideally choose grass fed dairy because it's richer in Omega-3 fats, vitamin E, beta-carotene, and CLA (Conjugated Linoleic Acid, a beneficial fatty acid).
8. Eat fish 5 or 6 times a week and poultry 4 times. Fresh or water-packed salmon and trout are healthy choices. Grill, bake or broil fish and avoid breaded and fried fish.
9. Limit red meat to no more than 4 times a month. When choosing red meat, make sure it's lean and keep portions small (about the size of a deck of cards).
10. Avoid high-fat, processed meats such as sausage and bacon.

Vitamins and Minerals

A healthy diet, like the Mediterranean diet, should provide you with all the vitamins and minerals you need. There are 2 types of vitamins:

- Fat-soluble
- Water-soluble

Fat-soluble vitamins

These are vitamins A, D, E and K. They are found in such fatty foods as milk and dairy products, eggs, vegetable oils and butter. We don't need to eat these food types everyday in order to get the vitamin benefit because our body stores fat-soluble vitamins in our liver and fatty tissue. We effectively build up a supply of them ready for use. If we store an over-abundance it can be harmful.

Water-soluble vitamins

These are vitamins B, C and folic acid. They are found in fruit, grains, vegetables, potatoes and dairy products. Water-soluble vitamins are not stored in our body and can be destroyed by heat or being exposed to the air. This means, of course, that they can be literally boiled out of our food. It's one reason why steaming or grilling certain foods is recommended.

Minerals such as calcium and iron help to:
- Build bones and teeth
- Control body fluid inside and outside cells
- Turn the food we eat into energy

We get minerals from such foods as fish, meat, cereals, dairy products and fruit.

Sometimes, though, some of us stop eating for a while:

Fasting

There is good evidence that fasting may be beneficial – and it is far from a recent practice. Fasting has been a part of our evolutionary history. As hunter-gatherers our ancestors often went for periods of time without food and this going-without produced protective responses that allowed them to adapt and survive.

A quite popular approach to fasting is known as *intermittent fasting*. This simply requires you to split either the day or the week into periods during which you eat and periods during which you fast. Given that we inevitably go without food when we sleep, some people choose to extend that period by missing out on breakfast. Although food is not allowed during the fasting time, drinks are.

Research into intermittent fasting suggests there are many possible benefits. For example, fasting seems to encourage important cellular repair processes, such as removing waste material from cells. It helps to fight inflammation that, as we have already said, seems to be a key driver of many diseases. It also increases the growth of new nerve cells, which could have benefits for brain function and increases levels of the brain hormone called brain-derived neurotrophic factor. A deficiency of BDNF has been associated with depression and other brain problems.

Despite the apparent positives, we would caution that fasting is not appropriate for the very young, people over 70 and those with illnesses who require a specific calorific intake. If you are uncertain whether or not fasting will be good for you, check with your physician. If you do make fasting a part of your own personal Process do ensure you keep well hydrated.

The next chapter is about cognitive function.

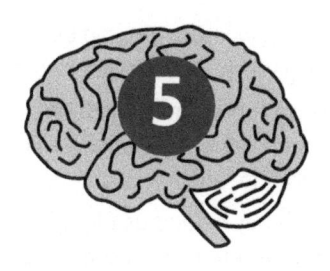

Cognitive Function

'Cognition reigns but does not rule.'

Paul Valery

Brain Priming – This chapter in focus

Here are the key facts and messages:

- Every day on average we have 70,000 thoughts.
- The frontal lobe is the primary driver of high-level thinking.
- Your frontal lobe is about 1/3 of your brain.
- The frontal lobe is often the first to show cognitive decline.
- Our frontal lobe synchronizes with the limbic system and the three other major lobes: temporal, parietal and occipital.
- Thinking faster, increasing memory capacity, and recall of facts and events starts right behind your forehead.
- Although cognitive decline starts for many in the fourth

decade of life, we now know this can be influenced – positively and negatively - by lifestyle choices.
- High level thinking coordinated by the frontal lobe is maintained through key elements of elimination/reduction, delegation/integration, and socialization.
- The latest research has helped us pinpoint the brain circuits for forming habits and to learn more about how we create memories.
- Cognitive overload is a part of modern life; however, our brain is made to adapt and we can help it do so. How we manage technology is one key part of this.

Thinking about thinking - and the so many other things we take for granted

Before we think even about thinking, let's take a moment instead to think about yesterday morning; to think about everything that happened from the moment you woke until midday. Think about all the things you did – even the apparently simple taken-for-granted things like remembering where the kettle is or where the keys are kept – and all the decisions you made and the judgments you exercised, and think too of the ways you gave attention to and interpreted what was happening around you – everything from how the weather looked to what people meant when they communicated with you and how best to respond. Think of all the things you had to *know* and all the predictions you had to make in order to manage yesterday morning as easily as you did. Think of all the feedback and learning you assimilated as you progressed through your morning.

If you review yesterday morning on a second-by-second, minute-by-minute basis you'll realize that even if you didn't apparently do too much your time was actually filled with an almost endless process of giving attention and interpreting, moving, remembering, communicating, reasoning, deciding and problem solving. You might also have done much, or all, of this whilst working to a specific schedule[1] or within a particular timeframe.

Yesterday John received a call on his mobile phone at 9.55am. It was from a client and John was pretty sure, based on their last conversation, what the client wanted to talk about. It was a conversation that John estimated would last at least 15 minutes. He had a meeting to go to that started at 10. John took the call, made the client feel valued and understood, progressed the topic, explained why he couldn't stay on the phone any longer, agreed a time when they could talk fully and walked into the meeting on time without giving any indication that it had been a near thing.

That's pretty much an everyday scenario, right? It seems so straightforward that it's unlikely anyone is thinking, *Well, of course John can manage that because he's a hugely experienced Clinical Psychologist*. Yet the truth is, even though we might all have been able to manage the demands of that situation, there was a heck of a lot going on! To highlight exactly what, let's just take those few minutes of John's morning step by step.

To begin with, he had to hear the ringtone on his phone and identify it correctly. That requires perception. He then recognized the number and, from a range of possibilities, evaluated the most likely reason for the call. That required both recall and complex reasoning. Motor skills came next when he operated and lifted the phone. A mixture of language – both speaking and understanding – and social skills were brought into play throughout the conversation. John also managed to give his

---

[1] The fact that you instantly understand what we mean by *schedule* and the fact that you can create and/or work to a schedule is due to you possessing a variety of interconnected cognitive abilities; it is a consequence of the so many things we take for granted.

attention to the competing demands of his caller and his meeting schedule, ensuring that he ended his conversation well and got to his meeting as planned.

In short, in those few minutes, John demonstrated a wide range of cognitive functions. These are the cerebral/brain-based activities that help us to gather information and develop knowledge, and so manage the myriad experiences and interactions we experience on a daily basis. They include perception, attention giving, memory, motor skills and spatial processing, thinking and reasoning, judgment and evaluation, language use, social skills and problem solving.

We use all of our cognitive abilities both consciously and subconsciously to help steer us through our day, and to help devise new and better days. They are abilities that are easy to take for granted when they are functioning normally. You are using some of them right now as you read and think about this book.

We referenced *thinking* in the sub-heading to this section rather than any of our other cognitive functions because we all recognize that we think frequently; we know that it's an activity that is common to just about everything we do, whether in our professional, social or personal lives. We are aware that we are thinking beings. It would be difficult not to be. If you think about it. Especially given that we have on average 70,000 thoughts a day.

In Chapter 6 we'll talk about the importance and inevitability of emotions and how they influence our behavior. It is true that emotions can overwhelm our cognitive functioning and, if we lose emotional control, we can lose with it our ability to use those cognitive skills and processes we tend to take for granted. After all, it's hard to think straight when our emotions are running riot. For now we'll focus on cognition and our vitally important cognitive functioning.

We can trace the origins of our word *cognition* back to the 15th century. It was used then to refer to *thinking* and *awareness*. Interest in the cognitive process, though, began a long time before that. As far back as the 3rd century BC the Greek philosopher Aristotle gave much of his attention to such cognitive aspects as memory, perception and mental imagery and how these affect human experience. Over subsequent millennia and as the field of psychology developed, cognitive research and, therefore, our understanding have grown significantly. Now cognitive science is a well-established inter-disciplinary field made up of psychology, neuroscience, linguistics, artificial intelligence, philosophy and anthropology.

The part of the brain that controls our important cognitive skills is the frontal lobe. We made reference to the frontal lobe in Chapter 1 and promised we would talk about it in more detail later. This is the later we were talking about:

The frontal lobe

It's located right behind your forehead and is divided into 2 hemispheres. The right hemisphere controls the left side of your body and vice versa. The frontal lobe not only controls planning, organizing, critical thinking, memory, problem solving and the attention process, it's also responsible for primary motor function (movement), the processing of emotion, complex decision-making and speech. However, these abilities are not accomplished by the frontal lobe alone. In order to direct our cognitive functioning, it connects and interacts with other areas of the brain via neural pathways, creating a vast network of reciprocal interconnections. Indeed, one way to think of the frontal lobe is as the brain's relay station. As we said in Chapter 1:

The frontal lobe is front and center when it comes to brain health and optimization.

Here's a visual reminder of how and where it fits:

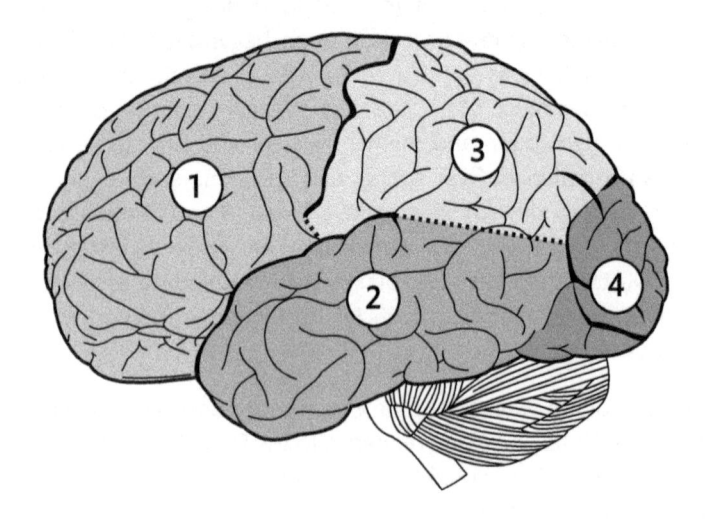

The frontal lobe is area number 1. The temporal lobe is number 2, the parietal lobe is 3 and the occipital lobe is 4.

The frontal lobe is the largest of the four major lobes of the cerebral cortex, making up nearly 1/3rd of your entire brain. It is positioned in front of the parietal lobe and above and in front of the temporal lobe.

What the diagram doesn't show is that the frontal lobe contains most of the dopamine-sensitive neurons. Dopamine is the neurotransmitter that is considered to be both excitatory and inhibitory. Although most commonly referred to in relation to feelings of reward and pleasure, dopamine is also associated with attention and short-term memory. It enables focus and is responsible for our drive to get things done.

You might think, because of the significant role the frontal lobe plays in our everyday performance, that it develops quickly; enabling us to manage our emotions, movements, communications, decision-making and thinking to our own advantage. You'd be wrong, though. The frontal lobe develops slowly. In boys the number of neurons in the frontal lobe increase until an average age of just over 12. In girls the age is just over 10. It doesn't stop there, however. The frontal lobe isn't fully formed and operational until a person is in their mid-late 20's.

Perhaps you guessed that? Perhaps if you are, or have been, a parent of teenagers you'd already worked that out? Research into frontal lobe development does much to explain why teenagers might make irrational decisions, have trouble controlling their emotions and/or communicating appropriately. The brain's relay station and the pathways to and from it are not complete during what can often be difficult teenage years and, consequently, the ability to manage some key aspects of cognitive functioning can be limited. So, if you ever experience a teenager demonstrating challenging, counter-productive or even potentially self-damaging behavior, you might:

a) Remind yourself that their frontal lobe is quite literally still a work in progress and that it's therefore unfair perhaps to expect the same levels of reasoning and self-control, particularly the dampening down of emotional responses, that we would from adults.

b) Take the opportunity – if, indeed, it exists – to explain to them something about what is actually happening inside their head.[2]

Paradoxically, given that the frontal lobe is slow to develop, the first signs of atrophy begin to occur in our mid 40's. Having said that we can, as we will discuss in the Process part of this chapter, actively do things to manage that decline. This is important given that our brain functions to ensure our survival – and a healthy, fully

---

[2] Although you needn't necessarily wait until teenage years. We think it's never too early to explain how and why the brain always wins.

functional frontal lobe is essential in this regard.

Although our frontal lobe evolved originally to control increasingly complex movement, its continual expansion has enabled us to do so much more, including thinking in many different ways, remembering, communicating, imagining and strategizing; all of which are vital in helping us achieve our goals. Indeed, the ability to remember past events and associated learning, whilst prioritizing and memorizing key elements of the present based on a plan for the future is as essential for our personal, professional and social development as it is for our survival. Recall and accurate prediction are vital to managing not only what we are doing in the moment, but also what we are intending to do in the days, months or years ahead.

Apart from the obviousness of our many thoughts and some of our other behaviors, much of our cognitive processing occurs subconsciously. This enables us to give attention to very specific stimuli, to filter our perception and attention-giving dependent on what's happening in our environment in relation to our current needs or future plans.

One of the other benefits of successful cognitive functioning is the interconnected sense of safety and calmness it creates. This feeling of security allows us to go inward, to reflect and ponder, to contemplate and create. It's a state that plays an important part in the creation of the cultural and artistic accomplishments we often associate with the cerebral cortex; those things that add unique value to our life experience and emphasize the unique qualities we possess as a species. We need to remember, too, that this part of our brain does more than enable creativity and expression. It also inhibits capabilities and responses that are either not needed as we mature (for example, the newborn's grasping reflex) or are deemed inappropriate (for example, a raging, emotional outburst in a business meeting).

It would be easy to imagine that our multi-faceted frontal lobe, evolving to 1/3rd of our entire brain size, enabling the highest levels of cognition and control, is disproportionately bigger than those of the other primates. This was certainly thought to be the case for many years. Not anymore. Research using magnetic resonance imaging has determined that the human frontal cortex is not in fact relatively larger than that of the other great apes. It does, though, put us top of the list when it comes to cognitive functioning. We know more, we keep learning more and, therefore, we can do more than any other species on the planet. Cognitive functions, including our inherent desire and ability to communicate and socialize,[3] underpin our survival and success. That's why we are going to direct our attention to them now, beginning with:

Attention

For most of us giving attention is such a basic commonplace activity it falls all-too-easily into the taken-for-granted category. Yet, as is so often the case, familiarity can blind us to complexity and variety. And attention has both. Here's a quick overview:

We can say we are giving attention when we focus appropriate cognitive resources on a specific stimulus as we simultaneously filter or ignore what we have determined to be irrelevant. We can think of attention as the allocation of our limited processing resources. And we could stop there surely? After all how complicated can it be? Well, actually, it's really complicated. That's why we said we are offering only a quick overview.

Attention has been - and is being - widely researched. Why is it deemed to be of such importance? For 2 reasons. Firstly, because it is a complex brain activity. Secondly, because what we give our attention to at any point in time directly influences our perspectives

---

[3] More about Socialization in Chapter 7.

and behaviors and, ultimately, our ability to adapt and survive. We live in an increasingly complex world, with a wealth of information available to us, bombarded by myriad stimuli every second of every day. How we manage our attention – how we allocate our limited processing resources – is central to our life experience.

According to different researchers studying the topic for different reasons there are different types and different models of attention. Here are just two:

Sohlberg and Mateer's clinical model identifies 5 different levels of attention, each more demanding than the last. Their hierarchy is:

1) Focused attention
This is quite simply the ability to respond deliberately to specific sensory stimuli.

2) Sustained attention
This is the ability to maintain both concentration and required behaviors whilst engaged in continuous and repetitive activity.

3) Selective attention
This is the ability to maintain focus and performance despite the presence of potentially distracting stimuli.

4) Alternating attention
The penultimate level is the mental flexibility to successfully and repeatedly shift attention from one task to another, even though the tasks have different cognitive requirements.

5) Divided attention
This is the highest level of attention. It is the ability to respond simultaneously to multiple tasks and/or multiple task demands.

Eric Knudsen offers a more general model based on 4 core

Cognitive Function

processes of attention and incorporating working memory:

1) Working memory

Working memory refers to our ability to store, analyze and use selected information over short periods of time. When we give attention to something, information associated with that something enters our working memory and is evaluated, enabling us to make decisions and plan how best how to act. For this reason, attention and working memory are inextricably linked.

Studies show that the information being processed determines the part(s) of the brain that are used. For example, tasks that engage the verbal working memory activate the ventrolateral prefrontal cortex and language areas in the temporal and parietal cortex on the left side, whereas tasks that engage the visuospatial working memory[4] activate the dorsolateral prefrontal cortex, the inferior parietal cortex on the right side and areas in the occipital cortex. The one area of the brain that is activated in all working memory tasks, operating as a form of executive controller, is the prefrontal cortex.

How do we decide what to give our attention to? The answer is:

2) Competitive selection

This is the process that determines which information gains access to working memory. As we have already said, there's an awful lot going on around and within us; it's a competitive process with our central nervous system processing extensively and automatically in order to direct our attention. One of the ways we do this is through:

---

4 Visuospatial skills are those that enable us to see and recognize objects and the spatial relationship they share with others.

3) Top-down sensitivity control

When facing this mixture of competing stimuli, we use the current content of our working memory to influence what – if any – new information is worthy of our attention. In this way we effectively regulate the relative signal strengths of the different information channels; prioritizing only those we deem most important. This internally controlled direction of attention is known as *endogenous attention*.

By way of contrast we are also influenced by:

4) Bottom-up salience filters

The salience, or saliency, of any stimuli is the manner and degree to which it stands out from those around it. Typically, the greater the contrast between the stimuli and its environment, the greater its saliency – and the more likely it is to attract our attention.

Of all our senses we tend to rely on our eyes predominantly to detect salience. For all sorts of very good reasons we are quick to spot something or someone looking out of place. However, our other senses can also play their part. Sudden, unexpected noises for example invariably demand our attention. This externally driven focus is known as *exogenous attention*.

For all of our undoubted abilities, we find it difficult to give attention to more than one stimulus simultaneously. We are therefore continually evaluating, integrating and prioritizing our internal and external influences.

One of those most powerful influences – the culture we grow up in – also, it seems, affects how we give attention. Research suggests there are societal differences in how people recognize and prioritize signals from the many sources of stimuli within a community.

In conclusion, then, giving attention really isn't the straightforward activity we might mistake it for. Which is probably no surprise given that it is inextricably linked to our other essential cognitive functions including:

Perception

This is the process of identifying, organizing and interpreting sensory cues in order to understand what is happening in our environment. Perception seems effortless. We differentiate a door from a wall, a cat from a crocodile, water from wind, a person we know from a complete stranger, so quickly and easily we don't even think about it. Actually for the vast majority of time we don't need to think about it. The process of perception – identifying, organizing, and interpreting – is usually a subconscious process. Which is why it seems effortless and immediate.

Perception begins when an object, referred to as the *distal stimulus* (or *distal object*), stimulates our body's sensory organs resulting in neural activity. The shift from sensory stimulus to neural activity is known as *transduction*. The neural activity itself is called the *proximal stimulus*, and the mental representation of the original distal stimulus it creates is called the *percept*.

According to the American psychologist Jerome Bruner whenever we come across a distal stimulus with which we are unfamiliar we:

a) Open ourselves to a range of differing informational cues in a desire to learn more about the subject.
b) Keep collecting information until we recognize some familiar cues that enable us to begin the process of categorizing the subject.
c) Become more selective and, therefore, restrictive as we search for cues that support our initial categorization. At this stage we actively ignore or distort any violations to our perception.

The situation we are in along with such internal drivers as our beliefs, expectations, emotions and needs also influence our perception. This top-down predisposition to perceive some things in a specific way occurs in the long-term and the short-term. Here are examples of both:

Long-term
Chris was in a crowded, noisy bar recently, yet when someone mentioned the name *Chris* he heard it despite the hub-hub. He turned automatically in the direction of the speaker. He is, like the rest of us, particularly sensitive to the sound of his name.

Short-term
A very hungry John was walking down a busy city street with traffic nose-to-tail and people hurrying about their business. He recognized instantly the smell of great Cantonese cooking as he passed a building with a window open. It was a Chinese restaurant. He was keen to eat and so he automatically focused on that specific stimulus.

Such predispositions, whether short or long-term, are called *perceptual sets*.

John's example reflects how motivation can influence our perception. Sometimes factors such as motivation or expectation can lead us to interpret experiences in ways that support our pre-existing bias. Just think how supporters of a sports team react whenever a referee penalizes one of their players, or how easy it is for a student to enjoy the classes of a teacher they like. In both cases the people involved are more likely to see and experience what they expect and want to. They have become, perhaps without realizing it, *primed* to perceive in a specific way.

Priming refers to the way in which an implicit memory influences our perception, leading us to activate specific associations and so reach specific conclusions. Beyond our own internal expectations, we can also be primed by the words and actions of others, our environment and our most recent experience. For example, a person who has just seen the words *goal* and *pitch* is likely to correctly unscramble *bllaftoo* more quickly than they would otherwise have done, because the first two words primed them for the third.

Priming can be achieved using visual, linguistic or even conceptual stimuli. Research suggests that the effects of priming can be both meaningful and long lasting. In one experiment researchers at the University of Toronto Canada showed participants a list of 96 words. A subsequent two-part test delivered 1 hour and then again 7 days after seeing the original list, required them to recognize words they had seen and also complete a series of fragmented words all of which had multiple possible completions. Unknown to the participants this latter task was primed by the inclusion of the target words in the original list. Unlike the recognition/recall task in which the results greatly diminished over the 7 day period, the priming effects – unconsciously influencing the participants to fill in the spaces to create words they had seen on the list – remained consistently strong.

As we mentioned in Chapter 1 perception, prediction and learning are linked. According to Chris Frith, Professor in Neuropsychology at the Wellcome Trust Centre for Neuroimaging at University College London, our perception is not of the world but of our brain's model of the world. In his excellent book *Making Up The Mind* he writes:

'Everything we know about the physical world, including what we know about our own bodies, comes through the brain...Our brain is continuously learning things about the world. From moment to moment it has to discover the identity of the things around it; should they be approached or avoided? It has to discover where these things are: are they nearby or far away? It has to discover how to reach for the fruit and avoid being stung by the wasp. Furthermore, this learning occurs without a teacher...

'We learn that certain signals tell us what is going to happen in the future. We learn that certain actions will cause things to happen in the future. Of course, it is not the signals that predict what is going to happen. It is the brain that does the predicting. We can see the brain predicting in this way if we look directly at activity in nerve cells.'

This mixture of perception, prediction and learning serves not only to keep us safe, it also influences our actions.

Motor skills

This term defines our ability to produce movement based on complex interactions between muscles, joints and nerves. Chris is using fine motor skills at the moment as he is writing this. John is using gross motor skills as he enjoys his morning run.[5] Despite the fact they are very different activities they both serve to highlight the way we use motor skills to achieve specific goals.

A variety of factors, some controllable and others not, contribute to childrens' motor skills development. Genetic traits are amongst the more obvious uncontrollable factors, culture and environment are amongst the more controllable.

Although many parts of our brain are involved in the development and performance of motor skills, 4 particular areas are worthy of mention:

---

[5] Neither has any desire to swop their activity for the other.

1) Prefrontal cortex

This covers the front part of the frontal lobe. Implicated in planning, decision-making and the moderating of social behavior amongst other activities, the prefrontal cortex plays a key role in the representation and pursuit of our internal goals. These can be as tangible as picking up a mobile phone or as abstract as planning a holiday.

The functions associated with the prefrontal cortex are often referred to as *executive functions*. These are the abilities that enable us to differentiate between conflicting thoughts, determine the most likely consequences of our actions and predict outcomes, as well as demonstrate socially acceptable behavior and create goal-focused orientations.

2) Motor cortex

This is an area that controls our goal-directed movements. It's located in the rear of the frontal lobe just before a furrow known as the central sulcus that separates the frontal lobe from the parietal lobe. The motor cortex is divided into 3 main regions, the primary motor cortex, the premotor cortex and the supplementary motor area; between them they control, set up and modulate our movements.

In order to do this our motor cortex first has to receive a variety of information from other lobes in our brain. This information ranges from that of a physical nature – where our body is located in space, for example – to that of a strategic nature based most probably on a clear understanding of a desired goal.

3) Basal ganglia

This is a group of interconnected regions situated at the base of the forebrain, close to the thalamus. Made up of two sides that are almost mirror images of each other, the basal ganglia incorporates the striatum, globus pallidus, substantia nigra, and subthalamic nucleus.

Apart from its association with such functions as motor control and cognitive coordination, the basal ganglia is important in the learning process and in the development and application of habitual behaviors.

Habits are a part of our daily lives. We are, it seems, in many ways and for significant periods of time, creatures of habit. And there are clear benefits to this. For all its brilliance our brain doesn't have unlimited energy. Habitual acts require less brain energy, so whenever we engage in a habit our brain can devote its resources to something else.

Although it's true to say that specific human performance techniques can be used to change and/or develop habits, they tend to form through associative learning. Simply put, once we realize what patterns of behavior work in a given context we are quick to repeat them. It's a 1-2-3 process:

1. We recognize something that triggers our subconscious response.
2. We behave in our habitual manner.
3. We get a reward.

By using some of the new imaging techniques we reviewed in Chapter 1 researchers are able to see some of the neural mechanisms that underlie habit formation. Essentially a repetitive neural loop is established when the prefrontal cortex communicates with the striatum and then with the midbrain. As part of this process the striatum receives input from dopamine-containing neurons, associating a sense of reward with the behavior. A new neural loop is formed each time the behavior is repeated and its value reinforced.

4) Cerebellum

As we mentioned in Chapter 1 the cerebellum, situated in the hindbrain beside the medulla, is significantly involved in coordinating movement. It receives information from the spinal cord and other parts of the brain and integrates these to create coordination, precision and timing.

Visual and spatial processing

Our ability to perceive the various objects in our environment, determine their nature and the spatial relationships they share and then understand how to manage our physical relationship with them helps us to, quite literally, make our way through the world.

We know more about the brain's visual system than we do any of our other sensory systems. We see an object whenever light is reflected off it in a straight line into our eyes. This light travels through the lens and is represented in neurons known as photoreceptors at the back of the retina. There are 2 types of photoreceptors: rods, which enable us to see in low light and cones which are more active in brighter light and also allow us to see color.

At this point our eyes are operating just like cameras, in that the images are the upside-down, mirror images of whatever we are actually looking at. Each retina contains millions of photoreceptors that turn the light into electric impulses. These impulses travel via the optic nerve and the thalamus to the primary visual cortex situated in the occipital lobe at the back of the brain. It is here visual perception takes place. En route from the optic nerve the neurons partially cross over, meaning that the right side of each eye is represented in the left half of the brain and vice versa.

The optic nerve also passes information to 2 nuclei in the midbrain. The first, known as the pretectum, controls the size of our pupils in response to light. The more intense the light, the more our pupils contract. The less light available, the more our pupils dilate. The second, the superior colliculus controls the way our eyes move in short jumps, called saccades, as we follow a moving object or scan for information. If you watch a person's eyes as they scan an environment you will actually see their saccadic eye movement, even though they will have no sense of it. For them – and us – it seems as if our eyes pan smoothly across our field of vision. Paradoxically, if they did we would experience extreme blurring. So instead our eyes move in small jumps capturing a sequence of still images that our brain stitches together seamlessly.

Actually our brain is so good at creating images of the world that it even adds in the details our eyes miss. And they do miss things. We have a blind spot in our eyes. It's a place where all of the nerve fibers that carry signals to the optic nerve converge leaving no room for light receptors. We don't experience this gap in our vision because our brain uses the information it does receive to fill in the missing details.

Perhaps even more amazing is the fact that our brain responds to things that appear in front of us even if we have no conscious awareness of having seen them! Researchers showed participants a series of faces including an angry face that was presented subliminally. Even though the participants didn't report having seen the angry face, activity in their amygdala increased whenever the face was presented. Sometimes, it seems, our brain sees more than we do.

Sometimes it helps us to visualize, to see things in our *mind's eye*. Mental imagery is an important part of how we think, create, plan, remember, imagine and solve problems. We'll talk more about mental imagery and visualization in Chapter 6.

Vision, which for many of us is just another aspect of our functioning we take for granted, is one more example of the governor helping us to make sense of it all.

Language

This not only helps us to make sense of our experience, it also enables us to share it. We use language to communicate with others and with our self. Over the years there has been much scientific debate about the nature of the relationship between cognition and language. For now, we'll just consider the brain's role.

As ever there is still considerable scope for further research, however studies show that most of our language processing functions are carried out in the cerebral cortex – where our other higher-order processing occurs. For over 90% of right-handed people specialized language areas reside in the left hemisphere of their brain. For almost 20% of left-handers the opposite is true and these areas are found in their right hemisphere. It also seems, however, that nearly 70% of us have some language abilities in both hemispheres.

Having said that, there are 2 specific and interconnected areas worthy of mention. Broca's area, found in the frontal lobe, is important in the production of speech. Wernicke's area, found in the upper part of the temporal lobe, is important in the understanding of speech. The two are connected by nerve fibers called the arcuate fasciculus.

As we'll discuss in Chapter 7 our brains are designed for us to socialize and communicate. They are both vital to our success and wellbeing. As is our memory.

Memory

Often people make the mistake of equating *memory* with *recall*. There is, though, more to it. After all, we can't recall, or remember, something unless it has been represented and stored successfully. Memory, then, in its fullest sense incorporates both retention and retrieval.

To go back a step further, we need to have experienced that particular something before we can begin the processing of coding and storing it. This experience will occur through our senses. We might see, hear, smell, touch or taste – or it might be any combination – and when doing so we are using different parts of our brain. The memory is coded and stored within these different parts according to the senses involved. Recall involves reactivating the parts stimulated during the original experience. Memory is not, therefore, stored in one specific place in our brain. When we remember something we are activating a brain-wide process. This means that if the brain is ever damaged some parts of the memory may survive – it's another example of the brain's incredible efficiency and resiliency.

In Chapter 3 we mentioned that we have different types of memory. These are managed by different brain structures. The following diagrams show the types and structures:

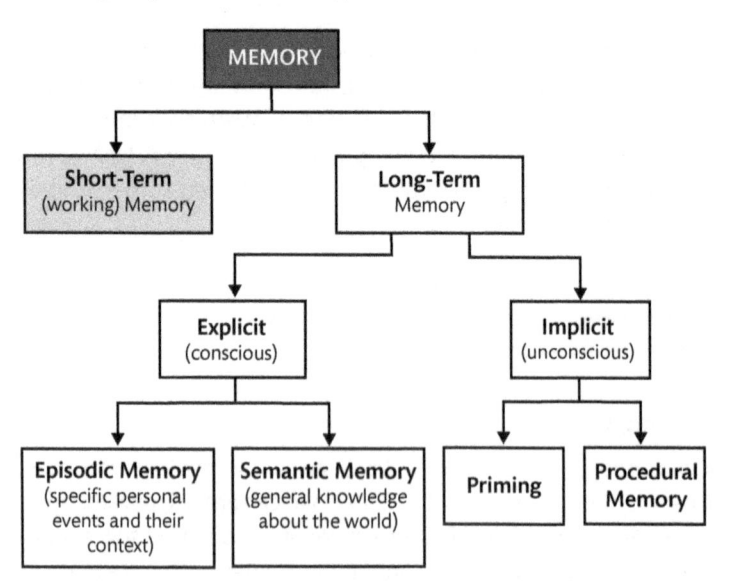

```
                        MEMORY
                       /      \
          Short-Term            Long-Term
        (working) Memory         Memory
                                /       \
                          Explicit      Implicit
                         (conscious)   (unconscious)
                         /      \        /      \
              Episodic Memory  Semantic Memory  Priming  Procedural
              (specific personal  (general knowledge               Memory
              events and their    about the world)
              context)
```

Image from http://www.brainwaves.com/memoryisplural.html

Striatum Putamen: Procedural memory

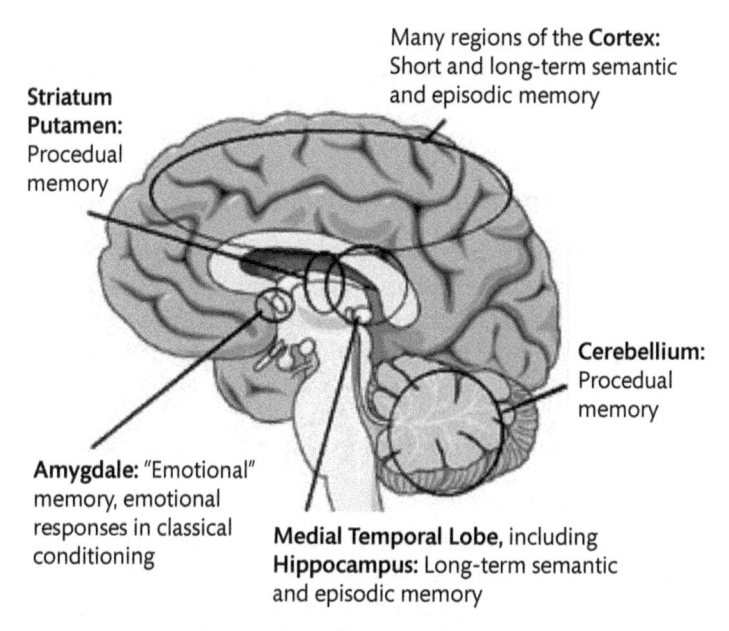

Many regions of the **Cortex:** Short and long-term semantic and episodic memory

Cerebellium: Procedural memory

Amygdale: "Emotional" memory, emotional responses in classical conditioning

Medial Temporal Lobe, including **Hippocampus:** Long-term semantic and episodic memory

Image adapted from pixshark.com

Despite the progress they are making, scientists are still in the relatively early stages of understanding how the parts of a memory are reassembled into a coherent whole. What we can say for certain is that the creation of memories is the result of a highly complex learning process.

It's a process that was originally thought to have at its core the repeated neural transmission of signals via the synapse. New research, though, is suggesting that the synapse might not be as important as first believed and that memories might actually be held in the neurons themselves.

One of the primary reasons researchers are able to learn so much more about our brain is the incredible and rapid development in technology. You might remember that in Chapter 1 we provided a brief overview of some of the ways researchers are now able to study the brain. Technology is changing our lives, bringing with it many benefits. There is a word of warning, however. It needs to be managed well:

Technology and cognitive functioning

Technology is a tool that many of us use on a daily basis. Its use is not limited to the office or the workplace. Just think of the last time you walked a city street and recall how many people were using their mobile phone as they strode out to their next destination or stood waiting for a bus, taxi or friend.[6]

Technology is a tool and we have to ensure it works for us and not against us.

Very few devices are designed to work with our brain in mind. In fact, many of our daily uses of technology actively stress our limbic and visual systems and decrease our frontal lobe response. Technology developers are often more concerned with how technology fits our hands than how it interacts with our brain.

As an applied sport scientist John is always studying welfare and performance, which he regards as 2 sides of the same coin, from the brain perspective. He is acutely aware that our everyday technology can be used positively to help us delegate or integrate tasks, thus freeing up valuable brain energy, or negatively resulting in an energy drain. Given that Albert Einstein once said, 'Never memorize what you can look up' it seems reasonable to think that the great man would have welcomed the delegation/integration potential of technology.

However, on a less positive note, there is evidence that when faced with questions we need to answer, our thoughts turn immediately

---

[6] If you can't recall it's probably because you were too busy on your mobile phone.

to our computer and the internet rather than to asking someone else. We are, it seems, increasingly *primed* to turn to technology for solutions. What's the potential downside? Well, as we'll discuss in Chapter 7, our brains are wired for us to socialize. Direct human interaction is an essential aspect of our life experience. It used to be at the heart of how we found the answers to those troublesome questions. Experiencing, coding and storing information – the creation of memory – was once a face-to-face social activity. Now, increasingly, we are living in a 2D, flat-screen world within which, amongst other things, we create thousands of friends and followers, share our day-to-day behaviors and experiences, shop, sell and seek for information. Because of technology our brains are experiencing a rate of change that is arguably faster than ever before. And our brains are malleable. Neuroplasticity means that our brains will inevitably adapt. The key questions are:

1. How will our brains change?
2. How can we best manage our own technology right now?

Although we can't offer you any definite answers to the first question, in the upcoming Process part of this chapter we do include some practical tips for making sure technology works for you.

Before that here's the usual reminder of the key points:

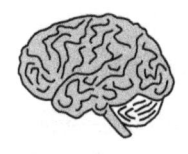

Summary

- Every day on average we have 70,000 thoughts.
- The frontal lobe is the primary driver of high-level thinking.

- Your frontal lobe is about 1/3 of your brain.
- The frontal lobe is often the first to show cognitive decline.
- Our frontal lobe synchronizes with the limbic system and the three other major lobes: temporal, parietal and occipital.
- Thinking faster, increasing memory capacity, and recall of facts and events starts right behind your forehead.
- Although cognitive decline starts for many in the fourth decade of life, we now know this can be influenced – positively and negatively - by lifestyle choices.
- High level thinking coordinated by the frontal lobe is maintained through key elements of elimination/reduction, delegation/integration, and socialization.
- The latest research has helped us pinpoint the brain circuits for forming habits and to learn more about how we create memories.
- Cognitive overload is a part of life; our brain is made to adapt and we can help it do so. How we manage technology is one key part of this.

The Process

Our recommendations

Value your cognitive functions. Avoid taking them for granted. Remember that whilst your brain is inherently resilient and adaptive it needs and uses energy and rest. Ensure you provide these.

Do this by:

1. Including in your daily schedule activities that help maximize frontal lobe performance.
2. Avoiding or, at least, limiting those activities that decrease your productivity and performance.
3. Being selective on how, when and why you use your brain's energy.
4. Understanding that by making appropriate lifestyle choices you can manage and potentially improve your cognitive functioning throughout your life.
5. Using our advice in the other chapters to help you achieve the above.

Maximizing frontal lobe activity

Before identifying and discussing some specific ways you can do this, a most relevant piece of advice from the late, great Bruce Lee:

> *'It's not the daily increase but daily decrease. Hack away at the unessential.'*

With that in mind here are our suggestions for becoming more effective and efficient:

Be physically active
Refer back to our advice in the Process part of Chapter 2.

Get enough rest
Refer back to our advice in the Process part of Chapter 3.

Eat plenty of food that's good for your brain and keep well hydrated
Refer back to our advice in the Process part of Chapter 4.

Be socially active – in the real rather than the virtual world

Social interactions provide a significant amount of cognitive stimulation and engage many neural pathways. Whenever you can, prioritize in-the-moment interpersonal communication, either face-to-face or on the phone, over emails and texts.

We offer lots more practical advice about socialization and communication in Chapter 7.

Be open to new experiences

Exercise your curiosity and creativity; stimulate your brain with newness.

Practice meditation and/or our Rapid Reset activity

Look ahead to the Process part of Chapter 6 for advice on how to do these.

Avoid (or at least, limit) multi-tasking

Multi-tasking doesn't make us more productive in the long-term. Actually, it can have the opposite effect. It seems that the increased stress caused by multitasking changes the function and structure of our brain and not for the better.

Researchers at the University of Sussex in the UK scanned 75 adults using an fMRI to examine their grey matter. Those who were frequent multi-taskers had less dense grey matter in their anterior cingulate cortex (ACC).

So, when multi-tasking is concerned - as with so many other aspects of our daily lives - just because we can doesn't mean we should. Multi-task sparingly.

Manage your habits

Do this by changing existing negative habits and/or creating positive new ones. Here are some ways you can approach this:

a) Make a detailed plan

Changing habits is possible because our brain is changeable and adaptable. By creating and implementing a plan based on small, measurable changes you make it easier for adaptation to occur. Also have appropriate others review the plan to ensure its value and timeliness.

b) Keep it simple

The more complex the behavior the longer it might take to become habitual, so keep your planning and goal-setting simple.

c) Link the new behavior to a routine or environmental cue

Associate the new activity to a pre-existing and positive behavior, routine or environmental stimuli. This use of associative learning will activate the structures of the medial temporal lobe including the hippocampus. Other areas of the brain including the motor-related areas of the frontal lobe, the prefrontal cortex, and the striatum are also thought to be involved. By creating a positive association between the new behavior and an existing cue, you can avoid an over-reliance on willpower.

d) Link a difficult task to a reward

You can also create a positive feedback loop by rewarding your own success. Be willing to reward yourself as you might others when goals are achieved or a particularly challenging part of the process has been managed well.

e) Repeat new behaviors and keep track of your progress

Contrary to the popular belief that successful new behaviors must be repeated daily, researchers have found that occasionally missing a day doesn't seem to affect the final outcome. Remember the brain likes consistency not perfection.

Log how many times the new behavior is performed and whether it is performed successfully or not. Self-surveillance allows you to keep important goals and obstacles to those goals within your focus, even when there is much information that can distract us.

f) Use peers for accountability

Begin the development of a new habit with an announcement to at least one significant other. Deliberately seek out other forms of external motivation. Depending on the habit you are creating this might, for example, be one of those times you can employ social media or other aspects of technology positively.

Moderate your alcohol consumption

The use of alcohol impacts the entire brain, including the frontal lobe. Research using magnetic resonance imaging (MRI) and positron emission topography (PET scanning) revealed that heavy drinkers showed a lower glucose metabolism, which is indicative of less frontal lobe activity and ability.

Learn to speed read

It's an extremely effective and efficient way to read. It's based on an understanding of how our eyes and brain work. It saves time and it aids recall.

Just take a moment to consider how much time every week you spend reading. Imagine being able to halve that time whilst still understanding and remembering everything you need to. Now work out how much time that would save you in a year. And then multiply that by however many years you deem appropriate. Now ask yourself *What could I do with all that free time?* Then realize 2 *other things:*

1. If you were able to speed read you would have got to this

point in the book ages ago;
2. Depending on how good you become, you can do better than halve your current reading speed.[7]

Here's a quick introduction into how to speed read:

a) Be motivated before you start reading

Know your purpose and its value. Identify the benefits and advantages of reading the material and create such an excited and motivated state that your entire body is affected. Approach reading the text just as you would any other vibrant opportunity.

We know that the pupils in our eyes change size according to the amount of light they are exposed to, the closeness of the object they are looking at, and the degree of motivation we feel. Therefore, the more motivated you are the more your pupils will dilate, the more words they will see at a single glance and the faster you will read.

There's obviously more to it than this. However, speed reading is a great example of how marginal changes can create significant differences in ability and outcome.

b) Understanding how your eyes move is key to increasing speed

Remember saccades, those small jumps our eyes make when we scan? When we read our eyes move across the page by making these small jumps. In-between each jump they pause very briefly to fixate on the word or words they are looking at. Once these words are comprehended our eyes make their next jump and the next fixation occurs. Initially many of us might only see one or two words in each fixation. We become faster at reading by:

---

[7] We suggest aiming for a speed of 1000 words per minute plus your required level of recall.

1. Increasing the number of words we see in each fixation.
2. Decreasing the pause between each jump.

c) Use your peripheral vision

It's highly developed. Our normal visual field is about 170 degrees, 100 of which are made up of peripheral vision. We can see many details to the left and right of our main focus of attention. This means we can actually see many words on a page – even a large page – without having to move our eyes from the centre. If you're not convinced, just stop reading and focus your gaze on the centre of a wall in the room you are in. Keep your gaze fixed and notice how much of the room you can see in your peripheral vision. Lots, right? Certainly far more than any page width.

d) Use a thin guide, or pointer, when you read

Move it in a smooth manner underneath the line you are reading. Begin by focusing on 2 word fixations.

e) Shorten the length of each pause

When you reduce the time by just a fraction of a second you are increasing your reading speed.

f) Increase the size of each fixation

When you can read comfortably and recall well focusing on 2 word fixations increase them to 3. Once you are comfortable with that go to 4 and so on. With practise you will be able to read 1 line in 2 fixations. When you can see an entire line in 1 fixation simply put the pointer in the center of the page and move it down.

g) Stop sub-vocalizing

Check whether or not you are sub-vocalizing – saying the words in your mind – as you read. If so, stop. Otherwise you will only ever be able to read as quickly as you can talk to yourself. In order to become a really fast reader you need to recognize words in the same way you do other shapes and objects: *Silently.*

Again, just take a moment to have a quick look around the room you are in.

Were you able to do it swiftly?

Did you correctly identify the many different objects, colours and shapes you saw? Did you experience a whole variety of stimuli?

Did you need to tell yourself what they were called before you could move on to look at or experience the next one?

Your answer to that last question is almost certainly *No*. We'd struggle to make our way through the world if we had to actively name in our mind every new stimuli we encounter. If you want to significantly increase your reading speed accept that words can be treated in the same way as all of these other things. You can see and understand them without having to resort to internal dialogue. You just need to practise. Your brain will adapt.

h) Avoid back-skipping

Sometimes we are tempted to re-read a word or phrase. This is known as back-skipping. It's a temptation that is best avoided for 2 reasons:

1. Most of the time the writer will refer back to that content in the next sentences or paragraph and that will either remind you or help you makes sense of it.
2. Your eye-brain system really is very good. Trust it and the inherent power of associative learning.

i) Create an ideal reading environment

The best reading light is natural daylight. So if possible read near a window. Failing that, place a lamp behind you so the light comes over the shoulder that is opposite to the hand you write with. Have general lighting in the room also.

Your desk should be approximately 20cms above your chair seat. The chair should encourage good posture by enabling you to have both feet flat on the floor and your back upright.

Your eyes should be approximately 50cms from the page. This makes it easier to focus on groups of words and lessens the possibility of eye strain.

When reading, rest your eyes by closing them for 2 minutes every 20-30 minutes. Also use eyes washes and blink deliberately.

j) Use skimming and scanning

When you skim a text you look through it very quickly with the intention of getting a general overview of the content and style. You scan to find specific information.

k) Preparing to read an unfamiliar text

Take the following 4 steps:

1. Be clear about your reading objectives and the associated benefits.
2. Spend approximately 2 minutes familiarising yourself with the content and writing style. Look at the contents page, chapter headings and sub-headings.
3. Spend between 5-10 minutes skimming the first paragraph of each chapter you are going to read.
4. Read the text.

Now our final 3 suggestions:

Use specific memory systems

There are a range of memory systems you can use to make recall easier. They are all based on 2 key elements:

1. Imagination
2. Association.

These are supported by the inclusion of:

1. Color
2. Humor
3. Exaggeration
4. Personal relevancy
5. Positivity
6. Sequencing/order

In the same way that facts and figures alone usually fail to motivate people to make significant changes,[8] so lists of names, numbers or other types of information usually fail to enable easy recall. The fact that we do remember so many things is due, of course, to our incredible brain. However, we can make life easier for it – and, therefore, us – by incorporating the above. Just as we can all learn to speed read, so we can all learn to remember more things more easily.

To do this we need methods that enable us to use our imagination positively, in ways that are directly relevant to our self and encourage associations to be made between the essential parts. Here's one memory system you can apply to achieve this:

A memory library

Take a few moments to sit quietly and visualize in detail a building you know well and that you have a positive connection to. Visualize the approach to the building. If, for example you have chosen your

---

[8] We'd suggest that's one of the main reasons why, when scientists simply share their research findings expecting the general public to change accordingly, they are often disappointed.

home, visualize the path, the garden, the garage etc. Notice the outside of the building. What color are the bricks? How many windows can you see? What do they look like? In your mind's eye approach the front door and be aware of how it looks, feels and sounds as you open it. Step inside. Take a good, careful look around the room you are in. What exactly can you see? Can you hear or smell anything? Associate with it as fully as you can. When you have done that walk into another room. Be equally aware of it. You can repeat this process with as many rooms as you choose.

Once you can take this internal journey with ease, always experiencing the same things in the same order, it's time to turn it into your personal memory library. How? By simply filling it with the information you need to store. Place the things you need to remember in, or on, very specific parts of the approach or inside of the building. If you have to remember such things as numbers, names or abstract concepts use your imagination to create a tangible representation of them. For example, you might write an equation in bright colors – ones you really like - on a large piece of paper, frame it and hang it on a wall. You might turn the number 4 into the image of a yacht (because 4 looks a bit like a yacht) and place it in the entrance to the building. To be reminded of a specific person you might think of a particular piece of clothing they wear frequently and put it in an appropriate place.

The key is to create powerful imaginary associations with the details or objects you need to recall – these can be exaggerated and humorous (in fact, it will really help if they are) – and to position them, sequenced deliberately, throughout your memory library. Ensure that different parts of your library contain related information. If you are visualizing a house the hallway might be where you store work-related details, the garage where you go to be reminded of things to do with travel, the kitchen might be reserved for family matters, and so on.

Over time and with practice you can extend your memory library to include as many rooms or areas as you need. Just always use your imagination to create personal, cheerful, positive and exaggerated associations that are sequenced and grouped deliberately. There are other memory systems, all based on the same principles, so if this one doesn't appeal to you do explore the rest.

Manage your technology

As discussed earlier in this chapter the brain does not have endless energy. Ultimately, then, when we talk about managing our brain we are talking about the proactive and positive management of its energy.

Each day our brain must decipher what is noise and what is important, yet the amount and density of stimuli and quasi-information that competes for our everyday attention is almost infinite.

If we do not control this data stream, we risk falling victim to it. Here are some ways you can ensure the technology in your life is really working for you:

a) Limit your screen-time

The vast majority of us cannot work in our modern world without some amount of screen time and for many of us that can mean hours each day. There is increasing research suggesting that extensive and repeated screen time influences a variety of brain regions, including those involved in emotional processing, executive attention, decision-making and cognitive control.

Whenever possible, limit your screen time.

b) Eliminate distractions from your PC

Although your PC is primarily a productivity tool, it can become a minefield of distraction due to advertising, cat videos, instant messaging, and multiple windows capabilities. Eliminate all you can.

c) Create systems that make life easy

Codify information and keep it in a database so that it is searchable and accessible.

d) Check email and voicemail only twice a day

Too-frequent checking reduces our daily productivity. Unsubscribe from email lists that are not directly relevant to your day-to-day work.

e) Reduce or eliminate addressing email first thing in the day or before bed

At the beginning of the day email can divert us from critical tasks and in the evening this action can increase frontal lobe activity, thus disrupting the slowing down process before bed. If you must answer emails in the evening allow yourself at least thirty minutes to slow down before going to bed.

f) Manage your mobile phone deliberately

Assess what is on your phone currently and remove any data and applications you do not use. Develop the habit of asking yourself, *Will I need this information and/or the mobile application I'm about to download?* before taking action.

g) Do not answer phone calls from unrecognized numbers

Avoid the risk of being surprised, of breaking your current concentration and of having to adapt. Reserve your energy. If it's important the caller will leave a message.

h) Turn your mobile phone off

If possible, spend a part of each day with your phone off or in a do not disturb format.

i) Turn off all ancillary technology when working on important tasks

Each time you are alerted by other information your brain has to adjust and then readjust.

j) Take breaks from technology

As you're now aware variety and rest are valuable to the brain, so give technology a daily break.

Organize your workload

Here are 6 tips:

1) Accomplish your most important tasks at the start of the day

Each day we start with a bank of energy. We should become accustomed to spending it like money. By accomplishing important work first thing, we increase our motivation and, therefore, our resiliency for what lies ahead.

2) When possible batch similar work together

By doing this we are more likely to access a flow state. Flow, as we mentioned in Chapter 3, is a functional brain state that enables us to be completely absorbed in an activity, with our thoughts and actions flowing easily and inevitably. It's a state of high efficiency.

3) Whenever possible reduce meetings and phone calls to 30 minutes

This allows you to give maximum attention. You can use the time saved for breaks or moving on the next important task.

4) Reduce distractions in meetings

If conducting meetings, do so in a space conducive to reducing distraction. If possible encourage those in attendance to turn off all technology that has the potential to damage efficacy, creativity and enjoyment of the task.

5) Write notes longhand

In recent studies, it was found that those who took notes on laptops performed worse in recalling information than those who took notes longhand. It seems just the act of putting information into one's own words improves our cognitive abilities.

6) Plan for tomorrow

End each day by readjusting your critical tasks for the next business or study day.

That brings us to the end of our thoughts about cognitive functioning. We are moving on now from this distinct and important aspect of human experience to another: *emotion*.

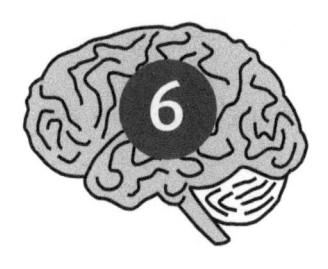

Emotional Management

'Genius is the ability to renew one's emotions in daily experience.'

Paul Cezanne

Brain Priming – This chapter in focus

Here are the key facts and messages:

- You brain perceives and acts upon emotional information.
- The emotional systems of the brain are the first to develop.
- We experience on average hundreds of emotional responses a day.
- Emotions allows us to survive and thrive.
- The brain, heart, and stomach work together to process emotions and responses.
- Emotional management has one of the largest effects on our overall health and performance.

- Consistent difficulty with managing emotions has long- term negative effects.
- Emotions can be managed for our wellbeing and in high stress situations.

You really are the emotional type

Honestly. You really are. Every one of you. Every one of *us*. Whether or not you have recognized this within yourself, dear reader, you are the emotional type.

But what does that really mean? Just what are emotions and what purpose do they serve? When you read our assertion about your essentially emotional nature how did you react? Did you deny, doubt or accept its truth? Did you automatically interpret it as a sign of weakness – perhaps, even, something you don't associate with your gender or profession or public image? Or did you translate it into something positive, associated with sensitivity, awareness or empathy?[1]

Whatever your instinctive response, whether you like it or not, it is true. We are all not only a little bit emotional; we are a lot emotional. And our forebears were, too. Being human involves being emotional. It's central to our life experience. Indeed, emotions are so prevalent and powerful it's a fair bet that Shakespeare must, at some point, have considered the line 'We are such things as emotions are made of' before dreaming of a different version.

So what is an emotion?

Actually, scientists find themselves struggling to produce a single, completely acceptable definition of emotion. So we'll work with

---

[1] How did you *feel*?

this one:

'An emotion is a complex psychological state that involves three distinct components: a subjective experience, a physiological response, and a behavioral or expressive response.'

Unlike many of us, psychologists differentiate between emotions and moods. Here's why: emotions are normally relatively short-lived, they are intense and the result of an identifiable cause; moods, however, tend to be less intense, longer-lasting and often arise without a definite stimulus.

In this chapter we are focusing on emotion because, for all the difficulty in defining them, emotions act as a highly efficient signalling system. Our challenge is to recognize and respond well to the signals.

We'll begin with the three component parts identified above:

The Subjective Experience

One of the challenges in defining, categorizing and understanding emotions is their subjective nature. Feeling an emotion is a personal thing. A stimulus that creates a certain emotion in one person might create a very different emotion in another. Just think, for example, of having to take a ride on the world's wildest rollercoaster. Just the thought will be enough to make some of you feel a tingle of excitement, others shiver with fear, and some experience nothing but disinterest.

Then, of course, we have to acknowledge that emotions are multi-dimensional; they are layered, creating a range of experience for us to define in our own, personal way. Think of the broad range of feelings we might experience under the heading of *happiness*. When for you does contentment turn into joy and joy into pure bliss? What are the differences you recognize as you move from one level of the emotion to the next? And how did you interpret the words we used to describe those emotional states? Can one person's joy be another person's *contentment*?

It becomes even more complicated when we realize that we often experience a mix of emotions at the same time. No doubt some of us who were thrilled a moment ago at the thought of an amazing rollercoaster ride would also admit that their excitement was tinged with – perhaps even fuelled by – some feelings of nervousness or fear. And then we can think of those big, life-changing events like starting school or university, or getting married or becoming a parent, that conjure up an incredible swirl of emotions. They create physiological responses, too.

The Physiological Response

Have you ever felt your heart race with excitement, or your stomach lurch with fear? Have you felt your mouth go dry or your palms sweat? Have you ever cried tears of joy or laughed with delight?

The odds are that you have – and that you have experienced and demonstrated all sorts of other emotions in your own unique way. Emotions create physical, often involuntary, responses. Our involuntary responses including heartbeat and breathing are controlled by the autonomic nervous system, itself a division of the peripheral nervous system. Amongst the best known of these involuntary responses is our body's flight or fight reaction in the face of a perceived threat. At such a time our body automatically changes to enable us to either flee to safety or address the matter head-on.

Although studies of the physiology of emotion tended to focus on such autonomic responses, more recently researchers have turned their attention to the role the brain plays in our emotional responses and experience. We'll turn our attention to this in just a moment, after we have considered the third component of emotions:

The Behavioral Response

This is simply the way we express the emotion, or emotions, we are feeling. When we are interacting with others, we tend to emphasize the importance of interpreting accurately the emotional expressions of others; we recognize this as a vital part of successful communication, of building relationships and, in turn, of being understood. The inability to either express our emotion appropriately or to interpret the emotion of others accurately can lead to anything from misunderstanding to dislike.

Although research suggests that, as human beings, we share some universal expressions, it's also the case that cultural norms influence strongly how we express and interpret emotions.

Whatever our universal commonalities or cultural differences, we do get many opportunities to both express and interpret emotions. In fact, on average, we all experience hundreds of emotional responses every day. That's right! Hundreds!

And there's more: not only do we have so many emotional experiences every day, we actually feel emotion *before* we rationalize. Daniel Goleman, author of the New York Times bestseller *Emotional Intelligence*, explains, 'The emotional brain responds to an event more quickly than the thinking brain.'

That's why we were able to say with such confidence that you really are the emotional type.[2] Here's how we create our much needed and frequently produced emotions:

The limbic system

Located within the temporal lobe situated on either side of the thalamus, the limbic system incorporates the hypothalamus, hippocampus and amygdala along with several nearby areas of the brain. It plays a key role in determining the nature of our emotions.[3]

The hypothalamus regulates how we respond to our emotions. One way to think of it is as the body's thermostat, regulating responses ranging from hunger, thirst, sexual satisfaction and aggression to blood pressure, digestion, breathing, pulse and other aspects of our autonomic nervous system. When, for example, your heartbeat increases and your breathing quickens as you feel a sudden rush of fear, your hypothalamus is at work.

The hippocampus appears to be essential in the converting of what is happening in our mind *now* into long-term memories. This is a vital task. Those of us with a fully functioning hippocampus probably take the ability to create new memories for granted. We have an experience, create and store an associated memory and access it as and when necessary to help us make decisions, share information or advice, and take appropriate action. Without

---

[2] Chris here: When talking to a friend recently about this very chapter he was quick to point out that he wasn't the emotional type. Yet in the next fifteen minutes he described situations in which he experienced empathy, guilt, doubt, impulsiveness and joy. Interestingly, it didn't occur to him once that these were emotional responses.

[3] The limbic system also has much to do with the formation of memories. (Refer back to Chapter1, The Governor, for a diagram of the limbic system.)

this ever-updated memory store, the world would seem a very different - a far less manageable - place. Individuals who suffer from a damaged hippocampus cannot create new memories and, sadly, can then rarely cope with the demands of everyday life.

The amygdala is made up of two almond-shaped masses of neurons. In Chapter 1 we described it as *the relay station for emotional processing*. Because of the amygdala's connections within the brain it not only operates as the center for self-preservation by identifying danger and threat, affecting our levels of fear, rage and aggression and creating a flight or fight response, it also influences our expressions of other emotions such as affection and love. People who suffer from lesions of the amygdala, lose their ability to experience associated emotional responses to stimuli. They will, for example, recognize another person but not know whether they like or dislike them.

Our brain, however, does not work alone in creating our emotions. It interacts with both the stomach and the heart. If you have ever wondered why we talk so readily about gut instincts or heart-felt emotions,[4] now you know. We are talking about a biological reality.

How does our brain do this? Via the amazing vagus nerve that we mentioned first in Chapter 4. Rooted in the cerebellum and the brainstem, the vagus nerve wanders[5] down into your abdomen, connecting with your heart and most other major organs along the way.

---

[4] Chris again: Those phrases are more examples of 'The Wisdom of the Village'.

[5] Vagus means 'wandering' in Latin. (It's also the source of such words as 'vague' and 'vagabond'.)

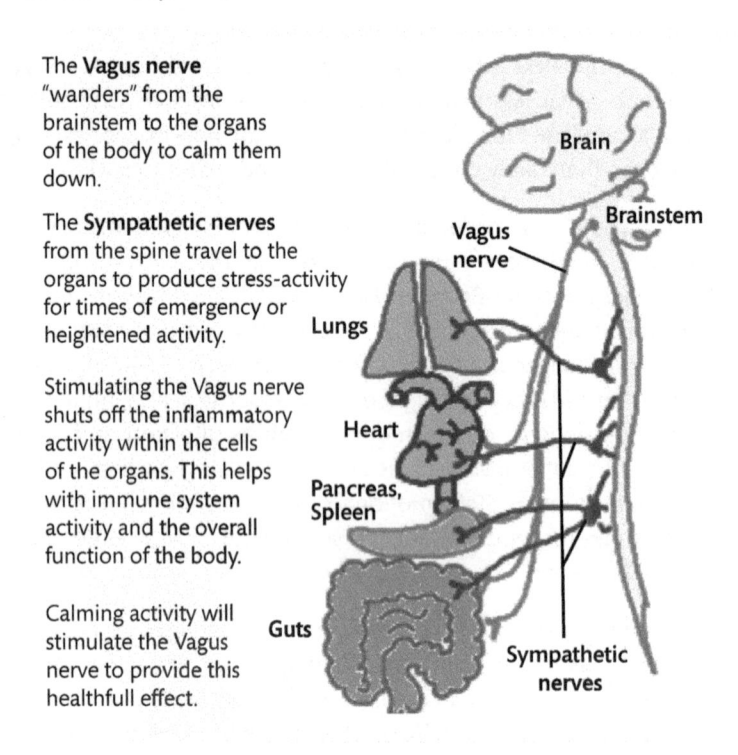

The **Vagus nerve** "wanders" from the brainstem to the organs of the body to calm them down.

The **Sympathetic nerves** from the spine travel to the organs to produce stress-activity for times of emergency or heightened activity.

Stimulating the Vagus nerve shuts off the inflammatory activity within the cells of the organs. This helps with immune system activity and the overall function of the body.

Calming activity will stimulate the Vagus nerve to provide this healthfull effect.

From: www.rawfoodsupport.com

The vagus nerve

Through its many connections, the vagus nerve is at the center of an ongoing interactive feedback loop between your brain and your gut. It is a genuine feedback loop because not only does the vagus nerve constantly provide information to the brain about the state of what is happening both within and around you, the brain also sends 'messages' in return to create and/or manage your responses in light of the information received. In this way we create our emotional states and associated actions.

A staggering 80-90% of the nerve fibers in the vagus nerve are dedicated to communicating this mix of emotional, contextual, internal and external information up to your brain! So when we talk about our so-called *gut instinct* we really are making reference to a significant biological process. And, since our brain is processing so much emotional information, it makes sense that this information is shared and sent to other sub-systems for action or decisions to be made.

These sub-systems, include the integumentary, skeletal, cardiovascular, endocrine, visual, neuromuscular, lymphatic, respiratory, digestive, excretory, reproductive, and immune systems.

The heart

Your heart is also connected to the brain via the vagus nerve and 40,000 sensory neurons all relaying information back to the *governor*. As the diagram on the next page shows we have a significant heart to brain communication system in operation. This connectivity has led researchers to call the heart the *little brain*.

Your heart communicates with the brain and the sub-systems of your body in four ways. These are via:

1. Nervous system connections from other systems (e.g.; stomach and neuromuscular).
2. Hormones produced in the heart.
3. Biomechanical information via blood pressure waves.
4. Energetic information from the electrical responses in the heart itself.

Heart to brain communication system

Amygdala
Storehouse of emotional memory comparing what is emotionally familiar with new information. Communicates to bottom frontal lobe.

Medulla
Contains nerve centers that control breathing circulation, etc.

Hippocampus
Intellectual memory. Decides most efficient response to situations. Communicates to top frontal lobe.

Sympathetic Afferents
(Flowing back to brain through spinal cord)

Cerebral Cortex
Thinks, strategizes, plans reflects, inspires and imagines.

Frontal Lobes
Determine appropriate behaviour and most effective responses based on information they receive.

Vague Nerve

Sinus Node

Heart's Intrinsic Nervous System

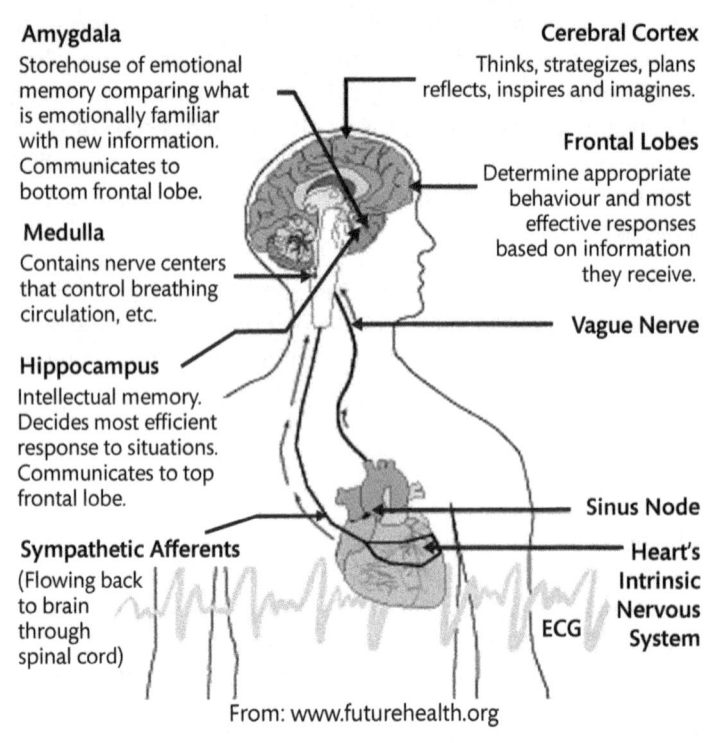

ECG

From: www.futurehealth.org

The purpose of emotions

Not only are we all emotional beings, we *need* to be emotional beings.

Why is this the case? Well, although the brain is the overall governor, our emotions play a vital role in determining just how we chart our way through life and respond to and manage the many different situations, challenges and opportunities we experience.

In fact, emotions are one of the brain's primary sources of information about safety, contentment, happiness, decision-making, wellbeing and, importantly, survival. Take, for example, an emotion as seemingly unpleasant as fear. In the right context fear serves to help protect us from danger, preparing us to flee or fight and, ultimately, to survive. A more obviously positive emotion such as love motivates us to build meaningful relationships and, if it's love for that most special person, often creates the desire to reproduce.

The emotions we create and how we manage them play a most significant role in determining how we perform internally and, then, externally.

Emotions motivate us to act

As mentioned above, emotions drive our behavior. It's also true that we seek out behaviors that create within us the emotions we most like. We do what we can to take actions that a) let us experience positive emotions and b) help us avoid, or at least minimize, negative emotions. For example, we choose hobbies that make us feel *good*. Whether *good* means excited or calm or clever, or any other type of emotion we value. And we instinctively seek to avoid situations that make us feel bored or sad or inadequate.

Emotions influence our decision-making

In fact, because we emote before we rationalize, emotions are a major influence on just about every decision we make from the moment we wake up to the moment we fall asleep. If you think you make only logical decisions, think again. Realize, too, that your emotions don't just influence you:

Emotions play a vital role in interpersonal communication

By expressing our emotions we give others valuable insights into how we are feeling and they, in turn, do the same for us.

Communication is our primary method of exchange. That's why we said earlier that our brain and gut really do communicate; it's because they exchange.

Through our interpersonal communication we exchange many things including emotion. The more clearly we understand how someone else is feeling, the more likely we are to adapt our communication to best reflect the way they are feeling. Apart from the words we use, we reveal our emotions through facial expressions, gestures, posture, breathing patterns and tone and pace of voice. These all help us to understand those around us, they allow us access to aspects of their internal world, and by doing so they give us the best chance of communicating – of exchanging – positively and well.

Emotions help us to survive

This is, of course, their most important function. It is the ultimate purpose of all the above. Emotions, managed well, enable us to avoid threat, defend ourselves if necessary, socialize and reproduce. The role emotions play in our survival is another, significant example of our brain working silently in the background to make sure that it – and we – *win*.

However, when emotions are misinterpreted or a person loses control of their emotional experience and expression, the costs can be serious. As the following demonstrates:

The costs of emotional mismanagement

Emotional stress has a huge negative impact across all parts of our society and economy. It costs us money. It limits creativity and growth. It impairs performance. It diminishes quality of life.[6]

In America, it's estimated that over 75% of all visits to a doctor are for stress-related problems. Apart from depression and anxiety, these range from such things as headaches and high blood pressure to skin disorders and heart problems. It's been determined that the effects of negative emotional stress costs the American economy more than $300 billion per year.

In the United Kingdom it's estimated that the yearly cost is £1.24 billion; the result of over 100 million days being taken off work due to stress-related illnesses.

This is hardly surprising given that long-term emotional stress actually changes our brain structure which, in turn, affects how our brain functions. Amongst other effects, the hippocampus – that part of our brain that regulates both emotions and memories – actually shrinks in response to extended periods of stress, and there are also detrimental changes to both the size and the connectivity of the amygdala.

Continual increased release of cortisol is believed to create a vicious circle of interaction between the hippocampus and the amygdala, reinforcing neural pathways that establish a fixed state of flight or fight.

Although in certain circumstances flight or fight is an appropriate and necessary response, it is not one we are supposed to maintain indefinitely. And that is precisely what long-term emotional stress does. The consequences can be significant. The number of stem cells that mature into neurons appears to decrease resulting in a loss of learning and memory and an increased likelihood of anxiety

---

[6] Think of our military personnel returned from active service. It's no surprise that some need our very deliberate and (what should be) readily available support. It is because the brain always wins that we can help. If we care enough.

or depression. Over time, the continual release of adrenaline scars our blood vessels and that, in turn, can increase the risk of heart attack or stroke.

And these are only a few examples of how our emotional wellbeing influences our overall wellbeing. Essentially, our emotional health is the primary driver of all beneficial changes in our brain and, indeed, all other parameters of health.

Let's just pause for a moment and give ourselves a chance to say that one more time:

> *Emotional health is the primary driver of all beneficial changes in our brain and in all other parameters of health.*

We really are emotional beings and the quality of our emotional health impacts significantly on many other aspects of our wellbeing and behavior, including:

- Mood.
- Quality of conscious thought.
- Feelings of innate energy.
- Our outlook day-to-day.
- Concentration and focus.
- Processing speed.
- Memory encoding and recall.
- Decision making.
- Quality and quantity of sleep.
- Perceptions of our physical appearance.
- Heart function.
- Arterial blood flow.

- Digestive efficiency.
- Endocrine communication.
- Overall growth and recovery/repair.

That's quite a list, isn't it? If you think about it, those behaviors are all impactful moment-to-moment functions that influence us all every day of our lives. For example, when was the last time you experienced a seemingly uncontrollable mood change, or realized that your ability to think clearly or concentrate had diminished? When was the last time you struggled to recall something when you needed to?

There are many good reasons, then, to learn how to manage our emotions positively and well. Thankfully, there are ways we can do this and by training or re-training our emotional patterns we can increase our brain health and optimize our performance.

Emotional management

According to Daniel Goleman, 'If your emotional abilities aren't in hand, if you don't have self-awareness, if you are not able to manage your distressing emotions, if you can't have empathy and have effective relationships, then no matter how smart you are, you are not going to get very far.'

There is a powerful truth in his performance-related assessment. It is both powerful and true because it relates directly to the brain and the relationship it shares with the stomach and the heart via the vagus nerve. If we lack emotional intelligence, if we are unable to manage our emotions coherently, our performance, progress and wellbeing will be inevitably limited.

At the time of writing, nearly 3,000 scientific articles have been published on emotional intelligence since the concept was first introduced and much has been learned. Goleman states that an individual with a high level of emotional intelligence is able to:

1. Recognize the emotion, or emotions, they are feeling at any given time so that they can a) manage them and b) avoid being overwhelmed by them.
2. Demonstrate high levels of self-motivation, complete tasks appropriately, and perform at their best when required to do so.
3. Recognize the emotional responses of others and use this awareness to manage relationships effectively.

Professor Victor Dulewicz and Dr Malcolm Higgs, eminent researchers and writers in the field of emotional intelligence, have suggested there are 7 essential components of emotional intelligence. These are:

- Self-awareness.
- Emotional resilience.
- Motivation.
- Interpersonal sensitivity.
- Influence.
- Decisiveness.
- Conscientiousness and integrity.

Self-awareness is the ability to recognize one's own emotional responses as they occur. Emotional resiliency is the ability to resist being swamped by these emotions. Without this combination, high-level performance is difficult to both maintain and repeat. An emotionally aware and resilient performer *uses* their emotions to enhance their behavior, managing to exercise and/or damp-down emotion as necessary in order to achieve their desired outcome. They find balance on the emotional 'high-wire' of expectation, necessity and need.

Emotional Management

The willingness to place oneself in such a challenging and precarious position is fuelled by a level of motivation commensurate with, and influenced greatly by, the degree of emotional commitment felt. Motivation is demonstrated through the willingness to take action in pursuit of a goal, even in the face of opposition or doubt.

Rarely, though, do we operate in isolation from others. In most scenarios we need to understand and relate to the needs, expectations, beliefs, fears, hopes and perceptions of others if we are to achieve our goals. To recognize and respond appropriately to these requires a high level of interpersonal sensitivity coupled with great communication skills. We need to be able to influence others positively and congruently.[7]

We also need to make the best decisions in the most-timely manner – sometimes in the face of ambiguous or incomplete information. Decisiveness is the ability and willingness to make these decisions, often by combining emotional gut instinct with the rational thought we discussed in Chapter 5.

In summary then, an emotionally intelligent person combines high levels of self-awareness and self-control with an understanding of others which they use to communicate, motivate and influence. The studies into emotional intelligence also conclude that whilst our level of emotional intelligence is mostly influenced by our early childhood experiences, it can be improved with training, guidance and coaching.

In his New York workshop, John turned his attention to the value of meditation and breath control as powerful ways of doing just this.

---

[7] More about communication and influence in Chapter 7 *Socialization*.

A Mindful Training Program

He introduced the topic with the warning that, 'Without proper training or, when necessary, *re-training* of our emotional patterns across our life span we are left following a predictable pattern with too-often negative consequences.'

Then, having described meditation as 'an emotion regulation, resiliency, and capacity builder,' he went on to say:

'Meditation as a training method is not new. Many have studied its impact and written about the methods that incorporate as much from the ancient past as they do from our modern scientific study. And the evidence is clear. It shows that the regular practice of meditative techniques changes not only the structure of the brain but also its function.

'Many of you may be surprised to know that the Dalai Lama has long been interested in neuroscience and what modern research methods might reveal about the brains of people who have spent years practicing meditation and other forms of mindful relaxation. At the heart of these techniques is breath rate and focusing on a relaxed, controlled breath.

'In response to the Dalai Lama's interest, The Center for Investigating Healthy Minds at the University of Wisconsin ran a simple experiment on eight Buddhist monks who had each spent an average of 34,000 hours in meditative training. The monks were asked to alternate between a meditative state and a neutral state and the scientists observed how their brains changed. What they saw surprised them. They actually observed high-amplitude gamma-oscillations, which are indicative of plasticity, in the brains of the monks. The implication being that their brains were ready for change and, in theory, more resilient than would normally be expected.

'There are many ways to meditate yet the ultimate goal is to slow down the cognitive processing of our conscious brain. This in turn slows both heart rate and stomach activity, and also reduces the vagus nerve reaction. The result is an increased ability to control our attention-giving and emotional responses.

'A common aspect of meditation techniques, as I'm sure many of you know, is a focus on controlled breathing which helps to reduce outward signs of stress such as high heart rate, sweating, increased stomach acid, muscle tightening, and increased thinking normally of an alarmed or negative nature.

'Buddhist monks have developed a breathing rhythm that has become known as *heart coherence*. This is the synchronization between the breath and heart rate, during which the heart speeds up on the inhalation bringing much needed oxygen and glucose to the brain and slows down again on the exhalation. The practitioners seem to experience maximum benefit at about six breaths per minute, during which they feel significant relaxation, a more controlled focus, reduced energy expenditure and a reduced heart rate.

'In essence, the ability to control our breath allows us greater management over both our central nervous system and peripheral nervous system. Research shows that this control impacts positively on our ability to create and/or maintain emotional coherence. As human beings we are, as far as we know, unique in our capability to do this. Our closest evolutionary cousin the Chimpanzee does not have this capacity and even less breath control appears to exist amongst Gorillas and Orang-utans.

'Breath control taught as a formal skill dates back thousands of years[8] and the knowledge of how and why it works is clear to us

---

[8] Another example of 'The Wisdom of the Village'.

today. It is ours to use or neglect. Jeff Lowe, the great mountaineer, a man used to managing his emotional state under pressure, says, "In a tight situation remember that deep breathing clears the mind and relaxes the muscles."

'The deep breathing he is talking about is diaphragmatic breathing – breathing from the lower abdomen rather than higher up in the chest. Breathing from the lower abdomen is a key advantage as blood flow is greater in the lower part of the lungs simply due to gravity. This is why diaphragmatic breathing can quickly change one's central nervous system response, bringing richer oxygenation of blood to the brain, halting any unwarranted stress response. In essence, the entire CNS system benefits from this simple change in breath rate, enabling us to remain calm with challenging, stressful, and typically uncomfortable dynamics.'

John then concluded this part of his workshop with a reference to the past, saying, 'In the words of the ancient proverb, "Life is in the breath. He who half breathes half lives."'

We'll conclude this half of the chapter with our usual summary, then we'll move on to some practical ways you can bring emotional management to life.

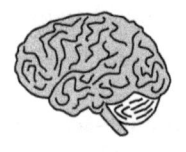

Summary

- You brain perceives and acts upon emotional information.
- The emotion systems of the brain are the first to develop.
- We experience on average hundreds of emotional responses a day.

- Emotions allows us to survive and thrive.
- The brain, heart, and stomach work together to process emotions and responses.
- Emotional management has one of the largest effects on our overall health and performance.
- Consistent difficulty with managing emotions has long- term negative effects.
- Emotions can be managed for our wellbeing and in high stress situations.

The Process

Our recommendations

Acknowledge and welcome the fact that you are an emotional being. Manage and/or create emotions that serve you best by enhancing your performance in every context and aspect of your life. Learn to use your emotions to help you achieve your desired outcomes.

Do this by:

1. Remembering that emotions, managed well, allow us to survive and thrive.
2. Developing the self-awareness to recognize accurately your own emotions as quickly as possible.
3. Developing and implementing strategies and techniques for managing your emotions on all 3 levels: the subjective, physiological and behavioral.

4. Distinguishing between empowering, productive emotions and those that are potentially damaging – and managing both accordingly

Managing your own emotions

The starting point is to realize that we can – and there are many very good reasons why we ought to - manage our own emotions. The fact that we emote before we rationalize means that, to some degree, our emotional response becomes: a) the lens through which we view any given stimuli and b) a key influencer on the nature and quality of our decision-making and subsequent behavior. Also, as Daniel Goleman observed, 'Emotions are contagious.' They are an essential part of our social fabric. How we are feeling at any given time ripples out and touches others. So we have a responsibility not only to ourselves but also to those around us to manage our own emotions positively and well.

And we can.

As ever, there are a variety of options available to us. All we have to do is select and implement those that best suit our personal needs. It is perhaps both obvious and appropriate to say that, as you read the following strategies, techniques and tips, just choose the ones that feel right. We'll begin with the key underlying principle:

Self-awareness leading to self-management

In a workshop Chris was giving about how to create personal learning states, the conversation turned at one point to meditation.

A student asked, 'Chris, when you meditate are you able to stop thinking?'

Emotional Management

'I can,' Chris replied. 'Only why do you ask?'

'Because I'd like to be able to do that. It must be a great feeling, having no thoughts in your mind.'

'That sounds like you have too many thoughts in your mind that create negative feelings,' Chris observed, 'otherwise you wouldn't be so keen to stop thinking. There is an obvious interaction that occurs between how we feel, think and act. Self-awareness – which can be developed through meditation as well as other techniques – is really the ability to recognize the nature of that interaction either as it's happening, or ahead of time and determine its value and appropriateness so we can then avoid, end, moderate or encourage it accordingly.

'Increasing our self-awareness means recognizing our personal strengths and weaknesses, along with such other things as our motivational and decision-making strategies, our communication patterns and, of course, our emotional tendencies.

'In my experience it's true to say that internal silence, the quiet observation of what is going on in our mind and body, can be a most positive and empowering state. It can help us to gain these insights into our self as well as others; it can also be restful and recuperative; it can underpin and aid creativity and both intra-personal and inter-personal communication[9]. However, it is equally true to say that how we manage our thoughts – and, especially, the nature and associated effect of the thoughts we repeatedly return to – is also a significant determinant in how we feel and perform.

'Repetition is an important part of how we communicate to create influence, and that's as true when we are communicating to our

---

[9] More about the relationship between silence and communication in Chapter 7, *Socialization*.

self as it is when communicating to others. The American author and poet, Henry David Thoreau, emphasized this point when he said, "As a single footstep will not make a path on the earth, so a single thought will not make a pathway in the mind. To make a deep physical path, we walk again and again. To make a deep mental path, we must think over and over the kind of thoughts we wish to dominate our lives."

'If we are aiming, then, to experience positive emotions we need to repeatedly use and revisit positive and useful thoughts. We need to actively create neural pathways that lead us into positive states.'

The question that came next was as obvious as it was important. 'How do we do that – especially in difficult circumstances?'

'Deliberately. Regard it as a skill and, like all skills, you need to train and develop it, beginning in situations that are stress free and progressing over time to ever more challenging scenarios. A simple and yet very powerful word we can use in our internal dialogue to create positive mental associations is the word *and*. All you do, at the end of any thought, is just use *and* to lead into a deliberately positive continuation. For example, you might be stuck in a traffic queue, frustrated by the delay, thinking to yourself, "I'm going to be late for work." Instead of developing that line of thinking and increasing your sense of frustration – risking it turning into something worse, like anger – simply use *and* to lead your thoughts in a different direction. You might think, "And this gives me an unexpected opportunity to think of the things I'm grateful for in my life." Or, "And this gives me chance to practice some diaphragmatic breathing." Or, "And this means I can review my plan for that meeting I have later today."

'We create meaning through the associations we make. The trick is to use our thoughts and emotions to create and establish useful associations. *And* can really help us to do this because as soon as we insert it into our internal dialogue it forces us to build from what we were thinking and move on to a new perspective. Of course, to make this work we have to associate *and* only with a shift towards something positive, something that makes us feel better than we were. And we can use this at any time. Even if we are feeling great, we can *and* our thoughts to memories, experiences, hopes, beliefs, in fact any aspects of our life that increases the intensity of the emotion and make us feel even better!

'Think of it in the way that Viktor Frankl[10] explained, that there is a space between stimulus and response and within that space lies the opportunity for us to choose how we will react. In one sense, improving our level of self-awareness means recognizing and using that space to accurately identify and then manage our emotions, thoughts and actions in the most productive of ways.'

Of course, taking control of our emotions can be a difficult task because, by their very nature, emotions tend to draw us in; we become caught up in the feelings we are experiencing; we risk losing sight of the space available to us. Emotions, whether positive or negative, can be seductive.

So here are some other ways, beyond the use of the word *and*, that you can use self-awareness to:

Manage negative emotions

Remember when we talked about neurotransmitters in Chapter 1? Amongst other things we said:

There are two kinds of neurotransmitters: excitatory and inhibitory. Excitatory neurotransmitters stimulate the brain and inhibitory transmitters calm the brain. Inhibitory neurotransmitters act to balance our mood when the excitatory neurotransmitters are active.

---

[10] An Austrian neurologist, psychiatrist and Holocaust survivor.

We're reminding you of this now to help us reinforce the following point:

Emotions are real chemical reactions in our brain.

By engaging in certain activities or behaviors we can influence and control that chemistry to our advantage. Here are a number of options:

Use your body, your physicality, to shift your focus.

Relax your body. Choose one muscle (or muscle group) at a time, tense it and then relax it very deliberately. Once it is relaxed repeat with different parts of your body until you are completely at ease.

Notice the nature and rhythm of your breathing and deliberately slow it down; use diaphragmatic breathing.[11]

Change your posture. We often physically express our emotions in an habitual manner; even without necessarily realizing it we might always use the same posture(s) to reflect a specific emotion. If we change our physicality we can disrupt, and begin to shift away from, the unwanted mind-body connection. In the same way, stop doing any movements you associate only with the negative emotion and very deliberately do something else.

Also if you find that, when a negative emotion is prevalent, your gaze keeps returning to or is fixed on the same spot, deliberately look elsewhere. If, for example, you naturally glance down and to your left when feeling an emotion such as doubt, look up and to your right and maintain that focus instead.

Use an object as a point of focus

Focus your attention on a single object, or image (or even a point

---

[11] More about this in a minute.

on the wall); be really curious about it, notice the details, shape and colors. You can then also imagine that your breath is engaging the object. To do this, breathe in slowly as if drawing air from just beyond or around the object and exhale slowly imagining your breath is returning to the same place. Again, use diaphragmatic breathing.

Carry a personal object with you that you use only as a state changer. It doesn't matter what the object is – as long as it is discreet enough to keep with you at all times – the important thing is that you associate it *only* with controlling and changing negative emotions. Take out and hold the object only when this is your goal, when using any of the above (or any other relevant) techniques. Over time, as the association builds, you might find that just holding the object will automatically begin the process of emotional control.

Use any other type of distracting technique

A distracting technique is anything that shifts your focus away from the cause of your negative emotion. You might, for example, engage in physical activity, listen to a particular piece of music, or identify and write down 2 or 3 different perspectives (plus the supporting evidence) to the one you are holding about your current situation.

Use visualization techniques

Visualization is a powerful form of mental rehearsal that can actually stimulate physical change. As an example of this, researchers from The Cleveland Clinic Foundation in Ohio asked one group of volunteers to visualize contracting their little finger, another group to visualize contracting their elbow, and a third group to actually perform maximal physical little finger contractions.

Each group performed their respective activity for 15 minutes every day for 5 days a week over 12 weeks. Not surprisingly, the group that had undertaken the physical training showed the greatest gain – an increase in finger strength of 53%. However, the groups that had only visualized the exercise also made significant improvements! Those who visualized contracting their elbows had improved their flexion strength by 13.5% and those who had visualized contracting their little finger had increased their finger abduction strength by an amazing 35%!

You can use visualization techniques both in the moment to help you change your state and, of course, ahead of time to rehearse how you will manage negative emotions.

Here are some progressive activities you can do to improve your ability to visualize:

a) Spend 30 seconds studying a picture, then close your eyes and remember it in as much detail as you can. Open your eyes and check how well you did. Notice what stood out to you and what you missed. Repeat using different pictures until your visualization is fully accurate.

b) Spend 30 seconds studying a 3D object then close your eyes and visualize it from all angles. As before, open your eyes and assess your accuracy. Again, repeat using different objects until you can visualize fully.

c) Spend 30 seconds studying a 3D object, put it out of sight and visualize it keeping your eyes open. Practice as required.

d) Visualize a scene, a place you know well, then visualize yourself in the scene. Watch yourself moving through the scene as if you are watching a film.

e) Repeat the previous visualization, only now see it through your own eyes, as if you are living in that moment. Notice if you begin to feel any associated emotions. (Ensure these are positive.)

f) When visualizing a future experience do so using the internal components you use to construct memories. In other words, use self-awareness to identify precisely how you remember positive memories.

Identify, for example, if they are in color – if so, how bright? Are the images in your mind moving or still? Are they in 3D? Do you see yourself in these images, or are you seeing them as if through your own eyes? Can you hear sounds and, if so, how loud are they? Give attention to all the details and construct your visualization using these.

Most of us tend to imagine something that is yet to happen differently from the way we remember something that already has. If we use our intra-personal communication to visualize a future event in precisely the same way we recall a past event, we can increase the positive impact of the visualization – we are coding from experience not imagination.

Identify negative triggers

A *trigger* is a stimuli that creates a specific emotional and physical response.[12] If we identify those triggers to which we respond negatively we can then plan to avoid them, and/or visualize responding differently if we do encounter them, and/or use any of the other techniques previously outlined when encountering them.

Actively reflect on your feelings and the ways you currently manage them

Differentiate between primary and secondary emotions; identify

---

[12] Triggers can be anything: individuals, places, memories, sounds, smells, tastes, imaginings, objects, activities etc.

which negative emotions occur first and if they, in turn, create subsequent emotions. Once you have clarified this relationship, use *and* or any other distraction technique to stop the chain reaction.

Model someone who manages their emotions well

Modelling involves uncovering and then adopting a person's subjective, physiological and behavioral strategies for achieving success. The aim is to identify what the person feels, thinks and does to be successful and to then adopt these yourself.

Choose the person, or people, you want to model carefully; they need to be able to achieve success – in this case, manage their emotions well – *repeatedly*. It's unlikely, however, that they will be consciously aware of everything they do to achieve this. So you will need to question, as well as observe, them.

Be aware that by asking direct questions you will uncover only what the person is consciously aware of. If they have achieved some level of mastery, expect that much of their *feel-think-do* processing will be subconscious. So if you can, watch them in action. You can also ask them to remember, to actively relive in their mind, a time when they managed their emotions well. When doing this, watch the person at least as closely as you listen to them, the likelihood is they will automatically demonstrate some of their physical behaviors as they relive the experience. Give attention to detail and sequencing; it isn't only the devil that's in the detail and the order in which we do things tends to influence the outcome, so notice both.

Understand, too, that you are an excellent modeller already. We started modelling others as children and, whether we realize it or not, we haven't stopped yet.

When thinking about managing negative emotions, let's remember that some emotions we don't enjoy feeling, like fear, are, in some situations, serving a useful, survival purpose. When we talk about negative emotions we are referring only to those that limit our performance, hinder our ability to achieve our desired outcomes, or threaten our wellbeing.

However, emotional management isn't just about managing negative emotions. What about the great, positive emotions we experience? What does managing those actually mean, and how do we go about that? Here are some practical tips to help you:

Manage positive emotions

Know what makes you feel good – and is good for you

Identify your personal triggers for positive emotions. Be clear about why and how these triggers and associated emotions add value to your life in both the short term and long term. Deliberately access and enjoy these triggers and their effects frequently.

Use visualization techniques

When those triggers are not present use visualization techniques to recreate the experience and the feeling. Realize and remember that we have the power to take control of our emotions, they are not only the result of current external stimuli; we can create them deliberately. So if you want to feel a particular emotion, avoid waiting for the necessary stimulus to occur in your environment, take a moment or two to recreate it by reliving the most powerful experience of it you've ever had through visualization.

Use your body, your physicality, to help create the emotion

Just as our body reflects negative emotion, so it does positive. Use any of the physical techniques outlined above to recreate and/or enhance your positive emotions.

Create and maintain close relationships

Researchers have suggested that having a close social network, and a harmonious relationship with your life-partner, enhances feelings of happiness and satisfaction. Remind yourself of the value of these relationships and work proactively to maintain them.[13]

Have great time management

In some respects, this is actually a product of great emotional management and awareness of both self and how we relate to others. There is a great difference between being busy under our own terms, especially if we are doing things that make us feel good, and being continually rushed from pillar to post keeping up with a schedule we don't agree with set by someone else. Aim to achieve the former. (Incorporating sufficient rest and recovery, of course.)

Invest in great experiences

Experiences stimulate our emotions. Great experiences stimulate great emotions. They also create memories we can then use as positive triggers. If we share these experiences with those who are close to us, we significantly increase the power of both the experience and the memory.

---

[13] More about relationship management in Chapter 7, Socialization and Communication.

With that said, let's introduce 3 more interconnected ways you can manage both negative and positive emotions. The first is:

Breathe!

This is an even more basic requirement than the one we included when talking about Physical activity and Rest and recovery, which was to *Move!*

With each breath we bring life to our brain and the processes that are important to our wellbeing, performance and survival. As we have already said, diaphragmatic breathing is one of the key components to meditation and mindfulness exercises. It impacts the brain and how we feel, most specifically by controlling the vagus nerve.

The diaphragm is a dome-shaped muscle located horizontally between the chest cavity and the stomach cavity. Diaphragmatic breathing is marked by expansion of the abdomen rather than the chest when breathing in. Here is a reminder of how it is performed:

1. Inhale gently and slowly through your nose, pushing your stomach *outward* as you draw air into your lungs.
2. Hold the breath (for a count of two).
3. Exhale gently and slowly through pursed lips, pulling your core inward, tightening your abdomen, keeping your chest as still as possible.
4. Repeat for 3-5 minutes.
5. Perform this routine as many times per day as your schedule allows (or demands). If you are new to this method, we recommend that you begin with at least 2 or 3 sessions daily.

If doing this sitting in a chair, place both feet flat on the floor, with your knees bent, and your neck and shoulders relaxed.

This type of breathing can feel a little unusual and awkward at first. However, it is worth persevering. And, if you do find it a little difficult, you might be comforted to know that you are actually remembering something rather learning something new. As a newborn baby you naturally breathed this way.

What you didn't know then is that diaphragmatic breathing influences your central nervous system and that slow diaphragmatic breathing can impact positively on:

- Mental tension.
- Heart rate.
- Breathing rate.
- Limbic system over-activity.
- Cortisol (the stress hormone) release.
- Adrenaline release.
- Pituitary stimulation.

It's because diaphragmatic breathing can be used to manage feelings of stress, anxiety and flight or fight that is it is taught to athletes, artistic performers and, of course law enforcement officers and elite military. This simple activity quite literally breathes life into our brains, halting any unwarranted stress response and facilitating over time a sense of appropriate calmness within challenging, demanding and, even, potentially dangerous environments and/or interactions.

Our next technique is one, like diaphragmatic breathing, we have already referred to:

Meditation

In Chris's learning states workshop the conversation returned to the topic of meditation on several occasions. Chris defined meditation as, 'A practice that can take many forms, incorporating breath control and a focus on a specific external or internal stimuli, with the aim of at least calming both mind and body and increasing awareness of what is happening in the instant.'

As he then explained, 'There are many different ways to meditate. Some encourage concentration on a single object such as a flower or a candle flame, or even your own reflection. Some are based on listening to a sound, or a piece of music or actually repeating a specific mantra. Other methods emphasis focusing on your breath, whether that is how you breathe naturally or deliberate diaphragmatic breathing. You can also meditate by spending time quietly reflecting on a specific question, or by simply letting your thoughts happen and observing rather than engaging with them. You can also let another person guide or lead your meditation. Finally, bear in mind that you can meditate standing, sitting, laying down or, even, when moving. You can, for example, practice most of the methods I've just mentioned whilst walking.'

In his workshop, Chris also talked about *sandwiching* his day between 2 meditation sessions. 'I know it's a strange way to think, or talk, about it,' he said. 'I've just always found that I experience the benefits of meditation most fully by incorporating it at the beginning and at the end of my day. First thing in the morning it helps to set the state for everything that is to follow and, as the final part of my preparing-to-sleep routine, it helps calm and relax my mind and body and, I feel, begin the process of consolidating any learning that has occurred previously.

'For people beginning meditation I'd recommend they first of all experiment to find the method that works best for them - begin with the one that instinctively appeals to you the most - and then *sandwich* the activities and experiences of each day between a minimum of 5 and a maximum of 10 minutes meditation. Over time this can be developed to two 20 minute sessions.'

If you don't have either the time or the inclination to use meditation sessions our third technique might be more appropriate for you. It's something John calls:

Rapid Reset

This is the deliberate inclusion into our daily schedule of very brief periods in which we actively enable our brain to recover from the demands being placed on it and re-energize.

Too many of us work through stress falsely believing that if we stop and take time to reset our emotional, physical and mental state we are wasting time. Nothing is further from the truth. Nothing matters more than energy management and efficiency.

If we push through stress too often (which actually means we are not listening to our brain communicating its needs) we induce periods of overtraining which weaken the central nervous system. Furthermore, after 45 minutes of intense work our ability to focus, move and make decisions drops significantly. So by implementing these opportunities for our brain to recover, we are actually improving our efficiency.

Rapid reset is an example of the type of behavior that John encourages and trains his elite performers to adopt. If you want to make it a part of your life, here's how you do it:

- Take one or two breaks per hour.
- Set a timer on your Smartphone for (at least) two minutes.
- Sit in a relaxed position.
- Close your eyes.
- Use diaphragmatic breathing to slow your respiration rate.

It's that simple.

If you want to use a variation, you can also use music. We know that music moves us, both physically and emotionally. Music has an intimate and powerful impact on our brain. We have all experienced hearing a song or a piece of music that has completely changed our mood. This happens because listening to music can create changes in our limbic system and how it then communicates emotions elsewhere. Music can, essentially, change our brain chemistry. And we can use that to help us create a rapid reset.

This Neuro-enhancing exercise is as simple as putting a playlist together of songs or pieces of music with a low tempo and giving yourself time to do the following:

- Take one or two breaks per hour.
- Sit in a relaxed position.
- Close your eyes.
- Use diaphragmatic breathing to slow your respiration rate.
- Listen to one or two of the songs or pieces of music.

The lower the tempo, or beats per minute, the more the music slows your brain, heart rate and respiration rate, and this in turn switches your central nervous system into recovery mode.

And that brings us to the end of this chapter. Time now to step through the door opened by our consideration of emotional management and move on to the closely connected topics of socialization and communication.

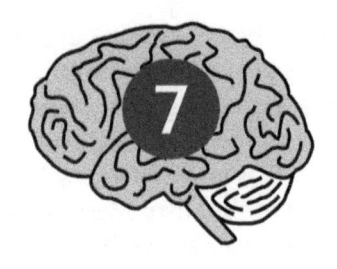

Socialization & Communication

'Man is by nature a social animal.'

Aristotle

Brain Priming – This chapter in focus

Here are the key facts and messages:

- We are social beings and our brain size reflects our sociability.
- Each and every interaction changes our neurobiology and reinforces the neuroplasticity of our brain.
- Social connections fulfil both our survival and higher order needs.
- Our need for social connectedness is essential to our overall development.
- Social interaction promotes general cognitive functioning.
- We have specialized social intelligence neural systems called mirror neurons.

- Words affect our brains and so affect our emotions and performance.
- Our face reveals our emotional state; being able to read other's emotions helps us to manage our relationship and interactions.
- Technology is changing our social world; we need to ensure we manage our use of technology deliberately and well.

Connections revisited

In Chapter 1 when we introduced you to the governor we talked about the importance of connections. We actually said this:

'Like every governor, our brain's power comes from its network and associated connections. Like every governor it fulfils its role best when it is given the support it most values.'

In many respects the way our brain operates, enabling us to learn, adapt and survive through the power of its potentially ever-changing neural networks, is a reflection of our need for – and the benefits we draw from – our social network and the associated connections we are able to make and maintain through that.

We are, as Matthew Lieberman, Professor of Psychology, Psychiatry and Biobehavioral Sciences at UCLA writes, *wired to connect*. Just as our neurons interact from synapse to synapse, reinforcing existing neural pathways and developing new ones, so we, as social animals, are drawn to interact with others, continually developing those relationships we feel most important and creating new relationships in response to our changing experiences and needs.

Let's just take a moment to consider one specific type of relationship: friendship. If we asked you, 'How many people alive on the planet today do you think have at least one friend?' what would your answer be? If you couldn't put a number on it, would you be confident in saying something like, 'The vast majority' or 'Just about everyone' or 'Well over 90%.' You would be right if you did. And you would probably expect to be. After all, just about everyone you know has a friend or two, don't they? In fact, it almost seems like a pointless question doesn't it?

Whilst we might debate exactly when an acquaintance becomes a friend, or when an occasional friend becomes a *real* friend, we all understand and experience the notion of friendship in one way or another. And it's this shared understanding – this universality – that stops the question being pointless and instead makes it really quite significant.

Just take another moment to consider what most of us regard as the inevitability of friendship. Think of it this way: someone you don't know eventually becomes someone you trust with your innermost secrets; someone who came to you as a stranger, turns into a person you turn to for advice or help, especially when the going gets tough; someone you were introduced to, or bumped into, or found yourself working with, ends up being one of the few people in your life who makes you feel understood, cared for and valued.

It might make more sense perhaps if this person was a family member, someone you shared blood ties with, had grown up next to, had known pretty much forever. Only friendship doesn't work like that. Our friends started out as people we would walk past on the street without giving a second glance. Only at some point, somehow, something happened and a relationship began, and you both worked on it enough to turn it into a *friendship*.

When you think of it like that, it's pretty incredible isn't it? Especially given that nearly every human being in every society in every culture on the planet goes out of their way - makes a deliberate effort – to create such relationships. Which, of course, is only one

Socialization & Communication

of the many different types of relationship we all establish. We have extremely complex social lives and, overall, we tend to manage them well. We are equipped to. Why? Because socialization is so important to us as individuals and as a species.

Our social interactions play a crucial role in developing our sense of self, our overall life experience and the outcomes we create. If managed well, social interactions enhance our wellbeing and the quality of our various behaviors. They do so because they always and inevitably influence our brain and, therefore, the anatomy and physiology of our nervous system. Conversely, if our social interactions are inappropriate or managed badly they can have a negative impact on both how we feel and how we perform.

However, our brain is not only influenced by our social interactions, it also drives our need for them. We have what we might think of as a *social brain*. We are truly wired to connect. And if you ever wondered why our brain is so large relative to our body size, the answer is coming up right now:

We have large brains in order to socialize.

In fact, the greatest indicator of brain size, particularly the outermost layer known the neocortex, is the size of the social group in which the species lives. The governor not only has its own internal network, it's also designed to encourage and ensure that we make the most of our own extensive social network. Which is something it's been doing for a very long time.

Scientists think that the first of our ancestors to have brains as large as our own lived 600,000 years ago in Africa. Known as *homo heidelbergensis*, they predate both homo sapiens and the Neanderthals and were, interestingly, the first hominids who worked collaboratively when hunting.

Now, of course, we collaborate in myriad ways. It makes sense that we do. Collaboration helps us to survive, to learn and maintain our dominance as a species. We have large brains so we can socialize in large groups. We socialize because successful socialization significantly increases our chances of having our physical and emotional needs met, of problem solving more successfully and, in the long-term, the survival of our species. Once again, the brain always wins.

In fact, socialization is so important to us, we even tend to think about our social life whenever we are alone and have a free moment or two. Have you ever stopped to consider why, if you are not involved in an active task that requires your brain's resources to be connecting in a specific way, it leads you to think so often about your social connections?

Although neuroscientists are obviously interested in what the human brain does when engaged in a whole range of activities and in response to an equally broad range of stimuli, they have also studied just what it does during those potentially more restful nothing-to-do-at-the moment times. They have identified what they now refer to as the *brain's default network*.[1] It's an interconnected and anatomically definable system that activates whenever we engage in such internal activities as daydreaming, recalling memories, or imagining the future, all of which are activities usually based around our social interactions. Hence we automatically spend at least some of our downtime seeking to make sense of the motives, goals and feelings of others – especially if they appear to differ from our own.

The question this raises is:

Do we instinctively think of social matters during our spare time because we experience so many

---

[1] Sometimes also referred to as the *default mode network*.

social interactions, or because our brain is built to do this?

At first glance it seems like a chicken and egg question - which came first? - and in one sense it is. Especially when you consider that, according to one study, 70% of our conversations are based on social matters. The good news, however, relating to this particular cause or consequence conundrum is that, because we can now study the brain using all those incredible tools and techniques we outlined in Chapter 1, researchers can offer us an answer. It is based primarily on the following 2 insights:

1. Newborn babies demonstrate default network activity, leading to the conclusion that this brain system exists and operates long before a person has any interest in the complexities of the social world.
2. The default network system activates even when people take only a brief rest from a demanding activity. In others words, even when we might expect a person's mind to stay focused on a task the brain automatically flips their attention back to their social interactions.

It seems, then, that the default network is an essential part of our brain's wiring, rather than the result of inevitable social activity. The default network is a powerful indication of the fact that we are inherently social beings and that creating strong social bonds provides many short and long-term benefits relating to our survival, our development and our sense of personal identity and self-worth.

Even in our fast-paced, technology-driven world, social connectedness is an essential part of who we are and how we live, learn, and love. The research professor, author and public speaker Brené Brown, defines *connection* as, '...the energy that exists between people when they feel seen, heard, and valued; when they can give and receive without judgment; and when they derive sustenance and strength from the relationship.' Whilst that might be the ideal, the need to be recognized, understood and belong is a most powerful one. It's a need that was being written about as far back as the 1950s by such pioneers as Dr Abraham Maslow and Dr Jerome Frank.

Maslow's Hierarchy of Needs theory, as shown below, is especially congruent with the latest neuroscience, emphasizing as it does the fact that if basic needs are not being met higher order needs are more difficult to attain.[2] As we have outlined throughout this book our brain cannot function at its best without relatively consistent sleep, hydration, nutrition, and physical activity. These basic aspects of human existence then empower us to connect socially and from these social experiences we develop and grow in a multitude of ways.

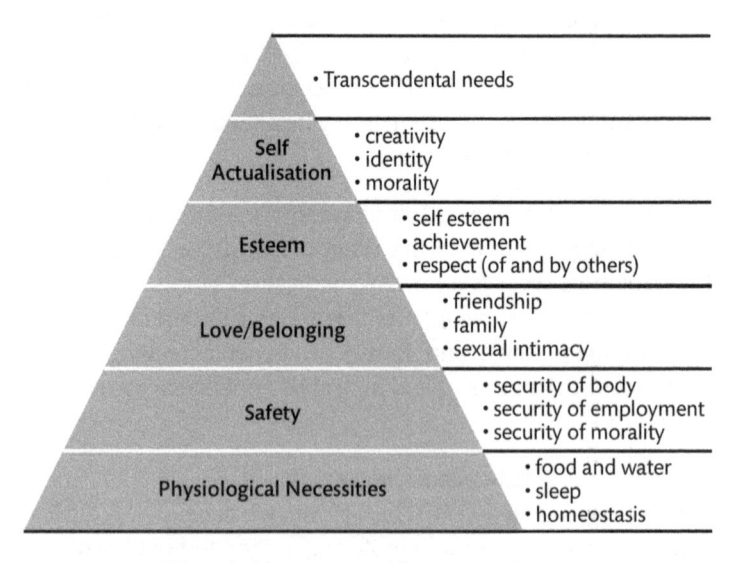

- Transcendental needs

Self Actualisation
- creativity
- identity
- morality

Esteem
- self esteem
- achievement
- respect (of and by others)

Love/Belonging
- friendship
- family
- sexual intimacy

Safety
- security of body
- security of employment
- security of morality

Physiological Necessities
- food and water
- sleep
- homeostasis

Example from: www.mirkocasagrande.com

---

[2] Of course a variety of needs can be met simultaneously.

Socialization & Communication

In a similar light Jerome Frank, who pursued the scientific mechanisms of psychotherapy in his book *Persuasion and Healing: A Comparative Study of Psychotherapy*, came to the conclusion that when working within any helping relationship it is the quality of the human connection, specifically the demonstration of genuineness in the interaction, an authentic and open stance, and the installation of hope, that is the primary driver of change. This viewpoint was reinforced by subsequent research in the 1990s. Frank's book, first published in 1961 is now in its 3rd edition and still has much to offer.

One of those reinforcing and developing Dr. Frank's work is Dr. Louis Colozino, who describes the human brain as "a social organ of adaptation", stimulated to grow through positive and negative interactions with others. Using the term the *social synapse* to describe the space through which humans communicate, Colozino states that communication stimulates the brain's social networks and that relationships actually influence the long-term construction of a person's brain.

The way in which our interactions influence our brain and the brains of those with whom we interact is determined, according to Colozino, by how we fill that communication space. It's something we do both consciously and subconsciously. We might, for example, choose to deliberately smile or wave or speak in a very specific way to someone else. We also, though, send out unconscious messages through our posture, gestures, or proximity, through our gaze or pupil dilation, through changes to our skin color or breathing. Colozino explains that:

'Contact with others across the social synapse stimulates neural activation, which influences the internal environment of our neurons. This activation in turn triggers the growth of new neurons as well as the transcription of protein, which builds neurons as they expand, connect and organize into functional networks. A basic assumption is that loving connection and secure attachments build healthy and resilient brains, while neglectful and insecure attachments can result in brains vulnerable to stress, dysregulation and illness.'

So through socialization and communication we become linked to each other, regulating and developing, just as the brain's neurons connect from synapse to synapse. As we mentioned in Chapter 1 there are specific neurons that help us create these links. They are called:

Mirror neurons

These were first identified during a study of macaque monkeys. Dr. Vittorio Gallese and colleagues at the University of Parma noted that specific neurons activated both when a monkey observed an action performed by another and when it made the same action itself. Because these neurons fire when observing a specific act and also when performing the act, they became known as *mirror neurons*. Evidence of mirror neurons has been found in the human brain too, in our motor cortex, somatosensory cortex, and parietal cortex as shown on the next page.

The fact that mirror neurons activate whether we are observing or doing has obvious implications for learning. As humans we learn by both observing and doing. (Amongst other ways.) Mirror neurons, then, might play an important part in how we develop new abilities and how we interpret and predict the behavior of others. Connected to this, because mirror neurons have also been found in the part of the brain known as Broca's area, the part responsible for speech production, they may also play their part in the learning and expression of language.

Beyond learning, mirror neurons might have a crucial role in helping us to bridge the social synapse and, perhaps, even

Socialization & Communication

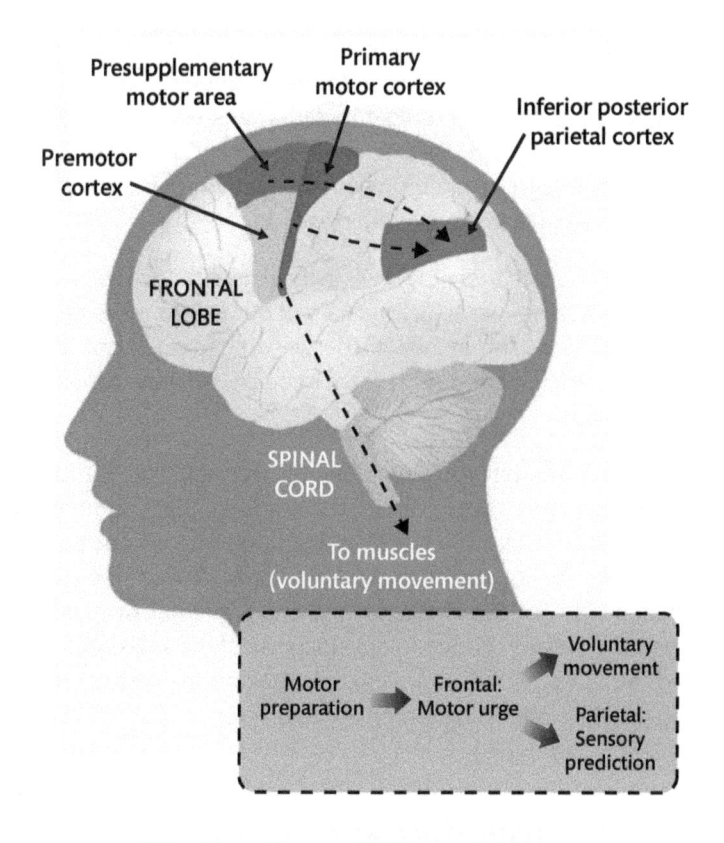

Diagram labels:
- Presupplementary motor area
- Primary motor cortex
- Inferior posterior parietal cortex
- Premotor cortex
- FRONTAL LOBE
- SPINAL CORD
- To muscles (voluntary movement)

Motor preparation → Frontal: Motor urge → Voluntary movement / Parietal: Sensory prediction

Picture from: dameunsilbidito.wordpress.com

empathize with others. Seeing emotional expressions of, for example, fear, sadness, or joy, can activate appropriate or similar responses within ourselves. We know from our personal, everyday experiences that observing and doing or feeling are closely linked. After all, it's nearly impossible to see a child looking sad and not be emotionally moved by the sight, isn't it? In all probability that's our mirror neurons in operation.

There is still much to be learnt about the role mirror neurons have in our development and interpersonal connectedness. That's why many researchers are examining them, asking questions about the various ways they influence us in terms of, amongst other things, our intentions, learning, empathy, self-awareness and language development and use. Despite this need for more research[3], it does seem that mirror neurons offer us yet another insight into how our brain influences everything we do.

And we do more than simply share in the emotional experiences of others. Sometimes we actually go out of our way to make people feel good. Even, sometimes, those we don't even know. Even, incredibly, when there doesn't seem to be any tangible benefit for us in doing so!

The chances are that you have done this yourself; that you know exactly what we're talking about. It's also likely that you've never questioned it before, that you've simply done your good deed and moved on. So let's ask the question now: Why are we willing sometimes to put the interests of others before our own? It's an important question about an essential part of the social glue that binds us. Guess where we are going to look for the answer?[4] First, though, a few interesting examples relating to:

Working together and putting others first

Sometimes we do things for others because we feel obliged to, because we feel that we owe them in some way. This sense of obligation is known as *reciprocity*. There has been much research

---

[3] And there's always the need for more research.

[4] You're right. It is, of course, the brain. Otherwise this book would have a different title.

Socialization & Communication

into the power of reciprocity.[5] One of the key findings suggests that when *Person A* feels they are in *Person B's* debt, they will not only repay, they will do so by offering something with a higher value than the original favor had. It seems that we don't feel satisfied repaying like for like. We need to express our gratitude by giving back more than we originally received.

However, what about those times when reciprocity is not at play? What happens then? You probably won't be surprised to know that in many cases we still often endeavour to make sure that all involved benefit equally or, even, that we put someone else's needs ahead of our own.

When participants in a study were asked to play a game known as the *Prisoner's Dilemma*, in which financial rewards are on offer and a willingness to trust and operate collaboratively with another is tested, over 60% of players deliberately chose to take a smaller reward for themselves - to share the prize equally with the other player - once they had been reliably informed of that player's intention to do the same. What makes their decision particularly interesting is, at that point in the game, they could have chosen to take all of the reward for themselves and left the other player with nothing! Yet they chose not to. They chose instead to think of the other's needs not just their own. They chose to behave in a way that many would regard as *fair*.

Other research used fmri scanning to study activity within the brain when people were asked to make decisions about giving money to charity. The study comprised 2 elements. Firstly, the participants were asked if they would like to receive a gift of $5. It was a no-strings-attached offering and, as you would expect, people were quick to take advantage of it. No surprises there. What happened next, though, revealed something very interesting. The

---

[5] If you want to know more about this research the work of Professor Robert Cialdini is a good place to start.

participants were then asked if they would sacrifice some of their newly acquired money in order for a donation of $5 to be made to a charity. The choice was simple: keep what you've got, or lose some of your wealth to let others benefit. Many chose the altruistic option. Again, perhaps, no big surprise there. When, though, do you think the reward regions in the participants' brains became most activated? When they received $5 for doing nothing or when they gave some away to help a charity? It was the latter. Giving, it seems, is more rewarding than receiving.

Maybe, you might think, this is due to feelings of social pressure, of the need to conform or at least to behave in ways we believe others would approve of? Well, actually it seems that it isn't. Different parts of our brain activate when we feel compelled to be complicit and when we are making genuine choices based on what truly feels right. When our decisions make us feel good it's because the brain's reward regions including the ventral striatum, an area situated in the forebrain and interconnected with the limbic system, are activated. These don't come into play when our decisions are driven by the need to comply with a social norm. Players in the *Prisoner's Dilemma* game who chose to win less for themselves in order to share equally with others demonstrated the same brain activity.

The lesson seems to be that working together and, indeed, giving to others even at our own expense, makes us feel good. They are rewards in their own right. Our brain ensures this is so.

Socialization brings other rewards, too. Simply being told by others that we are valued or appreciated activates our brain's reward system just as other, more tangible, rewards do. In fact, positive feedback impacts us so positively, there's a good argument for making it an integral part of our communication in the workplace, in education and in healthcare. As we will demonstrate later in this chapter, words really do matter because they influence our brain and, therefore, how we feel and perform. Positive words that signal recognition, affection or admiration really are good for us.

Teamwork is another benefit of socialization. It improves our problem-solving abilities, enables us to share knowledge, combine expertise, and learn through both imitation and instruction. It also increases opportunities for the sharing of positive feedback.

Positive and regular social interaction also improves our working memory and our ability to self-monitor. It can also help limit the likelihood of such problems as depression, especially in elderly and potentially lonely individuals. Our brain is not only wired for us to socialize, when we do socialize we actually improve our brain health and performance! It's a fabulous win-win situation.

There is, however, a potentially painful side to the governor's social wiring:

The pain of social rejection and loss

Given that we have evolved as a species to live, learn, work and survive collaboratively, it's no wonder that social rejection hurts. The fact that so many people still deny the existence of this particular type of pain or, worse still, believe that those who express it are weak-minded or overly sensitive, is a greater source of wonderment.

So let's be clear about it. The pain of social rejection hurts. It hurts just like every other pain. It hurts in just the same way that straining a muscle or breaking a bone hurts. But then it would do. You see, social pain and physical pain are both experienced when the same part of your brain is activated. It's called the *dorsal anterior cingulate cortex*. It's found towards the top and the front of the brain. Researchers have discovered that the more pain we feel, whether social or physical, the more the dACC is activated.

If you've ever felt bad because the beautiful person in the bar didn't want to know you, or because you weren't picked for the team or invited to the party, you were feeling a quite natural pain. It's a pain that, unlike the hurt of physical injury, often raises all sorts of unpleasant questions and doubts about our self-worth and sense of identity. Breaking your leg rarely, if ever, threatens your sense of belonging. Indeed, it can often bring welcome support. The pain of rejection, however, hurts and isolates. It's so powerful we don't even need to be rejected by people we know or like to experience it.

Researchers at Purdue University, Indiana, studied the brain responses of individuals who were quite literally taken out of the loop of an internet-based ball throwing activity. The participant believed they were engaged in a digital game with 2 unknown people that required them to 'throw' a ball back and forth amongst themselves. After a time, the others – who were, in fact, pre-programmed avatars rather than real people - began deliberately throwing the ball only to each other, excluding the subject who was then obliged to simply sit and watch. The result? Participants acknowledged feelings of anger and/or sadness about this unexpected rejection.

It seems we really don't like the pain of being left out. Even when that's by someone we have never met and never will. Even when it's only happening on a screen.

Neither do we like the pain of *loss*. And there is an unfortunate inevitability about the fact that, at times in our life, we are going to lose or be separated from loved ones. *Attachment theory* was first introduced in the 1950s as a way of explaining the behavior of orphans and other children without families who were living in orphanages during the Second World War. The distress caused by loss of attachment is a social distress. Think, for example, of the way a baby cries when it has no awareness of its parents or primary carers. These cries function as a signal for help, they alert the parent. They are vital, early stage examples of the dynamic, interactive communication loop that will last a lifetime.

It's tempting to assume that, for a baby, the need for attachment is based on the need for food rather than any aspect of socialization, that at this time in human development the focus is on nourishment and other basic need satisfaction and not human interaction. That's actually not the case. Babies, like other newborn mammals, are unable to care for themselves. They are totally dependent on others for their survival. Yet they are comfortable spending hours every day in the arms of their mother, touching her, holding on to her, because she feels like their mother not because she is the food provider. Even as newborns we have a need to be connected. And lengthy separation from parents not only increases levels of cortisol in young children, it can also lead to brain alterations in the orbitofrontal cortex, a region found in the frontal lobes of our brain that is believed to play a key role in decision-making, social adjustment and mood control.

Socialization, then, for all its many benefits, can also be a source of real, significant pain. However, there might even be a benefit in this – particularly the pain associated with rejection. After all, pain is a message that can often have a positive value. So what is the message caused by feelings of social rejection? Perhaps it's simply this: we need to avoid isolation because our chances of survival are best when we are part of a cohesive group. To encourage us to avoid this isolation, rejection *hurts*. The obvious way to escape the pain of rejection is to maintain acceptance within our group and, if that fails, to find and join another appropriate social set.

This need for social connectivity is so powerful that when not met it can impact seriously on our health. It's a statement of the obvious to say that our need for food, drink, warmth and shelter is immediately more important in the short-term than our need for relationships and human interaction. We can live for a lot longer without talking to someone than we can without drinking. Having said that, research suggests that a lack of appropriate, supportive social relationships is as much a threat to our health as smoking, high blood pressure, obesity and lack of physical activity.

As the poet John Donne wrote, *'No man is an island.'* We are happier and safer together. It makes evolutionary sense for us to build and live in societies. It is inevitable that the cultures we create that both bind and identify those societies influence us significantly

Culture and the brain

We might think of culture as the customs, beliefs and associated behaviors that are shared and accepted by those making up a society. These elements influence everything including how problems are defined and solved, the style of architecture that is preferred, the symbols used, the food that is eaten (and how it is eaten), the nature of family units, the structure and implementation of the law, religion, attitudes to others and approaches to social welfare. Given what we have already said about mirror neurons, the way our brain is influenced by social interaction and our inherent need for connectedness and belonging, it's fairly obvious that the culture we grow up in has a great deal to do with how our brain develops and functions.

Actually, we can be even more precise than that. It's the part of the society you grow up in and the way in which the overarching cultural values affect you that has the greatest effect on your brain. For example, research shows that continual money problems – the sort faced by people living in poverty-negatively affect problem solving and decision making, creating a loss in cognitive functioning equivalent to a 13 point drop in IQ. At the other end of the financial spectrum, there is evidence that economically privileged youngsters demonstrate higher rates of substance abuse, mood disorders and rule breaking than is the norm.

What also appears to be the case is that people from different cultures see the same situations differently; they view things from a different perspective, highlight or emphasize different factors and, sometimes, come to very different conclusions. This is hardly surprising given that different cultures place emphasis on different values and these, in turn, influence our neural activity. As an example of this, one study revealed a difference in brain activity between Western and Chinese participants when required to think of themselves and their mother. When asked to think of themselves the Western participants demonstrated activity in their medial prefrontal cortex, the part of the brain that is implicated in the processing of self-referential information. This brain region was not activated, though, when thinking of their mother. The brains of the Chinese participants showed no such separation, their medial prefrontal cortex activated when both thinking of themselves and when thinking of their mother.

Our brains, then, are influenced significantly by the culture, the society and the family they are born into. One thing these all have in common is:

Communication

As we said earlier communication is our primary method of exchange. We communicate with loved ones, colleagues and strangers. Through our communication we exchange ideas and information, beliefs, thoughts and feelings. We seek to explain ourselves to others and, in turn, gain insights into them. We learn, teach, sooth, encourage and persuade. We defend and promote those causes we support and oppose those we don't. We do all these things, and more, using a mixture of words, gestures, expressions and images shared through a variety of media and, often, face to face.

Sometimes we influence ourselves and those around us in ways we don't mean to. We misinterpret what we hear or see. We create an emotional response we don't intend. We hamper or limit performance when we meant to develop it. Sometimes we are reminded that it's a complicated thing, this communication process. It's pretty much non-stop and its nature and content can shift in an instant.

Thankfully, though, despite these challenges our wonderful brain coupled with our desire to interact positively and well, enables us to work together to make good things happen. How do we do this? Well, we tend to create an appropriate understanding of the words we hear and the gestures and expressions we see. We could do it an awful lot better, though.

Communication skills are identified as being of key importance in many contexts and yet most of us have had only limited training in how to improve those skills. We seem to operate on the assumption that, because we have the necessary kit - our senses and the ability to speak - and lots of opportunity to practice, we are automatically as good as we could be. That's a flawed premise. It's flawed in 2 regards. Firstly, deliberate skill development is dependent on progressive training not just repetition. Secondly, practice alone doesn't make perfect. Indeed, misguided practice can limit or damage ability rather than enhance it.

We manage our communications as well as we do because our brain helps us. As ever, it's there in the background doing everything it can to ensure we *win*. It's doing this despite the fact it's being influenced by the words and actions of both our self and others. Some words, it seems, are particularly influential.

Consider the word, *No*. According to research, just seeing or hearing the word causes the release of a variety of stress-producing

Socialization & Communication

hormones and neurotransmitters which, in turn, impair our language processing and communication as well as our ability to reason. If you say the word, go on to use other negative language, and then make matters worse by thinking about it, you run a very real risk, it seems, of disrupting your sleep, damaging your memory and negatively affecting your emotional management. It isn't just our communication that affects our brain. Spending time with people who use negative language on a regular basis can actually increase our own levels of anxiety and irritability and, even, feelings of prejudice towards others!

So, does positive language have the reverse effect? Thankfully, the answer appears to be *Yes*. Which, given the topic and the question, seems absolutely appropriate. There is one caveat though. According to psychologist and researcher Barbara Fredrickson and others, it takes 5 times more positive language to influence us as it does negative. The lesson appears to be, if you want to perform well and repeatedly, manage your intra-personal and interpersonal communications to ensure a minimum of 5 times more positive messages than negative ones.

The fact that words influence our brain and, therefore, our performance should come as no surprise. We are wired to socialize and communication is the way we do it; that's why we spend so much of our so-called *free time* reviewing, interpreting or imagining the communications of others. Our brain needs to be receptive to the myriad messages others share with us. It's essential to our wellbeing and our survival. Sometimes, though, as we've already suggested, that receptivity can work against us.

When Fabrizio Benedetti, a Professor of Physiology and Neuroscience at the University of Turin Medical School in Italy, told certain individuals about a link between high altitudes and an increased likelihood of headaches, those individuals experienced more headaches when skiing in the mountains than others unaware of the purported risk. This negative influence is known as *nocebo*. It's the opposite of the placebo effect.

Words, however, are not the only way we share messages and influence others. Facial expressions are also significant. Dr Paul Ekman pioneered the study of facial expressions and the insight they offer into emotions being experienced. If you've ever seen the hugely successful television series *Lie To Me* you've been introduced to his work already, albeit in a fictional manner.

We probably all know that non-verbal communication is a powerful part of face-to-face interactions and that facial expressions are central to this. We accept that we can all share or receive looks that are, amongst others, loving, threatening, quizzical, fearful or welcoming.

Ekman's study has revealed that some facial expressions and their associated meaning are universal; even people in societies that have no way of interacting with the outside world, such as tribes in the Amazon basin, use the same facial expressions as the rest of us to express certain emotions. They are just one more reminder of the fact that, whatever the differences created by our cultures and our own unique experiences, we share a common humanity. Even with people we never meet. Even with those in very different environments. And our brain is the powerful common denominator.

Ekman's work also focuses on what have become known as *micro-expressions*. These are essentially uncontrollable indications of emotion that flash across the face in a fraction of a second. Because we emote before we rationalize micro-expressions provide a clear although fleeting insight into what we are truly feeling. They reveal the emotion we might decide to disguise or the truth we might aim to deny. They are significant indicators of what is really being felt and, therefore, the real motivation for subsequent communication and behavior.

Socialization & Communication

Identifying expressions

Disgust
- Clenched nostrils
- Pursed lips

Happy
- Primarily a smile

Contempt
- Primarily tight lips raised slightly on one side

Rest

Sad
- Primarily a frown (or a furrowed brow)

Angry
- A flushed face
- An inward and downward brow movement
- A hard stare
- Flared nostrils
- Clenched jaw

Fear
- Widening eyes
- Dilated pupils
- Risen upper lip
- Brows draw together
- Lips stretch horizontally

Surprise
- Raised and curved eyebrows
- Stretched skin below the eyebrows
- Horizontal wrinkles across the forehead
- Open eyelids
- Dropped jaw
- Parted lips

Picture from 52-infographics.blogspot.com

Through training we can learn to recognize micro-expressions. Once developed, it enhances greatly our understanding of others and our ability to predict their likely responses.

One person who has used the interpretation of micro-expressions as a key part of his work is Daniel Gottman, Professor Emeritus of Psychology at the University of Washington. In his extensive study of how married couples communicate, fall out and make up, Gottman combined identification of micro-expressions with various psychophysiological data (for example sweating, heart rate, heart rate variability, and skin temperature), along with the coding of verbal content and statistical modelling to determine the likelihood of couples divorcing. How accurate was he?

With studies spanning from 1992 through 2000 Gottman and his colleagues were able to identify who was likely to divorce and who was likely to stay together with 90% accuracy! Our language, both verbal and physical, is clearly as revealing as it is influential.

The study of just how our brain is so significantly and frequently influenced by the myriad social interactions we experience is known as:

Interpersonal Neurobiology

Pioneered by Dr Dan Seagal and Dr. Allan Schore, Interpersonal Neurobiology encourages a multidisciplinary approach to seeking a better understanding of the brain and how it influences and is, in turn, influenced by our socialization and communication. Given John's commitment to the power of collaboration it's probably no surprise that this is an approach he endorses. In his explanation he draws on his own experiences working in the most elite, high performance environments:

'Whilst I believe that isolation is at times important to discover and control variables for greater understanding ultimately, to learn more, we must be willing and able to work in an integrated fashion. My work with high performers -especially in the military - requires this integration, bringing together multiple ways of understanding in order to provide the very best to each individual.

'It's important to emphasize that this team-based approach requires us, the experts involved, to focus on and be responsible for what we do best and nothing more. We all need to *own our lane and stay in it*. By this I mean we need to know enough to bring absolute value to the process, and at the same time we need to resist every temptation to step beyond the boundaries of our own expertise. Whenever we step outside our lane we stop serving our client and begin serving our ego.

'This integrative approach is not only relevant in the military. It's fundamental to developing our knowledge of the brain in relation to a wide variety of topics, including mental health, education, parenting, sport and organizational leadership.'

The study of Interpersonal Neurobiology is helping us to understand just how our social interactions influence our neurobiology and the neuroplasticity of our brain. For example, in the last chapter we mentioned that 80-90% of the nerve fibers in the vagus nerve are dedicated to communicating a mix of emotional, contextual, internal and external information up to your brain as part of an on-going interactive feedback loop. Much of this information comes from our social interactions and the environments in which they occur. The ability to interpret accurately social cues such as voice tone, facial expression, gesture and distancing is as important for ensuring our survival as it is for enabling us to develop relationships.

Dr Stephen Porges, the founder of the Polyvagal Theory, has highlighted the important role of the vagus nerve in social engagement. His groundbreaking work has shown that analysis of vagal nerve responses provides a platform for interpreting our social behavior within a bio-psycho-social context. Our brain is wired for us to socialize yet its primary purpose is to ensure our survival. Whether we are consciously aware of it or not – and we are usually not – we are constantly scanning and interpreting our environments and interactions for indications of safety or threat.

According to Dr Porges, whenever we feel safe and are therefore able to genuinely engage socially our metabolic demands reduce, facilitating health, growth, and restoration. When confronted by what we perceive to be a challenge, we respond initially by using facial expressions, language and tone of voice in an attempt to facilitate a negotiation. If that fails our relatively new – in evolutionary terms – social engagement system withdraws enabling us to engage in the more primitive responses of flight, fight or freeze.

This third response, *freeze*, which involves shutting down in the face of a seemingly inescapable or overwhelming threat, is our oldest defence mechanism. It occurs when our nervous system detects a most significant risk. How is this an example of the brain doing everything in its power to help us survive and *win*? Because when there's no other option our brain does whatever is necessary to help us disassociate from our current experience. Sometimes that might even mean we pass out. If we disassociate we will feel less pain, either physically or emotionally. We become numbed, even potentially to the point of unconsciousness.

Our need to socialize and our dependency on others, especially in our early most formative years, can unfortunately bring with it significant risks. As we have already discussed, social pain is as real, threatening and harmful as physical pain. Sometimes our interactions damage us. Sometimes they are repeated. The sad truth is, in some circumstances, they can be difficult to escape. If our social connections trigger dramatically or repeatedly our natural flight-fight-freeze defences they change our brain-heart-stomach responses and our vagus nerve reactions. These can, in turn, damage our ability to connect appropriately with important others at critical times of our development.

This is not the only risk, however. There's another form of social interaction that might be having a negative effect on our neurology, because it doesn't require and, therefore, doesn't develop the abilities we have been talking about. What is it? It's the use of social media.

Here's what Dr Porges has to say about it and its relationship to education :

'In this new world of social communication...we're stripping the *human interaction* from human interactions. We're going from a synchronous interactive mode, to an asynchronous mode[6]. Now we leave messages and read messages and form interactions that do not involve synchronous interactions. We are allowing the world to be organized based upon principles of individuals who have difficulty regulating in the presence of others, but regulate very well with objects.

'From a clinical perspective, many of the clinical disorders that are being treated are really about people who have difficulties regulating their state with others and gravitate to regulating with objects...What we know is that their nervous systems do not enable reciprocal social interaction – they have difficulties *feeling safe* and experiencing the beneficial physiological states that enable positive social behavior to be parallel to health, growth, and restoration. For them, social behavior is not calming but is disruptive.

---

[6] Synchronous communication occurs when both parties are present in real-time, for example in face-to-face or telephone conversations. Asynchronous communication occurs when this is not the case, for example texting or email.

'The problem is that our society, including our educational system, is emphasizing interactions with objects and not with people.

'Changes in education are moving away from face-to-face interactions. Schools are putting iPads in the hands of pre-schoolers and elementary school children. I was watching a recent newscast of a school where the administrators and teachers were so proud that in their first grade classroom, all of their students had iPads. As the camera captured the classroom, the kids were looking at the iPads, and were not looking at each other or the teacher.

'What is the consequence of this trend? This trend results in the nervous system not having appropriate opportunities to exercise the neural regulatory circuits associated with social engagement behaviors. If the nervous system does not have these opportunities, then the nervous system will not develop the strength and resilience to self-regulate and regulate with others, especially when challenged.

'If schools continue on this trajectory of "technological advancement," the children will not get the appropriate neural exercises to develop an efficient neural platform to support social behavior and to facilitate state regulation.

'...Under the pressure of our cognitive-centric, cortical-centric society, we seem intent on force-feeding everyone with more information without understanding that our nervous system needs to be in a specific physiological state to promote bold ideas, creativity, and positive social behavior.

'Rather than enabling opportunities for music and play with others such as team sports - all opportunities to exercise the social engagement system - we treat these as "extra" curriculum activity that would distract from cognitive activities with a goal of enforcing children to sit longer in the classroom.'

This is not to say that technology doesn't have a place in improving our lives. It clearly does. Our simple message is:

Make sure you use technology deliberately to enhance brain health and function. Know what to use and when to use it. And always prioritize looking into the eyes of another human being over looking at a screen.

Even if we never learn how to look and listen with the skill of researchers like Paul Ekman and Daniel Gottman, our ability to communicate well and to interpret the communication of others accurately is central to our life experience, the success or failure of our most meaningful relationships, and our brain's absolute need for us to socialize.

Before we discuss some practical ways of doing these things well, here's our usual reminder of the key facts:

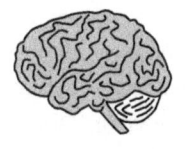

Summary

- We are social beings and our brain size reflects our sociability.
- Each and every interaction changes our neurobiology and reinforces the neuroplasticity of our brain.
- Social connections fulfil both our survival and higher order needs.
- Our need for social connectedness is essential to our overall development.

- Social interaction promotes general cognitive functioning.
- We have specialized social intelligence neural systems called mirror neurons.
- Words affect our brains and so affect our emotions and performance.
- Our face reveals our emotional state; being able to read other's emotions helps us to manage our relationship and interactions.
- Technology is changing our social world; we need to ensure we manage our use of technology deliberately and well.

The Process

Our recommendations

Manage how, when and with whom you socialize as deliberately and positively as you manage all the other vitally important aspects of your life. Remember, too, that you influence others just as powerfully as they influence you; manage this responsibility with the respect it deserves.

Do this by:

1. Identifying the influence that specific individuals or groups have on you and using this to guide the frequency and level of your interaction.
2. Spending as much time as possible with those people who make you feel great and add value to your life.

Socialization & Communication

3. Developing your ability to look and listen.
4. Developing your ability to deliver the right words congruently and well.
5. Managing your use of technology and social media.

Be proactive

Although we can't control the frequency, nature and content of all our social interactions as thoroughly as we can other aspects of our brain management Process, we can do much to ensure that it works for us rather than against us.

We are social beings; managed well our social interactions improve the quality of our lives in myriad ways. Indeed, for many of us our most valued relationships are at the heart of what makes life worth living. Socialization, then, isn't just necessary for our survival; it underpins our sense of personal identity and purpose. It is often through our relationships and the influence shared that we create and justify our own value; that we make sense of just *who* and *why* we are.

In the previous chapter we talked about the importance of emotions and emotional management. How, and with whom, we socialize and communicate impacts significantly on our emotional state. And our emotional state impacts significantly on how we perform in all aspects of our life. Our brain management Process is an interactive, iterative system in which all elements impact upon the other.[7] We can be as proactive in managing and improving our socialization and communication as we can all the other elements and, by doing so, realize that we are also impacting positively on those other elements.

---

[7] That's why the final S in Process stands for *Synergy*.

Having said that, to help us highlight some practical tips and techniques we're going to divide our social world into 3 parts: Our family, social and professional lives. Given the huge degree of influence that our family has on how we think, feel and act, it seems an appropriate place to start.

Family life

Research suggests the following tips for managing family life can add value:

Show affection

Just as we are more inclined to like people who demonstrate clearly that they like us, so research suggests that 47% of people are more likely to feel affectionate towards a family member who regularly expresses affection towards them. So if you want to feel the love, go first and make sharing positive feelings an inherent part of how you communicate.

Be positive - focus on the good stuff

Deliberately spend time thinking about all the good stuff in your life. Our level of happiness is, it seems, determined to some degree by what we think about most frequently. People who are satisfied with their personal and professional life tend to spend twice as much time thinking about the good stuff, as people who aren't.

Also do everything you can to be positive when things are proving to be difficult. Demonstrating such positivity can help reduce the stress felt by other family members by up to 60%.

Empower the children

According to scientists at the University of California children who plan their own schedules, set their own goals and evaluate their own work go on to have greater cognitive control over their lives. The lesson would seem to be, encourage and enable the children in the family to assume active responsibility for their behavior and performance.

Be willing to change

Studies suggest that our willingness to embrace change in both our family and professional life is associated with higher levels of overall satisfaction. They also indicate that individuals who are reluctant or resistant to change are less likely to communicate well with their family or to feel close to them.

Talk about the difficult topics

Mothers willing to discuss sensitive topics with their teenage daughters increase the likelihood of the relationship becoming closer in the future by as much as 36% according to research.

Engage the elders

Numerous studies have identified the benefits of actively involving the older generation in family life. Children who spend regular time with their grandparents are more likely to show concern for others, be socially able and do well in school than those who don't. There is also evidence to suggest that when mothers receive regular support from grandmothers their stress levels are decreased. This is an important finding given that our next tip is:

As a parent find ways to minimize your stress

When asked, children in 1,000 families said that above all else they wished their parents would be less tired and less stressed! Message to Mum and Dad: create a positive work-life balance; actively manage your stress levels and remember that, amongst all your many other responsibilities, you are a Role Model.

Have family rituals

Rituals help create feelings of belonging and security and can also increase the value we place on things. Rituals play an important role in helping us chart our way through uncertainty and change. Family rituals can do all of these things, with the added benefit of enhancing social cohesiveness.

One of the most obvious family rituals – and, if research is to be believed, one of the most significant – is the family dinner. Studies report that children who eat dinner regularly with the rest of the family have higher self-esteem, larger vocabularies and are less likely to drink, take drugs, or develop eating disorders. And these are just some of the benefits identified! Indeed, one survey determined that time spent eating meals at home was the single biggest predictor of children's academic achievement and behavior.

Rituals, of course, can also be used as part of our next tip:

Share the family history

Knowing the family history, including any ups and downs, can reinforce a child's sense of self-esteem. Being a part of something bigger, in this case a family unit that sticks together through good and difficult times, enhances both self-confidence and self-control. Finally, to further develop this feeling of belonging:

Socialization & Communication

Be part of a larger community

This takes us back to our inherent need to socialize. There are many positive impacts if families live in a neighborhood they really like, belong to meaningful groups and have many friends. John Donne could just as easily have written *No family is an island*.

Now that we are there, let's stay within the larger community. Here are some thoughts and tips for managing your:

Social life

Create and manage a positive social network

Too often when people talk or think about networking they are focusing either on a business activity intended to help achieve corporate objectives or the extensive use of social media. Whilst the latter might play a part in helping us to keep in contact with genuine friends who live far away, we are talking here about the value of relationships based on regular synchronous communication.

We've already said that it's good for our brain and, therefore, it adds value to our life if we prioritize spending time with people who:

- Use lots of positive language.
- Demonstrate that they value and appreciate us.
- Make us feel safe and secure.
- Activate our inherent desire to share, help and support.

We can add to that list, too. Spending time with people who make it easy for us to talk about the things that really matter can increase our happiness. And we don't just need to rely on family members for positive socializing. It's also what friends are for. Remember them? Those individuals who started out as complete strangers, who we met often by accident. Those people we made a real effort to get to know and, in turn, went out of our way to let them get to know us. *Friends*. It's worth managing our network of friends as carefully as we manage all the extremely important aspects of our life. Good friends really are good for us. We are really good for them. So be selfish in your pursuit and maintenance of such goodness. Keep in touch. Make things happen.

Here are 3 additional tips to help you to do this:

Go first

And keep going first if you have to. Take the initiative. Be proactive. Friendship is worth it. A positive social network is worth more than its weight in gold.

We can also go first by actively seeking out and joining particular interest groups or volunteering to support causes that move and motivate us.

Emphasize quality over quantity

Avoid the mistake of measuring the value of your social network by how many people you know. Measure it instead by the quality of the communication you share. Remember, influence is inevitable. Spend time with people who are good for you. And enjoy being good for them, too.

Reduce your social media use to the required minimum

Use it primarily to communicate with genuine friends or family members you are unable to meet with on a regular basis. And do remember that the more time we spend using social media the less time we have to do those things that encourage actual socialization. As we discussed in Chapter 5 technology offers benefits providing we manage and control our use of it.

Make clear your boundaries

We all have them. Physical, emotional, contextual. Be willing to share them. Be aware enough to recognize and respect the boundaries of others. The nature and level of the boundaries we set with another says much about the nature of that relationship. It's important we get it right, both socially and in the workplace.

Which is where we're going next as we consider socializing, communicating and our:

Professional life

Communication in the workplace is at least as important as it is elsewhere. We spend a great deal of our life at work, spending a great deal of that time communicating with others about work-related issues. The workplace can be filled with internal politics fuelled by strategic decisions, inter-department rivalry or personal agendas. It can also be a positive and motivating environment. To a great extent it all depends on the quality of the communication and the relationships that are built.

A survey of 1,400 British employers conducted in 2006 by the integrated accounting firm KPMG and the Chartered Institute of Personal Development revealed that communication skills were regarded as more important to employers than any other. These results were reflected in a survey of 1,500 MBA graduates in the USA who also identified Communication as the single most important business skill.

Here, then, are some tips for communicating well in the workplace. Before we introduce them do bear in mind that they:

a) Are all attitude and skill-dependent. If you want to make any, or all, a natural part of how you communicate you will need to practise.
b) Are all transferable and equally valuable in our family and social interactions. (Although the first 3 tips need a degree of translation in order to apply them to parenting or other social leadership situations).

1) If you are a leader in the workplace ensure you have well developed communication and social skills

Research suggests that these are highly valued by those being led. The ability to create a sense of team or community, to communicate in ways that demonstrate interest, understanding and care, that express value and appreciation, is as significant as contextual expertise.

2) Create safe environments and interactions

As we have already said, we communicate best when we feel safe. That's as true in the workplace as it is elsewhere. It's important to note that safety does not equate with a lack of challenges. Rather it relates to creating a culture in which people feel empowered to keep learning, take risks, make mistakes and feel adrenalized. We create such a culture through a clear sense of identity and purpose communicated congruently through appropriate systems and structures and, importantly, consistent interpersonal communications.

3) Provide and encourage regular social breaks in the workplace

Given our need and desire to socialize and the many, associated benefits to wellbeing and performance, why wouldn't you?

Socializing, like rest, are two productive ways to enhance workplace commitment and productivity.

4) Give attention

Specifically, give *skilled* attention. This takes us back to the point we made earlier about the need for us to continually develop our ability to talk, look and listen with clarity and insight. Just because we do these things regularly doesn't mean we are particularly skilled.

To help with this, whenever your aim is to create rapport do the following in your interpersonal communication:

a) Use the language of the other person right back at them; hear their key words or phrases and incorporate these into your reply.

b) Identify their starting position and meet them there; recognize, for example, the other person's beliefs, fears, knowledge, desires, current emotional state and address these either directly or indirectly.

c) Remember always that influence is inevitable *and* emotional; know what emotion you need to create within the other; know how to create it and how to recognize it when you have.

d) Remember, too, that the most influential communication is based around a compelling narrative; it's a narrative that is of relevance to your audience, shares relevant and clear key messages, uses facts and/or figures to emphasize its truth, and is memorable.[8]

---

[8] John here: If you want to learn more about how to create and share a compelling narrative and about other essential aspects of communication and influence read *Campaign It!* co-written by Chris and Alan Barnard, published by Kogan Page (2012).

5) Create dialogue not discussion

There is an important difference between the two. Discussion is what happens when opposing points of view are put forward and defended. The aim is to prove oneself right and the other party wrong. The emphasis is on winning. Dialogue has a different purpose. A dialogue is a sharing of words, ideas and perspectives with the intention of broadening everyone's understanding. It is cooperative and developmental rather than combative.

Two tips for helping to create a dialogue are:

a) Avoid the use of the word *but*. It's a word that denies everything that has gone before. It's heard a lot in discussions. *But* is one of those words we hear coming before it arrives. It's like a train pulling in at a station. *'I really appreciate your point of view and I've taken on board everything you've said, BUT...'* After which the speaker's argument is put forwards and the verbal battleground is established. Instead:

b) Do use the word *and*. It's a building word, one that forces you to acknowledge – if not agree with – everything you've just heard. A commitment to using *and* changes the very structure and fabric of an interaction. Use it. *And* find out for yourself.

For reasons we've already shared, avoid also using negative language, especially when accompanied by negative gestures and expressions.

Avoid, too, using the word *don't* when giving instructions. It's difficult to process a negative, so we tend to focus on what follows. If, for example, we say to you, *Don't think of the color of your front door right now* it's almost certain that you already have. We created the opposite outcome to the one we intended simply by using the wrong word at the start.[9] If we want you to avoid thinking of your

---

[9] We also supported *don't* with the power of *now*.

front door how should we go about it? Easy. Avoid talking about it in the first place.

Do, however, use any positive words especially when accompanied by smiling, encouraging, open gestures.

The words *do, now, because* and *just* also have power and need to be used with good intentions. *Do* is the polar opposite of *don't*. It opens the way for clear direction. For example, *Do think of a person you love right now. And enjoy the feeling it creates.* Pretty straightforward, isn't it?

The use of the word *now* in both our *Don't* and *Do* sentences adds to the immediacy of each instruction and makes them harder to ignore. *Now* is a great word for helping people focus *because* it speaks to the instant, about what needs to be addressed immediately. And *because* is influential because it's almost invariably followed by an explanation or a reason, and we are so used to this we sometimes simply accept what we hear without sufficiently rigorous thought. *Just* saying the word *because* can, it seems, influence people to agree to a request, even when no good reason has been offered.

As used in the previous sentence, *just* implies that something is simple or easy. The request from a teenage daughter to her father, *Dad can you give me $10 towards my night out?* is softened by the inclusion of *just* – *Dad can you give me just $10?* Suddenly it doesn't seem like such a big deal anymore. It becomes even more difficult to resist when some of the other words are brought into play: *Dad can you give me just $10, because I do want to make sure I have enough money for a taxi to come home and I know you want me to be safe...*

And that brings us safely to the end of this chapter. It's time now for the final element of our brain management Process: *Synergy*.

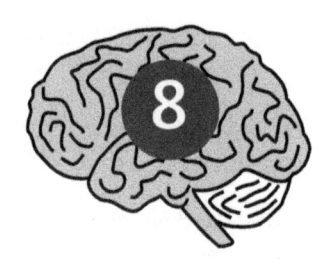

Synergy

'Growth is never by mere chance; it is the result of forces working together.'

James Cash Penney

Base the creation, implementation and development of your personal brain management Process on the following principle and guidelines:

The principle

It's through combinations and associated synergies that we create the most value. Aim therefore to create a Process that combines:

- Physical activity.
- Rest and recovery.
- Optimum nutrition.
- Cognitive function.

- Emotional management.
- Socialization and communication.

Guidelines

1. Take time to assess your current situation. Consider the nature, quality and impact of your:
   - Levels of physical activity.
   - Patterns of rest and recovery.
   - Nutritional intake.
   - Cognitive performance.
   - Emotional and Social behavior.
   - Daily schedules and routines.
   - Life/work balance

   Identify areas of personal strength and weakness. Use your evaluation to direct your Process planning.
2. Start by implementing any part, or parts, of the Process you feel to be most appropriate and/or most appealing. Whilst the aim is to actively incorporate and manage all of the elements we have covered in this book, it's important to accept that we have to start somewhere. So make the beginning easy for yourself.
3. Determine and implement simple specific changes. Set objectives that are:
   - Specific
   - Measurable
   - Achievable
   - Realistic

- Time framed.
4. Make these changes a part of your life *now* rather than part of an intended future plan.
5. Build off success. Progress is always easier when we recognize accomplishment. That's why we recommend implementing and achieving simple, measurable changes.
6. Aim for consistency and not perfection. The former is achievable. The latter isn't. And consistency is always influential.
7. Be curious. Remember that scientific research is ongoing; make learning even more about your brain a natural part of what you do. After all, it is the most amazing thing we know. And it is yours.

The final conversation.

'Education, therefore, is a process of living and not a preparation for future living.'

John Dewey

Our final conversation about this book was a mixture of the usual good-natured and excited questioning followed by one particular moment of reflection. The ending began when Chris asked John:

'If this was a workshop, how would you close it?'

'By reminding everyone of the central point: the brain always wins. We have to realize and remember that all training is dependent on the brain and, in turn, influences the brain. It either builds health and neurological growth or it challenges our brain's resiliency. We function as a top-down or brain-first entity. Whatever the nature of our behaviors – whether they are personal or professional, in business or in sport, law enforcement or the military, politics or parenting, healthcare or socializing - we should be thinking first and foremost about how we best impact brain growth, learning, and resiliency.

'The bottom line is brain health and high performance are inseparable. That leads us to 2 conclusions:

1. 'Every learning or training program should be based on this understanding, focusing throughout on how the brain is affected in only the most positive of ways.

    'To do anything else is to gamble with people's health, talent, and goals.
2. 'As individuals we can take responsibility for our own brain management. There's enough information available now, being provided on an almost daily basis by scientists around the world. Our brain has been vital to our evolution and success as a species. It's central to our humanity. We owe it to our self and others to make the most of what we've got.'

Then, in his usual fashion, John ended his answer with a reminder and a question of his own:

'When we first met you were interested only in what worked and not in the science of why things worked. Has that changed at all?'

'Massively. I'll never stop looking for wisdom in the village. It's just that from now on I'll also be turning to science for all the latest insights. And, because of our work together, I've changed quite a few of my own routines and behaviors. My personal brain management Process is well in place thank you very much and I'm experiencing the benefits already. Which reminds me that this wasn't always about brain management.'

'Wasn't it?'

'No. Some of your original emails had a glorious typo in the title. Remember? They didn't read The Brain Always Wins they read Brian Always Wins! For months I loved the fact that I was writing a book about how best to look after Brian!'

'Thanks for reminding me! Mind you, that's probably as good a place as any to end. Hopefully our readers leave us with a developed understanding and appreciation of their brain and how they can manage it to improve their lives.'

'Yes. All that's left for us to do now is write our acknowledgements.'

'And there are lots of people we both really need to thank.'

'Especially Brian.'

'Absolutely. Where would we be without Brian?'

'Now that really is a very good question...'[1]

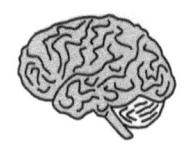

A final thought:

'More is not better; being better at the Process is better.'

John Sullivan.

---

[1] If you ever see a couple of guys in a restaurant chatting, laughing and frantically scribbling notes, wearing T-shirts that read 'Brian always wins' it's bound to be us. Please do pop over and say 'Hi'.

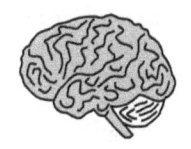

About the authors

John Sullivan is a leading sports scientist and one of the top sports psychologists in the US. His specialities include human performance technology, central nervous system measurement/assessment, recovery training, talent identification, concussion assessment and rehabilitation, and mental health concerns. John has spent 15 years working with the NFL and has provided clinical sport psychology and sport science support to numerous Super Bowl teams and Champions. Alongside working with the NFL, John also works as a consultant to the US Special Forces, providing oversight on welfare, recovery, cognitive abilities and performance. John has also consulted internationally within British Premier League football and Premiership rugby, and has co-authored chapters of the National Collegiate Athletic Association (NCAA) Sports Medicine Manual.

Chris Parker began his study of interpersonal and intrapersonal communications in 1976. It became a lifelong study that has underpinned four decades of work in a variety of professional roles and contexts. A Licensed Master Practitioner of Neuro-Linguistic Programming, Chris is a highly experienced management trainer, business consultant, lecturer and writer. He has provided training in communications and influence for a wide range of clients including blue-chip organisations, Local Education Authorities, public and private leisure providers, sportsmen and women, politicians, actors and healthcare professionals.   He has taught on undergraduate and postgraduate programmes throughout the UK and Europe, and has worked with many individuals to help create personal and/or professional change.

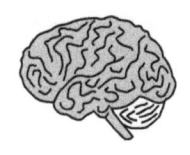

More than just a book

Because brain health and resiliency is so very important to all of us, we want to provide you with more learning and support than we can offer in one book.

So, if you want to share in more information and insights and gain even more practical advice on how best to create and run your own brain management Process, join us at The Brain Always Wins website.

Here we provide a range of constantly updated sources and resources that include:

- Apps and other practical – and often free – brain-related technology.
- YouTube films.
- QR Codes linking you directly to other relevant websites.
- The latest academic research.
- Additional recommended reading.

To visit our website and join our Brain Always Wins community, just go to:

www.thebrainalwayswins.com

You can also listen in to our weekly podcast in which the conversations and stories that underpin this book are developed and other brain-related topics are introduced. You can access the podcast from the website.

And if you want to contact us directly, to ask a question, make a comment or share your experience, you can also do this via the website.

We look forward to hearing from you!

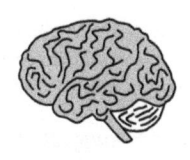

References

Chapter 1 The Governor

Page 3 **Our brain is optimally efficient, capable of using the smallest number of connections...** Gulyás, A., Bíró, J. J., K rösi, A., Rétvári, G., & Krioukov, D. (2015). Navigable networks as Nash equilibria of navigation games. Nature Communications Nat Comms, 6, 7651.

History of Neuroscience. (n.d.). Retrieved March 04, 2016, from https:/faculty.washington.edu/chudler/hist.html

Chapter 2 Physical Activity

Page 30 **Our ability to gain or maintain on a day-to-day basis is largely based on the quantity and quality of this stimulation...** Johnson, N. F., Gold, B. T., Bailey, A. L., Clasey, J. L., Hakun, J. G., White, M., . . . Powell, D. K. (2015). Cardiorespiratory fitness modifies the relationship between myocardial function and cerebral blood flow in older adults. NeuroImage.

Page 31 **For example, an analysis3 of more than 1,200 participants...**

Spartano, N. L., Himali, J. J., Beiser, A. S., Lewis, G. D., Decarli, C., Vasan, R. S., & Seshadri, S. (2016). Midlife exercise blood pressure, heart rate, and fitness relate to brain volume 2 decades later. Neurology.

Page 31 **More recent research suggests that people who are fit in their forties seem to retain more brain volume two decades later ...** Presented at the American Heart Association Meeting in Baltimore Maryland U.S.A., March 4th 2015 by Nicole Spartano, Ph.D., postdoctoral fellow, Boston University School of Medicine, Boston; Joseph Masdeu, M.D., director, Nantz National Alzheimer Center, and neuroimaging, Houston Methodist Neurological Institute, Houston.

Page 33 **These findings were supported by a report presented in 2010...** Dr. Ode and Jennifer Flynn at the American College of Sports Medicine's 57th annual meeting.

Page 33 **a study in Scotland looked at the relationship between physical activity levels and academic performance...** All enrolled in the Avon Longitudinal Study of Parents and Children (ALSPAC).

Page 33 **This positive relationship between exercise and educational accomplishment...** Danbert, S. J., Pivarnik, J. M., McNeil, R. N., & Washington, I. J. (2014).Academic success and retention: the role of recreational sports fitness facilities. Recreational Sports Journal, 38(1), 14-22.

Page 36 **a study of 200 patients at eight memory clinics in Denmark has shown that intensive aerobic exercise can even have a positive cognitive effect...**Gunhild Waldemar, MD, Congress of the European Academy of Neurology (EAN). Abstract O3105. Presented June 22, 2015.

Page 36 **There is also significant evidence that exercise can aid in the management of cancer ...** Cormie, P., Nowak, A. K., Chambers, S. K., Galvão, D. A., & Newton, R. U. (2015). The Potential Role of Exercise in Neuro-Oncology. Front. Oncol. Frontiers in Oncology, 5.

Jones, L. W., Mourtzakis, M., Peters, K. B., Friedman, A. H., West, M. J., Mabe, S. K., ... Reardon, D. A. (2010). Changes in Functional Performance Measures in Adults Undergoing Chemoradiation for Primary Malignant Glioma: A Feasibility Study. The Oncologist, 15(6), 636-647.

Cramp, F., & Daniel, J. (2008). Exercise for the management of cancer related fatigue in adults. Cochrane Database of Systematic Reviews.

Cormie, P., Galvão, D. A., Spry, N., Joseph, D., Chee, R., Taaffe, D. R., . . . Newton, R. U. (2014). Can supervised exercise prevent treatment toxicity in patients with prostate cancer initiating androgen-deprivation therapy: A randomised controlled trial. BJU International BJU Int, 115(2), 256-266.

Page 38 **What we have come to know from research is that, rather than causing damage or over-training, stimulation is the key....**

Flann, K. L., Lastayo, P. C., Mcclain, D. A., Hazel, M., & Lindstedt, S. L. (2011). Muscle damage and muscle remodeling: No pain, no gain? Journal of Experimental Biology, 214(4), 674-679.

Page 44 **Please use the Physical Activity Readiness Questionnaire (PAR-Q)**

Chisholm DM, Collis ML, Kulak LL, Davenport W, Gruber N. (1975). Physical activity readiness. British Columbia Medical Journal 17: 375–378.

Chisholm DM, Collis ML, Kulak LL, Davenport W, Gruber N, et al. (1978). PAR-Q Validation report: the evaluation of a self-administered preexercise screening questionnaire for adults, Ministry of Health, Vancouver.

Page 48 **Even moderate physical activity can result in favorable brain, physiological, and biochemical outcomes...**

Gupt, A. M., Kumar, M., Sharma, R. K., Misra, R., & Gupt, A. (2015). Effect of Moderate Aerobic Exercise Training on Autonomic Functions and its Correlation with the Antioxidant Status. Indian J Physiol Pharmacol, 59(2), 162-169.

Goldsmith RL, Bloomfield DM, Rosenwinkel ET. (2009). Exercise and autonomic function. Coronary Artery Dis; 11(2): 129–135.

Chapter 3 Rest and Recovery

Page 58 **Researchers at the University of Rochester Medical Center (URMC) for Translational Neuromedicine have discovered yet another clue...**

Iliff, J. J., Wang, M., Liao, Y., Plogg, B. A., Peng, W., Gundersen, G. A., ... & Nagelhus, E. A. (2012). A paravascular pathway facilitates CSF flow through the brain parenchyma and the clearance of interstitial solutes, including amyloid -. Science translational medicine, 4(147), 147ra111-147ra111.

Page 63 **In the UK that figure is slightly less at 42%...** Foundation, N. S. 2013 Bedroon Poll Summary of Findings. Retrieved from http://sleepfoundation.org/sites/default/files/RPT495a.pdf

Page 64 **More shocking still, researchers at Pennsylvania State University...** Vgontzas, A. N., Liao, D., Pejovic, S., Calhoun, S., Karataraki, M., Basta, M., ... & Bixler, E. O. (2010). Insomnia with short sleep duration and mortality: the Penn State cohort. Sleep, 33(9), 1159-1164.

Page 67 **Now, though, researchers at the University of California Berkeley...** Goldstein-Piekarski, A. N., Greer, S. M., Saletin, J. M., & Walker, M. P. (2015). Sleep Deprivation Impairs the Human Central and Peripheral Nervous System Discrimination of Social Threat. The Journal of Neuroscience, 35(28), 10135-10145.

Walker, M. P., Brakefield, T., Hobson, J. A., & Stickgold, R. (2003). Dissociable stages of human memory consolidation and reconsolidation. Nature, 425(6958), 616-620.

Yoo, S. S., Gujar, N., Hu, P., Jolesz, F. A., & Walker, M. P. (2007). The human emotional brain without sleep—a prefrontal amygdala disconnect. Current Biology, 17(20), R877-R878.

Page 71 **Not surprisingly, research shows that physicians...** Lockley, S. W., Barger, L. K., Ayas, N. T., Rothschild, J. M., Czeisler, C. A., & Landrigan, C. P. (2007). Effects of health care provider work hours and sleep deprivation on safety and performance. The Joint Commission Journal on Quality and Patient Safety, 33(Supplement 1), 7-18.

Page 73 **The Centers for Disease Control and Prevention** Insufficient Sleep Is a Public Health Problem. (2015). Retrieved March 04, 2016, from http://www.cdc.gov/features/dssleep/

Better sleep. (n.d.). Retrieved March 04, 2016, from http://www.nhs.uk/LiveWell/sleep/Pages/sleep-home.aspx

Page 73 **In Canada a study estimated...** Daley, M., Morin, C. M., LeBlanc,

M., Gregoire, J. P., & Savard, J. (2009). The economic burden of insomnia: direct and indirect costs for individuals with insomnia syndrome, insomnia symptoms, and good sleepers. Sleep, 32(1), 55-64.

Page 73 **American researchers found that 15% of employees...** Léger, D., Guilleminault, C., Bader, G., Lévy, E., & Paillard, M. (2002). Medical

and socio-professional impact of insomnia. Sleep, 25(6), 625-629.

Page 75 **When faced with a series of creative problems...** Cai, D. J., Mednick, S. A., Harrison, E. M., Kanady, J. C., & Mednick, S. C. (2009). REM, not incubation, improves creativity by priming associative networks. Proceedings of the National Academy of Sciences, 106(25), 10130-10134.

Page 80 **Researchers from the University of Illinois...** Ariga, A., & Lleras, A. (2011). Brief and rare mental "breaks" keep you focused: Deactivation and reactivation of task goals preempt vigilance decrements. Cognition, 118(3), 439-443.

Page 81 **The results supported what the researchers called...** Dijksterhuis, A., Bos, M. W., Nordgren, L. F., & Van Baaren, R. B. (2006). On making the right choice: The deliberation-without-attention effect. Science, 311(5763), 1005-1007.

Chapter 4 Optimum Nutrition

Page 96 **For example, according to Fernando Gomez-Pinilla...** Gómez-Pinilla, F. (2008). Brain foods: The effects of nutrients on brain function. Nature Reviews Neuroscience Nat Rev Neurosci, 9(7), 568-578.

Page 98 **We share a symbiotic relationship...** Geurts, L., Neyrinck, A., Delzenne, N., Knauf, C., & Cani, P. (2014). Gut microbiota controls adipose tissue expansion, gut barrier and glucose metabolism: Novel insights into molecular targets and interventions using prebiotics. Beneficial Microbes, 5(1), 3-17.

Chen, X., D'Souza, R., & Hong, S. (2013). The role of gut microbiota in the gut-brain axis: Current challenges and perspectives. Protein Cell Protein & Cell, 4(6), 403-414.

Page 98 **For example, a study published in 2013...** Tillisch, K., Labus, J., Kilpatrick, L., Jiang, Z., Stains, J., Ebrat, B., . . . Mayer, E. A. (2013). Consumption of Fermented Milk Product With Probiotic Modulates Brain Activity. Gastroenterology, 144(7).

Page 100 **The more we interact with others...** Montiel-Castro, A. J., González-Cervantes, R. M., Bravo-Ruiseco, G., & Pacheco-López, G. (2013). The microbiota-gut-brain axis: Neurobehavioral correlates, health and sociality. Frontiers in Integrative Neuroscience Front. Integr. Neurosci., 7.

Page 100 **Researchers are gathering increasing evidence...** Gareau, M. G., Wine, E., Rodrigues, D. M., Cho, J. H., Whary, M. T., Philpott, D. J., . . . Sherman, P. M. (2010). Bacterial infection causes stress-induced memory dysfunction in mice. Gut, 60(3), 307-317.

Wall, R., Marques, T. M., O'sullivan, O., Ross, R. P., Shanahan, F., Quigley, E. M., . . . Stanton, C. (2012). Contrasting effects of Bifidobacterium breve NCIMB 702258 and Bifidobacterium breve DPC 6330 on the composition of murine brain fatty acids and gut microbiota. American Journal of Clinical Nutrition, 95(5), 1278-1287.

Page 104 **According to the authors of this research...** Smyth, A., Dehghan, M., O'donnell, M., Anderson, C., Teo, K., Gao, P., . . . Yusuf, S. (2015). Healthy eating and reduced risk of cognitive decline: A cohort from 40 countries. Neurology, 84(22), 2258-2265.

Page 104 **It's actually the conclusion...** Zeevi, D., Korem, T., Zmora, N., Israeli, D., Rothschild, D., Weinberger, A., . . . Segal, E. (2015). Personalized Nutrition by Prediction of Glycemic Responses. Cell, 163(5), 1079-1094.

Page 106 **Incredibly, other research suggests...** David, L. A., Maurice, C. F., Carmody, R. N., Gootenberg, D. B., Button, J. E., Wolfe, B. E., ... & Biddinger, S. B. (2014). Diet rapidly and reproducibly alters the human gut microbiome. Nature, 505(7484), 559-563.

Page 106 **An 8 year long study...** Cherbuin, N., Sargent-Cox, K., Fraser, M., Sachdev, P., & Anstey, K. J. (2015). Being overweight is associated with hippocampal atrophy: The PATH Through Life Study. Int J Obes Relat Metab Disord International Journal of Obesity, 39(10), 1509-1514.

Page 109 **One relatively small study...** Cassani, R. S., Fassini, P., Silvah, J., Lima, C. M., & Marchini, J. (2015). Impact of weight loss diet associated with flaxseed on inflammatory markers in men with cardiovascular risk factors: A clinical study. Nutrition Journal Nutr J, 14(1), 5.

Page 109 **In a separate study...** Zick, S. M., Turgeon, D. K., Vareed, S. K., Ruffin, M. T., Litzinger, A. J., Wright, B. D., . . . Brenner, D. E. (2011). Phase II Study of the Effects of Ginger Root Extract on Eicosanoids in Colon Mucosa in People at Normal Risk for Colorectal Cancer. Cancer Prevention Research, 4(11), 1929-1937.

Page 110 **Even mild dehydration...** Adan, A. (2012). Cognitive performance and dehydration. Journal of the American College of Nutrition, 31(2), 71-78.

Page 121 **Research has shown that this traditional Mediterranean diet...** Valls-Pedret, C., Sala-Vila, A., Serra-Mir, M., Corella, D., Torre, R. D., Martínez-González, M. Á, . . . Ros, E. (2015). Mediterranean Diet and Age-Related Cognitive Decline. JAMA Internal Medicine JAMA Intern Med, 175(7), 1094.

Estruch, R., Ros, E., Salas-Salvadó, J., Covas, M. I., Corella, D., Arós, F., ... & Lamuela-Raventos, R. M. (2013). Primary prevention of cardiovascular disease with a Mediterranean diet. New England Journal of Medicine, 368(14), 1279-1290.

Salas-Salvado, J., Bullo, M., Babio, N., Martinez-Gonzalez, M. A., Ibarrola-Jurado, N., Basora, J., . . . Ros, E. (2010). Reduction in the Incidence of Type 2 Diabetes With the Mediterranean Diet: Results of the PREDIMED-Reus nutrition intervention randomized trial. Diabetes Care, 34(1), 14-19.

Page 123 **For example, fasting seems to...** Alirezaei, M., Kemball, C. C., Flynn, C. T., Wood, M. R., Whitton, J. L., & Kiosses, W. B. (2010). Short-term fasting induces profound neuronal autophagy. Autophagy, 6(6), 702-710.

Page 124 **It helps to fight inflammation...** Johnson, J. B., Summer, W., Cutler, R. G., Martin, B., Hyun, D., Dixit, V. D., . . . Mattson, M. P. (2007). Alternate day calorie restriction improves clinical findings and reduces markers of oxidative stress and inflammation in overweight adults with moderate asthma. Free Radical Biology and Medicine, 42(5), 665-674.

Page 124 **It also increases the growth of new nerve cells...** Lee, J., Duan, W., Long, J. M., Ingram, D. K., & Mattson, M. P. (2000). Dietary Restriction Increases the Number of Newly Generated Neural Cells, and Induces BDNF Expression, in the Dentate Gyrus of Rats. Journal of Molecular Neuroscience JMN, 15(2), 99-108.

Chapter 5 Cognitive Function

Page 131 **Research into frontal lobe development...** Giedd, J. N., Blumenthal, J., Jeffries, N. O., Castellanos, F. X., Liu, H., Zijdenbos, A., ... & Rapoport, J. L. (1999). Brain development during childhood and adolescence: a longitudinal MRI study. Nature neuroscience, 2(10), 861-863.

Page 133 **Research using magnetic resonance imaging...** Semendeferi, K., Lu, A., Schenker, N., & Damasio, H. (2002). Humans and great apes share a large frontal cortex. Nat. Neurosci. Nature Neuroscience, 5(3), 272-276.

Page 133 **We can think of attention as...** Anderson, J. R. (2004). Cognitive psychology and its implications / John R. Anderson. New York: Worth.

Page 134 **Sohlberg and Mateer's clinical model identifies...** Sohlberg, M. M., & Mateer, C. A. (1989). Introduction to cognitive rehabilitation: Theory and practice. New York: Guilford Press.

Page 134 **Eric Knudsen offers a more general model...** Knudsen, E. I. (2007). Fundamental Components of Attention. Annu. Rev. Neurosci. Annual Review of Neuroscience, 30(1), 57-78.

Page 135 **For example, tasks that engage the verbal working memory...** Schumacher, E. H., Lauber, E., Awh, E., Jonides, J., Smith, E. E., & Koeppe, R. A. (1996). PET Evidence for an Amodal Verbal Working Memory System. NeuroImage, 3(2), 79-88.

Page 135 **... the right side and areas in the occipital cortex** Smith, E. E., Jonides, J., & Koeppe, R. A. (1996). Dissociating Verbal and Spatial Working Memory Using PET. Cerebral Cortex, 6(1), 11-20.

Page 135 **The one area of the brain...** Miller, E. K., & Cohen, J. D. (2001). An integrative theory of prefrontal cortex function. Annual review of neuroscience, 24(1), 167-202.

References

Page 136 **Research suggests there are societal differences...** Chavajay, P., & Rogoff, B. (1999). Cultural variation in management of attention by children and their caregivers. Developmental Psychology, 35(4), 1079-1090.

Page 139 **Unlike the recognition/recall task...** Tulving, E., Schacter, D. L., & Stark, H. A. (1982). Priming effects in wordfragment completion are independent of recognition memory. Journal of Experimental Psychology: Learning, Memory, and Cognition, 8(4), 336-342

Page 140 **We can see the brain predicting...** Frith, C. D. (2007). Making up the mind: How the brain creates our mental world. Malden, MA: Blackwell Pub.

Page 144 **Even though the participants didn't report ...** Whalen, P. J., Rauch, S. L., Etcoff, N. L., McInerney, S. C., Lee, M. B., & Jenike, M. A. (1998). Masked presentations of emotional facial expressions modulate amygdala activity without explicit knowledge. The Journal of neuroscience, 18(1), 411-418.

Page 147 **New research, though, is suggesting...** Chen, S., Cai, D., Pearce, K., Sun, P. Y., Roberts, A. C., & Glanzman, D. L. (2014). Reinstatement of long-term memory following erasure of its behavioral and synaptic expression in Aplysia. ELife, 3.

Page 152 **Those who were frequent multi-taskers...** Loh, K. K., & Kanai, R. (2014). Higher Media Multi-Tasking Activity Is Associated with Smaller Gray-Matter Density in the Anterior Cingulate Cortex. PLoS ONE, 9(9).

Page 154 **Research using magnetic resonance imaging...** Wang, G. J., Volkow, N. D., Roque, C. T., Cestaro, V. L., Hitzemann, R. J., Cantos, E. L., . . . Dhawan, A. P. (1993). Functional importance of ventricular enlargement and cortical atrophy in healthy subjects and alcoholics as assessed with PET, MR imaging, and neuropsychologic testing. Radiology, 186(1), 59-65.

Page 164 **In recent studies, it was found ...** Mueller, P. A., & Oppenheimer, D. M. (2014). The Pen Is Mightier Than the Keyboard: Advantages of Longhand Over Laptop Note Taking. Psychological Science, 25(6), 1159-1168.

Chapter 6 Emotional Management

Page 166 **Whether or not you have recognized this ...** Cornelius, R. R. (1996). The science of emotion: Research and tradition in the psychology of emotions. Prentice-Hall, Inc.

Chow, S., Ram, N., Boker, S. M., Fujita, F., & Clore, G. (2005). Emotion as a Thermostat: Representing Emotion Regulation Using a Damped Oscillator Model. Emotion, 5(2), 208-225.

Page 167 **An emotion is a complex psychological state ...** Hockenbury, D. H., & Hockenbury, S. E. (2010). Discovering psychology. Macmillan.

Page 167 **One of the challenges in defining ...** zard, C. E. (2009). Emotion theory and research: Highlights, unanswered questions, and emerging issues. Annual review of psychology, 60, 1. zard, C. E. (2013). Human emotions. Springer Science & Business Media.

Darwin, C., Ekman, P., & Prodger, P. (1998). The expression of the emotions in man and animals. Oxford University Press, USA.

Schore, A. N. (2015). Affect regulation and the origin of the self: The neurobiology of emotional development. Routledge.

Barrett, L. F., Mesquita, B., Ochsner, K. N., & Gross, J. J. (2007). The experience of emotion. Annual review of psychology, 58, 373.

Page 168 **Although studies of the physiology of emotion ...** Bailenson, J. N., Pontikakis, E. D., Mauss, I. B., Gross, J. J., Jabon, M. E., Hutcherson, C. A., ... & John, O. (2008). Real-time classification of evoked emotions using facial feature tracking and physiological responses. International journal of human-computer studies, 66(5), 303-317.

Kandel, E. R., Schwartz, J. H., & Jessell, T. M. (Eds.). (2000). Principles of neural science (Vol. 4, pp. 1227-1246). New York: McGraw-hill.

Nummenmaa, L., Glerean, E., Hari, R., & Hietanen, J. K. (2014). Bodily maps of emotions. Proceedings of the National Academy of Sciences, 111(2), 646-651.

Page 169 **This is simply the way we express the emotion...** Strack,

References

F., Pauli, P., & Weyers, P. (2016). Emotion and Behavior. Frontiers in Psychology, 7, 313.

Dolan, R. J. (2002). Emotion, cognition, and behavior. science, 298(5596), 1191-1194.

Page 169 **That's right! Hundreds!** Trampe, D., Quoidbach, J., & Taquet, M. (2015). Emotions in Everyday Life PLOS ONE PLoS ONE, 10(12).

Page 180 **Professor Victor Dulewicz and Dr Malcolm Higgs** ... Higgs, M., Dulewicz, V. (1999). Making sense of emotional intelligence. NFER-NELSON Publishing. Berkshire.

Page 181 **In his New York workshop...** Hill, C. L., & Updegraff, J. A. (2012). Mindfulness and its relationship to emotional regulation. Emotion, 12(1), 81.

Tang, Y. Y., Hölzel, B. K., & Posner, M. I. (2015). The neuroscience of mindfulness meditation. Nature Reviews Neuroscience, 16(4), 213-225.

Page 182 **Then, having described meditation ...** Khalsa, S. S., Rudrauf, D., Davidson, R. J., & Tranel, D. (2015). The effect of meditation on regulation of internal body states. Frontiers in Psychology.

Kox, M., Stoffels, M., Smeekens, S. P., van Alfen, N., Gomes, M., Eijsvogels, T. M., ... & Pickkers, P. (2012). The influence of concentration/meditation on autonomic nervous system activity and the innate immune response: a case study. Psychosomatic medicine, 74(5), 489-494.

Page 191 **As an example of this ...** Ranganathan, V. K., Siemionow, V., Liu, J. Z., Sahgal, V., & Yue, G. H. (2004). From mental power to muscle power—gaining strength by using the mind. Neuropsychologia, 42(7), 944-956.

Page 196 **Researchers have suggested ...** Rüesch, P., Graf, J., Meyer, P. C., Rössler, W., & Hell, D. (2004). Occupation, social support and quality of life in persons with schizophrenic or affective disorders. Social psychiatry and psychiatric epidemiology, 39(9), 686-694.

Chapter 7 Socialization

Page 203 **We are, as Matthew Lieberman ...** Lieberman, M. D. (2013). Social: Why our brains are wired to connect. Oxford: Oxford univ. press.

Page 203 **In fact the greatest indicator of brain size ...** Shultz, S., & Dunbar, R. (2010). Encephalization is not a universal macroevolutionary phenomenon in mammals but is associated with sociality. Proceedings of the National Academy of Sciences, 107(50), 21582-21586.

Page 207 **Especially when you consider that ...** Dunbar, R. I., Marriott, A., & Duncan, N. D. (1997). Human conversational behavior. Human Nature, 8(3), 231-246.

Page 207 **Newborn babies demonstrate ...** Gao, W., Zhu, H., Giovanello, K. S., Smith, J. K., Shen, D., Gilmore, J. H., & Lin, W. (2009). Evidence on the emergence of the brain's default network from 2-week-old to 2-year-old healthy pediatric subjects. Proceedings of the National Academy of Sciences, 106(16), 6790-6795.

Page 208 **Frank's book, first published in 1961 ...** Frank, J. D., & Frank, J. B. (1993). Persuasion and healing: A comparative study of psychotherapy. JHU Press.

Page 209 **One of those reinforcing and developing ...** Cozolino, L. J. (2010). The neuroscience of psychotherapy: Healing the social brain. New York: W.W. Norton & Co.

Page 209 **A basic assumption...** Cozolino, L. J. (2010). The neuroscience of psychotherapy: Healing the social brain. New York: W.W. Norton & Co.

Page 210 **Dr. Vittorio Gallese and colleagues ...** Gallese, V., Fadiga, L., Fogassi, L., & Rizzolatti, G. (1996). Action recognition in the premotor cortex. Brain, 119(2), 593-609.

Page 216 **Researchers at Purdue University ...** Williams, K. D., Cheung, C. K., & Choi, W. (2000). Cyberostracism: Effects of being ignored over the Internet. Journal of Personality and Social Psychology, 79(5), 748-762.

Page 216 **Attachment theory was first introduced ...** Bowlby, J. (1982). Attachment and loss. New York: Basic Books.

Page 217 **Yet they are comfortable ...** Harlow, H. F. (1958). The nature of love. American Psychologist, 13, 673-685.

Page 217 **And lengthy separation from parents ...** Hanson, J., L., Chung, M., K., Avants, B., B., Shirtcliff, E., A., Gee, J. C., Davidson, R., J., & Pollak, S. D. (2010). Early stress is associated with alterations in the orbitofrontal cortex: A tensobased morphometry investigation of brain structure and behavioral risk. Journal of Neuroscience, 30(22), 7466-7472.

Page 218 **Having said that ...** House, J. S., Landis, K. R., & Umberson, D. (1988). Social relationships and health. Science, 241(4865), 540-545.

Page 218 **...13 point drop in IQ** Mani, A., Mullainathan, S., Shafir, E., & Zhao, J. (2013). Poverty impedes cognitive function. Science, 341, 976–980.

Page 218 **At the other end of the financial spectrum ...** Racz, S. J., McMahon, R. J., & Luthar, S. S. (2011). Risky behavior in affluent youth: Examining the co-occurrence and consequences of multiple problem behaviors. Journal of Child and Family Studies, 20, 120–128.

Page 219 **The brains of the Chinese participants ...** Zhu, Y., Zhang, L., Fan, J., & Han, S. (2007). Neural basis of cultural influence on self-representation. Neuroimage. 2007 Feb 1;34(3):1310-6.

Page 220 **According to research, just seeing...** Talarovicova, A., Krskova, L., & Kiss, A. (2007). Some assessments of the amygdala role in suprahypothalamic neuroendocrine regulation: a minireview. Endocrine regulations, 41(4), 155-162.

Page 221 **Spending time with people who use ...** Duhachek, A., Zhang, S., & Krishnan, S. (2007). Anticipated group interaction: Coping with valence asymmetries in attitude shift. Journal of Consumer Research, 34(3), 395-405.

Page 221 **The lesson appears to be ...** Fredrickson, B. L., & Losada, M. F. (2005). Positive Affect and the Complex Dynamics of Human Flourishing. American Psychologist, 60(7), 678-686.

Page 221 **When Fabrizio Benedetti ...** Benedetti, F., Durando, J., & Vighetti, S. (2014). Nocebo and placebo modulation of hypobaric hypoxia headache involves the cyclooxygenaseprostaglandins pathway. Pain, 155(5), 921-928.

Page 225 **Dr Stephen Porges, the founder of ...** Porges, S. W. (2011). The polyvagal theory: Neurophysiological foundations of emotions, attachment, communication, and self-regulation. New York: W.W. Norton.

Page 227 **Here's what Dr Porges has to say ...** Retrieved from http://files.nicabm.com/Trauma2012/Porges/NICABM-Porges-2012.pdf

Page 235 **Spending time with people who ...** Mehl, M. R., Vazire, S., Holleran, S. E., & Clark, C. S. (2010). Eavesdropping on Happiness: Well-Being Is Related to Having Less Small Talk and More Substantive Conversations. Psychological Science, 21(4), 539-541.

Page 241 **Just saying the word because ...** Langar, E., Blank, A., & Chanowitz, B. (1978). The mindlessness of ostensibly thoughtful action: The role of "placebic" information in interpersonal interaction. Journal of Personality and Social Psychology, 36, 635-642.

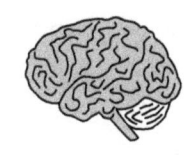

Index

adrenaline 178
alcohol 104, 121
Alzheimer's 27, 30, 35, 41, 106, 120
amygdala 12, 21, 144, 170, 171, 180
attention 131–36
   alternating 134
   bottom-up salience filters 140–1
   competitive selection 140
   divided 139
   exogenous 141
   focused 138–9
   selective 139
   sustained 139
   top-down sensitivity control 140
avocados 118
axon 13

bacteria 99–101
balance 8
basal ganglia 7, 8, 9, 10, 141
BDNF (Brain-derived neurotrophic factor) 31
Benedetti, Fabrizio 221
blind spot 144
blood pressure, high 120
Brain
   Broca's area 145, 210
   comparison with chimpanzees 4–5
   control areas 8–9
   evolution 2–6
      reasons for 3
   facts about 1–2, 27–8,
   prediction 22–3, 132
   protection 6
   stem 7, 8, 11
   structure and functions 6–11
   study of, history of 6

breath control 181–3, 199–201

CAT (Computerized Axial Tomography) scanning 18
cerebellum 7, 8, 11, 25, 143, 147
cerebrum 10
chimpanzees 4, 183
chocolate 256
   dark 118
cholesterol 120
chronic traumatic encephalopathy (CTE) 58
coffee 118
cognitive function 125–64
   emotional control 128
   facts 125–26
   language 145
   memory 145–48
   motor skills 140–3
   recommendations 150–64
      managing your technology 161–3
   technology 148–9
   vision 143–4
collaboration 206
Colozino, Dr. Louis 209–210
communication 219–24
   negative language 220–1
   non-verbal 222–4
   micro-expressions 222–4
   positive language 221
   professional life 237–41
   skills 220
connections
   in the brain 3, 13, 20–1,
   social 203–12

cortex 6, 7, 17, 147, 210–11
   cerebral 10, 130, 132, 174
   motor 141, 211
   neocortex 205
   occipital 135
   parietal 135
      inferior 135, 211
      pre-frontal 12, 35, 135, 225
      dorsolateral 135
      motor skills 140, 142
      ventrolateral 135
   primary sensory 7
   somatosensory 210
   temporal 135
cortisol 66, 111, 177
cranium 6, 7
culture 218

Dalai Lama 182
decisiveness 180, 181
dementia, vascular 30
dendrites 14
distal stimulus 137
dopamine 16, 17, 99, 111, 130, 142
dorsal anterior cingulate cortex 215
DTI (Diffusion Tensor Imaging) 20
dura 6, 7

ECoG (Electrocorticography) 19
EEG (electro-encephalography) 18
Ekman, Paul 222
emotion
   behavioural response 169–70
   decision-making 175

definition 166-77
interpersonal communication 175-6
managing 179-181
multi-dimensionality 168
physiological response 168-9
purpose of 174-76
subjectivity 167-8
survival 176
emotional health, quality of 178
emotional intelligence 174-6,
Emotional Intelligence 169
emotional management 165-201
    costs of mismanagement 176-9
    facts 165-6
    managing your own emotions 186-201
        close relationships 196
        creating associations 188-89
        identify negative triggers 193
        modelling 194
        positive emotions 195-201
        negative emotions 189-94
        rapid resetting 200-1
        time management 196
    mindful training program 182-84
    recommendations 185
emotional resiliency 180
endorphins 34
enteric nervous system 96-7
epinephrine 16

fasting 123-4

fatigue 37
fMRI (Functional Magnetic Resonance Imaging) 19, 67
forebrain 9
Frank, Jerome 209
free radicals 115
Frith, Chris 139
fruits 115-16, 117

GABA 15, 99
garlic 118
Giffords, Gabrielle 20-1
Goleman, Daniel 169, 179
Gottman, Daniel 224
grey matter 10
guidelines for creating a Process 243-4
gut instinct 173

habits 142
    managing 152-4
heart 173, 174
heart coherence 183
heart rate 46-7, 53-55
High Intensity Interval Training (HIIT) 51-2
hindbrain 11
hippocampus 12, 106, 170-1, 174, 177
homo heidelbergensis 205
hydration 110-13, 118-20
hypothalamus 10, 12, 170

iEEG (Intracranial EEG) 19

immune system 98
interconnections in the brain 3, 129
interpersonal neurobiology 224-9
interpersonal sensitivity 180-1

Krioukov, Dmitri 3

language 7, 9, 145
limbic system 9, 11, 35, 170-3
lobes 6-8
   frontal 6-7, 11-12, 35, 125-6, 129-50, 174, 211
      decline of 131-2
      development of 130-1
      functions of 131
      managing habits 152-4
      maximizing activity 151-2
      sense of security 132
   occipital 7, 8
   parietal 7, 130
   temporal 7, 8, 11, 130
      medial 147
Lowe, Jeff 184

Making Up the Mind 139
Maslow's Hierarchy of Needs 208
meditation 182-3, 198-200
Mediterranean diet 121-2
medulla oblongata 11, 174
MEG (magneto-encephalography) 19
melatonin 85
memory

cognitive function 145-8
hydration 111
library 159-61
short-term 8, 69, 130
sleep and storing memory 68-72
verbal 8
visual 8
working 135
meninges 6
mental imagery 144
microbiome 98-101
microscope, fiber-optic 21
midbrain 10-11
mindful training 182-84
minerals 122-3
motivation 180
motor skills 140-3
movement, importance of 28-29
MRI (Magnetic Resonance Imaging) 19, 20, 106
muscle coordination 8, 25
muscle memory 25

napping 74-5, 79-80
Neanderthals 205
neocortex 205
nervous system 14
   dysfunctions 15
neurons 3, 13-14
   dopamine sensitive 130
   mirror 17-18, 210-212
   social interactions 209
neuroplasticity 20-1, 31
neurotransmitters 14-18, 189
nocebo 221

norepinephrine 16, 17
nutrition 93–124
   alcohol 121, 154
   amino acids 118
   antioxidants 108, 115, 116, 118
   betacarotene 117
   blood glucose levels 105–6, 118
   brain-healthy diet 111–20
   cognitive abilities 104–5, 102
   communication with brain imbalance in 101–3
   facts 93–4
   fat 96
   fatty acids 96, 108
   gastrointestinal system 96–101
   general tips 120–121
   inflammation, foods to fight 108–10
   intestines 97
     bacteria 97–101, 105–6
     hydration 110, 112
   mood 99–100
   neurodegenerative disease 107
   recommendations 114
   saturated fat 120
   superfoods 107–8
   Omega-3 96, 108, 116
   Vitamin C 117
   Vitamin E 116
   Zinc 117

obesity and cognitive decline 106–7
olfactory bulb 12
optic nerve 143, 144

organizing your workload 163–4
over training 39–41, 53

pain 215–8, 226
   of loss 216
   of rejection 215–16
percept 137
perception 137–40
   perceptual sets 138
   priming 138–9
Persuasion and Healing: A Comparative Study of Psychotherapy 209
PET (Positron Emission Tomography) 19, 20
physical activity 27–55
   academic performance 33–4
   anxiety 35
   benefits to brain 27–8, 30, 32–4
   cancer therapy 33, 36
   cooling down 51
   depression 35
   emotional health 34–5
   fitness trackers 54–55
   learning 32
   managing 42–55
     frequency 45
     intensity 45, 46–7, 51–2
     time 45, 47
     training, different types of 42–3, 47–50
   measuring performance 52–5
   memory 31
   mental toughness 36–41
     definition 37
   risks of lack of 29–31

warming up 50-51
Physical Activity Readiness Questionnaire (PAR-Q) 44
pineal gland 84
Polyvagal Theory 225
pons 11
Porges, Dr Stephen 225, 227
predictive coding 22
pretectum 143
principle governing creating a Process 242-3
Proprioceptive Neuromuscular Facilitation (PNF) 50
Prisoner's Dilemma 213, 214
probiotics 99
proximal stimulus 137

rapid resetting 200-1
recall 145-6
resting 77-83
    breaks 80-1
    breathing exercises 81-2
    meditation 82-3
    movement 81
    music 83
    see also napping

saccades 144
Seagal, Dr Dan 224
Schore, Dr Allan 224
Scientific 7 Minute Workout 52
sedentary lifestyle 28
self-awareness 179, 180, 185, 186-90,
serotonin 15, 17, 99, 111

skull (cranium) 6, 11
sleep
    aiding return to sleep 80-90
    benefits of 56-59
    brainwaves 59-61
    circadian rhythms 83-4
    counting sheep 90
    darkness, importance of 84-5
    depression 66
    deprivation 63-74
        accidents caused by 71
        costs of 63-5
        decision-making, impact on 72-3
        disasters caused by 69-71
        economy, effect on 73-4
        medical errors caused by 71-2
    emotional management 67-8
    golden chain 57-8
    growth hormone 58, 61
    importance of 62
    light, using to improve sleep 84-5
    mood 65-6
    napping 74-5, 78-80
    preparations for sleeping well 86-9
        anxiety management 88
        exercising 87-8
        pre-sleep routine 91-2
        shift work 90-1
        snacking 87
        travelling 91-2
    recommendations for managing 76-7
    stages 61

index

REM (rapid eye movement) 61
storing memory 68-72
stress 65-7
social interaction 202-41
  being proactive 231-2
  collaboration 205-6
  communication *see* communication
  disassociation 226
  face-to-face 228-9
  facts 202-3
  family life, managing 232-5
    change 233
    children 233
    elders 233
    history 234
    minimize stress 234
    positivity 232
    rituals 234
  friendship 203-4
  positive feedback 215
  professional life, managing 237-41
    creating dialogue 239-40
    negative language 240
    safe environments 238
    skilled attention 239
    social breaks 238-9
  putting others first 212-15
  reciprocity 212-13
  recommendations 230-2
  rewards 214
  social brain 205-6
  social connections 203-12
  social life, managing 235-7
    boundaries 237
    networks 235-6
    positivity 235-6
    social media 227-9
    teamwork 215
  social rejection 215-18
  social synapse 209-10
soma 14
spatial information 7
spatial processing 143-4
SPECT (Single Photon Emission Computed Tomography) 20
speed reading 154-8
spinal cord 6, 7, 8, 11, 12, 14
stem cells 177
stimulation, importance of 38
stress
  dealing with 28
  emotional 176-7
  family life 234
  innoculation 37
  negative language 220-1
  nutrition 99
  residual 88
  sleep 65-6, 88
striatum 142, 147
superior colliculus 144
synapse 14, 147
sympathetic afferents 174

tea, green 118
techniques for examining the brain 18-22
tectum 10
tegmentum 10
thalamus 10, 12
training, different types of 42-3,

47–51
  cardiorespiratory 47–9
  flexibility 50
  resistance 49
transduction 137
transmission of messages 14–17

vagus nerve 99, 171–3, 174, 225, 227
vegetables 115–6, 117
visual attention 111
visual processing 143–44
  systems 8
visualization techniques 191–3, 195
vitamins 116–17, 122–3

water *see* hydration

yoghurt 99–100

index

Urbane Publications is dedicated to developing new author voices, and publishing fiction and non-fiction that challenges, thrills and fascinates. From page-turning novels to innovative reference books, our goal is to publish what YOU want to read.

Find out more at

urbanepublications.com